LEADERSHIP

IN EMPOWERED SCHOOLS

ఈ

LEADERSHIP

IN EMPOWERED SCHOOLS

Themes from Innovative Efforts

Second Edition

Paula M. Short
University of Missouri System

John T. Greer

Merrill
Prentice Hall

Upper Saddle River, New Jersey
Columbus, Ohio

Library of Congress Cataloging-in-Publication Data
Short, Paula M.
    Leadership in empowered schools : themes from innovative efforts /
Paula M. Short, John T. Greer.—2nd ed.
        p. cm.
    Includes bibliographical references and index.
    ISBN 0-13-019945-1
    1. Educational leadership—United States.   2. School management and
organization—United States.   3. Teacher participation in administration—
United States.   4. Educational change—United States.   I. Greer, John T.   II. Title.

LB2805.S584   2002
    371.2'00973—dc21   2001030583

Vice President and Publisher: Jeffery W. Johnston
Editor: Debra A. Stollenwerk
Editorial Assistant: Mary Morrill
Production Editor: Linda Hillis Bayma
Production Coordination: Ann Mohan, WordCrafters Editorial Services, Inc.
Design Coordinator: Diane C. Lorenzo
Cover Designer: Jeff Vanik
Cover art: SuperStock
Production Manager: Pamela D. Bennett
Director of Marketing: Kevin Flanagan
Marketing Manager: Krista Groshong
Marketing Coordinator: Barbara Koontz

This book was set in Century by Carlisle Communications, Ltd. It was printed and bound
by R.R. Donnelley & Sons Company. The cover was printed by Phoenix Color Corp.

Pearson Education Ltd., *London*
Pearson Education Australia Pty. Limited, *Sydney*
Pearson Education Singapore Pte. Ltd.
Pearson Education North Asia Ltd., *Hong Kong*
Pearson Education Canada, Ltd., *Toronto*
Pearson Educación de Mexico, S.A. de C.V.
Pearson Education—Japan, *Tokyo*
Pearson Education Malaysia Pte. Ltd.
Pearson Education, *Upper Saddle River, New Jersey*

10 9 8 7 6 5 4 3 2 1
ISBN 0-13-019945-1

To the memory of John T. Greer for his profound
contributions to educational administration

and

to Linda Greer, JD, for her outstanding support
for the publication of the second edition of this book

ABOUT THE AUTHORS

Paula M. Short is Associate Vice President for Academic Affairs for the University of Missouri System and Professor of Educational Leadership and Policy Analysis at the University of Missouri–Columbia. She received the Ph.D. in Educational Administration and Supervision from the University of North Carolina at Chapel Hill. She has served as a teacher and administrator at the building, district, and state levels of K–12 education and has been in higher education for 16 years. She is the recipient of the 1993 Jack Culbertson Award, given nationally to a junior professor for outstanding contributions in educational administration research, and the 1993 Association of Secondary School Principals (NASSP) Distinguished Service Award for her contributions to the NASSP Assessment Center Project. Paula is Past President of the University Council for Educational Administration (UCEA), the National Council of Professors of Educational Administration, and the Southern Regional Council for Educational Administration.

Paula served five years as editor of the *Journal of School Leadership*, is series editor of the *School Leaders Library* published by Technomic Publishing Company, and serves on the editorial board of *Educational Administration Quarterly*. She served as a member of the American Association of School Administrators National Commission on Standards for the Superintendency and the Council of 55 that developed the publication *Preparing Students for the 21st Century* and has served two terms as a member of the National Policy Board for Educational Administration. Paula has published five books, four book chapters, and more than 60 scholarly journal articles on leadership, empowerment, collaboration, and organizational change. Her teaching and research interests include empowerment, collaboration in higher education, organizational change, and leadership.

John T. (Jack) Greer was Professor of Educational Policy Studies at Georgia State University. After serving as a teacher and administrator in public schools, he joined the faculties of the University of Arizona and the University of Nebraska. Jack served as the President of the National Council of Professors of Educational Administration (NCPEA), President of the University Council for Educational Administration (UCEA), Chair for the Southern Regional Conference of Professors of Educational Administration, and Chair of the Latin

American Committee of the Southern Association of Colleges and Schools. He served on the editorial board of *Educational Administration Quarterly.* Jack's untimely death was a tremendous loss to the field of educational administration. His interest in empowerment and the autonomous school had a profound effect on the research reported in this book. He is deeply missed by students, colleagues, and friends.

PREFACE

The last two decades have produced a sustained effort to restructure public education. Site-based management, charter schools, learner-centered communities, and teacher empowerment have been the focus of much of the reform effort. The call for change has advanced notions about roles, culture, and norms within school organizations. Ideas about leadership have expanded as schools attempt to build learning organizations with empowered participants. While much has been written about school restructuring, there is a need for a better understanding about how to build empowering environments in schools based on empirical findings rather than rhetoric or opinion.

This book addresses that need by using two large national studies conducted over six years in 26 schools, as well as other research, to provide an empirical base for drawing conclusions about leadership in schools that are restructuring and striving to provide empowering environments for faculty and students. Professors and students of educational leadership should find the material in this book useful in the study of leadership and organizational change. Practitioners should find key dimensions of leadership useful in their application to the real world of practice.

This new edition builds on the historical view of restructuring and empowerment as a context for understanding the two national studies and describes the current landscape of school restructuring. It presents the key dimensions of empowering leadership gleaned from research as well as an in-depth discussion of the leadership dimension. Leadership assessment instruments have been added to this new edition, as well as a chapter on leader reflection, critical to leadership understanding and development. New case studies from the schools that participated in the studies have been added to illustrate the leadership dimension. Not all cases show success; some are included to illustrate how the principal's failure to exercise particular leadership dimensions created less-than-desired results in the school's effort to create an empowering organization. Some cases are more in-depth than others, encouraging the reader to spend time reflecting and problem solving around the case scenario. The shorter cases give the reader the opportunity to pick up ideas quickly. Also new are "Voices from the Field," a series of descriptions of empowerment efforts in the voices of those who experienced them firsthand.

Questions for discussion follow each of the in-depth case studies and should be useful in focusing discourse and debate regarding the

PREFACE

leadership dimension and the particular school context described in the case. Finally, each chapter concludes with helpful references.

This new edition should be useful to students as well as practitioners who have a commitment to the constant search for better ways to build schools that meet the needs of all students.

ACKNOWLEDGMENTS

The research reported in this book was supported with a grant from the Danforth Foundation of St. Louis, Missouri. I greatly appreciate the support of the foundation in efforts to better understand leadership in empowered schools. I also want to thank Linda Greer, Jack Greer's wonderful wife, for her interest and support in the publication of this second edition. In addition, I would like to acknowledge the contributions of those educators who wrote case studies and shared their "Voices from the Field" for the second edition of this book. Those individuals are Amy Miller, Pandora Gilboa Elementary School, Pandora, OH; James K. Walter, Texas A&M University—Corpus Christi; Michael L. Supley, Education Study Center, Kingsville, TX; Betty Chong, Cape Girardeau School District; Rose Talent, Southeast Missouri State University; Cynthia MacGregor; Southwest Missouri State University; James Machell, Central Missouri State University; Carol Maher, University of Missouri-Columbia; Nancy Colbaugh, Weller Elementary School; Barbara Crossland, Hollister Elementary School; Bruce Johnson, Stanberry R-II School District; Deborah A. Myracle, New Madrid County R-1 School District; and Judy K. Statler, Jackson R-2 Public School District. I particularly want to express deep appreciation to George Petersen for his major contributions to the revision of this book.

My appreciation also goes to the reviewers for this second edition, who lent their expertise to give helpful suggestions for making this a better book: Martha Bruckner, University of Nebraska at Omaha; Donna M. Carney, Edinboro University of Pennsylvania; Carol Carter-Lowery, Central Connecticut State University; Stuart E. Gothold, University of Southern California; and Thelma Moore-Steward, California State University, Long Beach.

Finally, I would like to express my appreciation for the support and advice of my editor, Debbie Stollenwerk, who encouraged the development of the second edition of this book, and Ann Sleper for her technical skills in producing the manuscript.

Paula Myrick Short
University of Missouri System

DISCOVER THE COMPANION WEBSITE ACCOMPANYING THIS BOOK

The Prentice Hall Companion Website: A Virtual Learning Environment

Technology is a constantly growing and changing aspect of our field that is creating a need for content and resources. To address this emerging need, Prentice Hall has developed an online learning environment for students and professors alike—Companion Websites—to support our textbooks.

In creating a Companion Website, our goal is to build on and enhance what the textbook already offers. For this reason, the content for each user-friendly website is organized by topic and provides the professor and student with a variety of meaningful resources. Common features of a Companion Website include:

For the Professor—

Every Companion Website integrates **Syllabus Manager™**, an online syllabus creation and management utility.

- **Syllabus Manager™** provides you, the instructor, with an easy, step-by-step process to create and revise syllabi, with direct links into Companion Website and other online content without having to learn HTML.
- Students may log on to your syllabus during any study session. All they need to know is the web address for the Companion Website and the password you've assigned to your syllabus.
- After you have created a syllabus using **Syllabus Manager™**, students may enter the syllabus for their course section from any point in the Companion Website.
- Clicking on a date, the student is shown the list of activities for the assignment. The activities for each assignment are linked directly to actual content, saving time for students.

- Adding assignments consists of clicking on the desired due date, then filling in the details of the assignment—name of the assignment, instructions, and whether it is a one-time or repeating assignment.
- In addition, links to other activities can be created easily. If the activity is online, a URL can be entered in the space provided, and it will be linked automatically in the final syllabus.
- Your completed syllabus is hosted on our servers, allowing convenient updates from any computer on the Internet. Changes you make to your syllabus are immediately available to your students at their next logon.

For the Student—

- **Topic Overviews**—outline key concepts in topic areas
- **Web Links**—a wide range of websites that provide useful and current information related to each topic area
- **Readings**—suggested readings for further study of certain aspects of the topic areas
- **Trends and Issues**—links to relevant sites about the trends and issues of educational administration
- **Education Resources**—links to schools, online journals, government sites, departments of education, professional organizations, regional information, and more
- **Electronic Bluebook**—send homework or essays directly to your instructor's email with this paperless form
- **Message Board**—serves as a virtual bulletin board to post—or respond to—questions or comments to/from a national audience
- **Chat**—real-time chat with anyone who is using the text anywhere in the country—ideal for discussion and study groups, class projects, etc.

To take advantage of these and other resources, please visit the *Leadership in Empowered* Schools: *Themes from Innovative Efforts*, Second Edition, Companion Website at

www.prenhall.com/short

CONTENTS

CONTENTS

STIMULATING RISK TAKING AND INNOVATION   85

6

USING CRITICAL EVENTS TO FRAME NEW OPPORTUNITIES   107

7

REFRAMING SCHOOL ISSUES   129

8

EMPOWERING TEACHERS   145

9

EMPOWERING STUDENTS   171

10

EVALUATION OF EMPOWERING LEADERSHIP   185

11

REFLECTION IN EMPOWERED SCHOOLS   201

INDEX   213

Context of Restructuring and Empowerment

The 20th century was the century of growth and development for public education in the United States. Borrowing liberally from the work of organization theorists, school leaders attempted to create organizations that resembled those found in private industry. Such efforts were not without foundation, for the schools were showing the same growth and expansion curves as private-sector companies. During this period, the schools went from serving a largely rural population to serving an urban population: large, multischool districts were formed, universal education was extended through the secondary school, and students with special needs became members of all school populations.

This book incorporates the results of two national studies. In the first, the Empowered School District Project (Short, Greer, & Melvin, 1994), we studied the process of teacher empowerment in nine schools scattered across the country from Utah to Georgia. In the second, the Arizona Restructuring Project (Greer, Allen, & Slawson, 1994), we studied school restructuring based on the establishment of multiage, multigrade classrooms in elementary and secondary schools in 17 Arizona schools. Since our research efforts revealed that the secret of success in the 26 schools studied was a high level of teacher involvement and commitment, it made sense for us to draw upon both studies for this book, gleaning generalizations and insights regarding teacher empowerment.

In the following two sections, the topics of restructuring and empowerment are treated in historical order to provide some perspective on the current emphasis on empowerment within the restructuring movement.

RESTRUCTURING

Historical Perspective

The 20th century was a century of education reform (Kastle, 1990). Beginning with the national reform effort of the 1890s, the schools were subjected to a constant stream of innovations aimed at helping them meet the challenges imposed by larger enrollments and limited resources. This reform effort established two themes for the public schools: efficiency and individual growth (Kastle, 1990). Although little attention was paid to the individual growth theme until the progressive education movement of the 1920s, the efficiency theme was embraced immediately by the nation's school leaders.

The progress of the efficiency movement during the first half of the 20th century has been documented by Callahan (1962). The leading exponent of efficiency theory was Frederick Taylor, the leader of the scientific management movement. Taylor (1916) believed that all work could be studied, designed, and measured. Through such efforts, the most efficient work behavior for every job could be established. Such thinking had wide appeal among school administrators who were facing the problem of educating ever-increasing numbers of students. It also coincided with the measurement movement in psychology that was sweeping the nation. Psychologists were developing tests and other measures that enabled them to establish a student's mental capacity and levels of achievement.

These two factors—scientific management and the measurement movement—created what Callahan (1962) called the "Cult of Efficiency." The idea was to increase levels of student achievement given the limited resources available, and these levels could be established through measurement.

The efficiency movement spotlighted the bureaucratic pattern of organization. Max Weber (Gerth & Mills, 1946) emphasized the benefits of organizing according to a legal system of authority, by which he meant that an organization should be run by trained individuals according to preestablished rules. The structure of the organization would be pyramidal, and the work of individuals would be supervised by higher-ranked persons. When such an organization was established, Weber held that it was both the most efficient and the most effective method for coordinating the work efforts of large numbers of people. He called such an organization a *bureaucracy* (Gerth & Mills, 1946).

The appeal of the bureaucratic model obviated any consideration of alternate patterns of educational organization. Boards of education, superintendents, and central office administrators became the decision makers for all of the schools included in their districts, just as boards of directors, presidents, and headquarters personnel became the decision makers for entire corporations. Bureaucracies, whether they were in education or in private industry, were efficient and therefore good.

Individual schools within a district were also organized as small bureaucracies. Principals were hired as leaders, with teachers and staff members as subordinates. It was the principal's responsibility to carry out the wishes of the central office and to guide the school staff in working with students.

With the exception of two short periods when attention was paid to the inclusion of students from diverse racial and ethnic groups and students with disabilities (Kastle, 1990), the twin themes of efficiency and measurement characterized the approach of the schools during the second half of the 20th century just as they had during the first half. The only difference was that the name of the efficiency movement was changed to the *accountability movement*. The objectives, however, remained the same: guaranteed results in student achievement and efficient use of financial resources.

Although the antecedents of restructuring and empowerment were visible in schools as early as the 1930s, the terms themselves entered popular usage as parts of the reform effort of the 1980s. Educators have long been influenced by the efficiency model of management, and rather than focusing their attention on finding more productive, alternate methods of organizing the instructional effort, school leaders directed their efforts toward perfecting the bureaucracy. Thus, written school board policies became popular in the 1950s, more attention was given to the homogeneous grouping of students, and measurable results became synonymous with learning.

As soon as it was introduced during the reform effort of the 1980s, *restructuring* quickly became the buzzword of the entire education establishment. Any change in grouping, instruction, or organizational arrangements became known as the school's restructuring effort.

For the purposes of this book, we have adopted a narrow definition: *Restructuring* means changing the basic organizational structure of the school. Examples of restructuring include ungraded primary units that eliminate grade designations and schools-within-a-school that collapse departments into larger academic structures. In essence, restructuring means changing the common "factory model" of the school, in which schools resemble an assembly line, into something different.

Models of Restructuring

District Restructuring

Restructuring occurs at the district and the building levels. Most of the attention in this book is given to efforts at the building level, but two forms of district restructuring must be mentioned.

Site-Based Management. Site-based management has become synonymous with restructuring. At its core is power sharing: Outsiders—district officials and boards—share power with insiders; administrators share power with staff and educational professionals; and they share power with parents, students, and the public (Goldman & Dunlap, 1990).

According to Goldman and Dunlap (1990), site-based management has at least three independent meanings. First and foremost, it implies decentralization of the decision-making process from the district to the building level, without implying how much is enough. School districts already differ substantially in decentralization. In some, individual schools are controlled tightly from district or regional headquarters; in others, each school is essentially self-managed. Note, however, that decentralization *to* the building level does not necessarily imply decentralization *at* the building level. Schools already differ greatly with regard to the extent of their curriculum standardization and teacher autonomy, so site-based management could have different meanings in different places.

Second, site-based management implies an attempt to match educational programs to specific characteristics of students, teachers, and the community in which the school is located. Substantial differences in curricular strategies among school buildings, even within the same district, are not only permitted but encouraged (Goldman & Dunlap, 1990).

Third, for many educators site-based management implies participative management. It allows use of the knowledge and energy of participants—teachers, parents, and students. In a recent study by Johnson and Scollay (1998), however, these researchers found that of parents, teachers, and principals on site-based councils (teams), all saw the principal as exercising the most influence on the council and parents as exercising the least. Johnson and Scollay's instrument for measuring site-based council influence is shown in Figure 1.1.

Figure 1.1
Instrument to Measure Site-Based Council Influence

School Code _____

Personal Code _____

School-Based Council Influence Scale

Each member of your council, including yourself, has been assigned by name to one of the following designators: Principal; Teacher 1; Teacher 2; Teacher 3; Parent 1; or Parent 2, etc. This assignment is found on the instruction sheet attached to the envelope enclosing this form. You must refer to this list when responding to the following items; otherwise your responses will be invalid and will have not value. However, do not write any names on this sheet. Destroy the council member list when you have finished with this form. Do not return it to the investigators.

In column 2, rank order the council members from having the most influence (1) on decisions made by the council to the least influence (11). Write your ranking in the blanks under column 2.

In column 3, rate each council member on the following statement: "The person named influences the decisions made by the council." Use the following scale for your rating:

1	2	3	4	5
Disagree Strongly	Disagree Moderately	Neither Agree nor Disagree	Agree Moderately	Agree Strongly

In column 4, give each council member an attendance rating by indicating the percentage of meetings attended.

1. Role on Council	2. Influence Ranking (1–11)	3. Influence Rating Circle the appropriate number.	4. Percentage of Meetings Attended Circle the appropriate number.
1. Principal			
2. Teacher 1			
3. Teacher 2			
4. Teacher 3			
5. Teacher 4			
6. Teacher 5			
7. Teacher 6			
8. Parent 1			
9. Parent 2			
10. Parent 3			
11. Parent 4			

Note. From *School-Based and Decision-Making Councils: Conflict, Leader Power, and Social Influence in Vertical Teams* by P.E. Johnson and S.J. Sculley, 1998. Unpublished manuscript. Reprinted with permission.

The logic behind site-based management is unassailable. The problem rests with the amount of autonomy the district is willing to give the school and its staff. Unfortunately, a growing body of evidence suggests that central administrators are unwilling to give schools complete freedom to make the decisions needed by their students (Greer, 1993). Formula-based financial allotments, centralized purchasing of instructional materials, and standardized personnel programs have all been used to weaken the effectiveness of site-based management programs.

Wohlstetter (1995) cited several reasons why site-based management fails:

It is adopted as an end in itself. Site-based management will not self-generate improvement in school performance. It is simply a means through which school-level decision makers can implement various reforms that can improve teaching and learning. Research by Wohlstetter (1995) indicated that in schools visited there was little connection between site-based management and the reform of curriculum and instruction and that school councils often got bogged down in issues of power—who can attend meetings, who can vote, and so on—and had no time or energy left to confront issues of school improvement.

Principals work from their own agendas. They tend to dominate discussions and set the agenda for meetings. They impose their own agendas on the council. Wohlstetter (1995) found that these tactics often led to power struggles between teachers and the principal over who controlled the school, and in some cases, the faculty rejected the principal's unilateral plan for change.

Decision-making power is lodged in the single council. Councils often were composed of a small group of committed teachers who did not have broad representation. These councils tended to get bogged down in establishing power relationships. There were always feelings of alienation among faculty members, and often factions developed between "them" (the empowered) and "the rest of us."

Business proceeds as usual. The schools Wohlstetter visited assumed that site-based management can be put in place with average levels of commitment and energy. In fact, site-based management is a time-consuming and complicated process that places high demands on all individuals involved. The schools that struggled with site-based management had simply layered it on top of what they were already doing. Schools did not redesign schedules so that teachers could interact during the regular day. There were strong feelings of isolation among teachers because of the lack of meetings that would allow them and the stakeholders to discuss specific projects or tasks.

Charter Schools. The charter school movement started in the United States with the passage of charter legislation in 1991 in Minnesota. By 1997, more than 30 states had passed legislation enabling the establishment of charter schools. Currently there are approximately 800 charter schools in the United States, with many more being established annually. Although charter schools vary, most share common principles of choice. The expected outcome is improved educational experiences for students. Charter schools are independent public schools that are released from state and local rules and regulations of public education. This freedom is intended to help educators and the community to create and deliver programs tailored to achieve educational excellence and meet critical needs of the community. The charter concept incorporates the ideas of the early 1960s, when choice and creative alternative educational programs gave students different opportunities to learn. The overall goals of charter schools are aligned with the goals of all choice programs: to increase student achievement, expand educational opportunities for families and children, expand professional opportunities for educators, and stimulate change in the larger educational system. The concept is public school choice modeled on the tenets of the free market system (Center for Educational Reform, 2001).

In a national study of charter schools (National Institute on Student Achievement, Curriculum, and Assessment, 1998), researchers learned that most charter schools focus on attracting parents and students by focusing on academics. However, an equally important attraction is a supportive environment often based on small school size (93%) a safe environment (90%), and a value system (88%). Newly established charter schools appear to be established to realize an alternative vision for public education (National Institute on Student Achievement, Curriculum, and Assessment, 1998). The most frequently cited reason for beginning a charter school is to gain autonomy from the school district or to bypass various regulations. Private schools that convert to charter status do so to seek public funds so they can stabilize their finances and attract students, often students whose families could not afford private school tuition.

Building Restructuring

A number of restructuring experiments have been conducted in the nation's schools during the last half century. The primary motivation for such experiments is to break the tenacious grip of the "factory model," a term that likens the school's pattern of organization to a factory's assembly line. Students are grouped according to age and ability into groups of 25 to 30. Each group moves along the assembly line while a teacher ministers to its preestablished educational needs for a 9-month period. At the conclusion of the period, each student is judged as capable or not capable of moving on with the group and its new teacher. This 9-month cycle continues throughout the student's school career. Students who are not allowed to move on are judged as failures and removed from the assembly line. They are then recycled through the same 9-month experience, often with the same teacher.

This pattern of organization has disturbed many educators because of its insensitivity to the needs of individual students. Additionally, the lockstep format has seemed to discourage joint or cooperative teaching and learning efforts among teachers and students.

In spite of the difficulties involved, some restructuring efforts have been established in schools across the country. The following models are not all-inclusive, but they include the most prevalent efforts developed in the second half of the 20th century: the middle school, the ungraded primary classroom, and the school-within-a-school.

The Middle School.   Educators interested in adolescents recognized that a unique institution was needed to better serve students of this age. The junior high school, patterned after the high school, was thought to be too impersonal to respond to the psychological, emotional, and educational needs of early adolescents. The middle school evolved as a distinctly different educational institution to provide for those needs.

The middle school philosophy is focused on helping students as they pass from childhood to adulthood. Individualized attention is provided through strong counseling and advising programs. The faculty is organized into interdisciplinary teams so that an entire team of teachers is in contact with a group of students throughout much of the day. Short-term elective classes are provided to broaden the students' intellectual and leisure interests.

The middle school is a true model of school restructuring. The basic structure of the school has been changed by the elimination of academic departments and the establishment of interdisciplinary teams. It is true that most middle schools still retain the graded format so that students are divided into, for example, sixth-, seventh-, and eighth-grade groups, but the traditional 45 or 50-minute class periods have been replaced with more flexible blocks of time.

However, not all traces of the factory model are eliminated in the middle school model. The assembly line, for example, is still in evidence as students progress from one grade to another. Nevertheless, breaking out of the restrictions that academic departments impose on a school and freeing the school from never-changing class schedules are significant restructuring accomplishments.

The Ungraded Primary Classroom. Another restructuring effort in many elementary schools throughout the nation is the *ungraded primary classroom*. This format calls for children in kindergarten through grade 2, or in grades 1 through 3, to be taught together. The 3-year experience enables the child to grow and mature at his or her own rate. It also eliminates the promotion process and its attendant anxieties during the first 2 years.

Children in ungraded primary classrooms may be taught by one teacher or a team of teachers. The major difference between the two settings is the size of the student group and classroom. The dynamics of the classroom, however, are largely the same in both settings. Thematic teaching is very much in evidence, and students work independently and with others in a variety of groups.

The ungraded primary classroom is another good example of a restructuring model. During the 3 years, the graded assembly-line approach is discarded. In its place is a classroom setting where children and teachers work together for an extended period.

The School-Within-a-School. The idea of dividing a large school into smaller, more personal units originated in the late 1950s. The early models were designed as miniatures of the large school. Students were randomly assigned to one of the small units as entering freshmen and joined with the school's sophomores, juniors, and seniors to form the school-within-a-school. The early experiments varied in the degree of independence given to each small school. In some schools, the faculty was divided into small-unit faculties and taught the students of the small unit almost exclusively. In other situations, the small school was the setting for activities such as the extracurricular program, counseling, homeroom, and so forth. These early school-within-a-school efforts would not satisfy the restructuring definition given earlier because they did not change the basic academic department structure of the schools. Departments continued to exist even though their members might be assigned to smaller units. The students continued to be described as freshmen, sophomores, juniors, and seniors and enrolled in classes established for their grade levels.

Later versions of the school-within-a-school model did depart from the miniature school model just described. These small units were designed to serve students with unique educational interests or needs. Some were organized to provide specialized types of education, such as technical or global education, while others were designed to provide experiences for at-risk students that would keep the students in school and, at the same time, prepare them for the world of work they were about to enter. These special-focus schools-within-schools had their own faculties that were drawn from the larger school's faculty. The smaller faculties represented a variety of academic disciplines that worked together offering interdisciplinary programs tailored to the interests and needs of the students. A final feature of the special-focus schools was that students were not divided by grade levels. They were assigned to classes according to their interests or needs and worked together regardless of age.

Certainly these later schools-within-schools satisfy our definition of restructuring. Academic departments are eliminated within the small school, faculty members teach and work together regardless of their academic discipline, and the graded format of the traditional school is discarded.

Why Restructure?

The foregoing discussion provides a partial answer to the question of why a school should want to restructure. The school bureaucracy imposes terrible restrictions on professional educators who seek to work with individual students. Board of education policies, pupil/teacher ratios, and the accountability mentality that makes standardized test scores synonymous with learning all serve to create a learning environment that encourages sameness and discourages individuality.

There are other minuses connected to traditional school and classroom structures. The efficiency and accountability movements have placed heavy emphasis on outcome and performance measures. Sacrificed are the students' opportunities to grow and mature naturally. In fact, all of the models of restructuring listed in this chapter were developed to offset the harmful effects of the efficiency/accountability movements on the individual. The middle school was developed, at least in part, to meet the social and emotional needs of the adolescent. The ungraded primary was designed to provide young children with the opportunity to grow and develop naturally in a nurturing environment. The school-within-a-school was a response to the special interests and needs of segments of the high school student population.

Further support for the thesis that restructuring efforts are educators' responses to the insensitivity of the traditional school can be found in the results of a recently completed multiage, multigrade restructuring project in Arizona (Greer et al., 1994). One of the concluding activities of the project called for the directors to interview key participants in all of the project schools. In school after school, the researchers saw evidence of what was later judged to be a theme of the entire 4-year, 17-school project: In multiage, multigrade classrooms, students are more mature, are more independent, and possess a higher level of self-esteem than students in traditional classrooms.

The Arizona project researchers were also impressed by the participants' observations regarding the effects of multiage, multigrade classrooms on students, teachers, principals, parents, superintendents, and board of education members. The observations of all these participants focused on affective aspects of schooling. Typical comments were "Students develop a sense of family, and the classrooms become something more than typical school classrooms; they become 'homes' " and "Very few discipline problems exist. The classroom is viewed as a place of safety and students don't have to 'act out' " (Greer et al., 1994, pp. 12–13).

About the only comments that referred to the academic achievement of students were statements that implied criticism of the traditional academic program, such as the following: "If we had not had the ungraded classrooms, a number of our kids would have never made it. The ungraded classrooms gave the kids time to mature and develop." " 'Difficult' students and those who are disabled with learning problems seem to thrive in these [ungraded] classrooms" (Greer et al., 1994, p. 16).

Thus, the answer to the question of "Why restructure?" revolves around providing opportunities for *individuals* to develop and mature as independent learners. Although it was not planned as such, this response coincides with the second objective of the 1890s education reform effort (i.e., fostering individual growth), which was ignored by those interested in efficiency and accountability (Kastle, 1990).

PARTICIPANT EMPOWERMENT

Historical Perspective

Even casual readers of the organization theory literature will recall that the Western Electric studies of the late 1920s and early 1930s redirected the focus of organization research. The individual worker, particularly as he or she worked with other persons, became the center of attention. The new research thrust became known as the *human relations movement*. Extensive studies on the nature, leadership, and work behavior of groups were conducted throughout the 1940s and early 1950s. Within this environment, interest developed in workers' having a voice in organizational decision making. The topic came to be known as *participative decision making*.

Two hoped-for outcomes motivated those interested in participative decision making: increased worker productivity and worker satisfaction. Both concepts came from the findings on human behavior in work settings that resulted from the Western Electric and similar studies. These findings focused on the small work groups that were parts of the larger organizations. It was found that such groups were the primary influence on the behavior of workers. They influenced the amount of work that members produced and the members' feelings about the organization (i.e., morale) and provided a set of relationships with other workers engaged in similar types of work.

Researchers assumed that increased productivity would result if workers' opinions and insights were included in the decisions related to production. They also assumed that decision participation would increase the job satisfaction of workers and increase their commitment to the organization.

Participative decision making was evaluated extensively throughout the 1940s and 1950s. Frost, Wakely, and Ruh (1974), after reviewing the bulk of the evaluation research, concluded that participative decision making programs could result in greater organization effectiveness, individual performance, and job satisfaction. There were, however, several studies that failed to support these findings and led Frost and colleagues to add a note of caution to their conclusions.

A more systemized approach to participative decision making, known as the *Scanlon Plan*, emerged during the late 1940s and 1950s (McGregor, 1960). In many respects, the success of the Scanlon Plan in companies throughout the United States provided the examples and rationale used as a theoretical base for the empowerment research reported in this book.

According to its originator, Joseph Scanlon, the Scanlon Plan was more of a management philosophy than a plan for organizing a company. The heart of the plan was management's recognition that workers could aid in making decisions that would make the company more efficient and effective. The Scanlon Plan provided a format for involving workers in decisions and the changes brought about by those decisions.

Although the versions of the Scanlon Plan varied from company to company, the heart of the plan called for regular meetings of persons engaged in similar kinds of work. The meetings were held on company time and were focused on identifying improvements that would make the company more efficient and effective. As changes were suggested by the work groups, they were submitted to screening committees that reviewed the ideas and decided which ideas should be implemented. When an idea was successful and resulted in an improved operation, the originating work group was rewarded by receiving a bonus, a portion of the money the innovation had earned for the company (McGregor, 1960).

A number of companies adopted the Scanlon Plan. Even today, it is possible to find traces of the plan in some of these same companies. Like participative decision making, the Scanlon Plan attracted many researchers. In contrast to most of the studies of the time, Lesieur and Puckett (1958) studied three companies that had been organized as Scanlon Plan companies for more than 10 years. Their conclusions were that the plan improved efficiency and productivity, increased labor–management cooperation, and increased employee willingness to accept technological change.

Frost and colleagues (1974), after reviewing the bulk of Scanlon Plan research, generally supported the conclusions of Lesieur and Puckett (1958). They also described several companies that had abandoned the plan. Two reasons were listed as contributing to the plan's failure. First, some of the companies failed to see the plan as a philosophy of management (McGregor, 1960), and second, in others the plan was never fully implemented and failed because of technical difficulties.

It is interesting to note that the heart of the Scanlon Plan was the work group. Within the group, ideas for improvement were generated. The work group was highlighted again by researchers and students of organizations 25 years later, when it became known as the *self-managing work team*. Again, it was the source of ideas for organization improvement. The self-managing team is described more fully in Chapter 8 as a part of the discussion of empowering teachers.

A few years after the self-managing work team was described, there was yet another round of interest in the work group. This third occurrence was included in the literature describing Japanese industry. Ouchi (1980) and other writers described "quality circles" as a major source of ideas regarding the improvement of Japanese companies.

Versions of Empowerment

Empowerment is a catchword of the education reforms of the 1980s. Based on the historical perspective of empowerment just given, it is tempting to declare that *empowerment* and *participative decision making* are synonyms. Such a statement cannot be made, however, because there are two distinct versions of the empowerment process, each governed by its advocates' different perception of power.

The first version of the empowerment process draws upon the labor–management tradition. Power is conceived as a finite commodity within an organization. In a school, for the teachers to become empowered (i.e., to gain power), the principal must lose or give up power. Thus, the empowerment issue that was a part of the Los Angeles teacher strike of 1989 was settled by the board of education's establishing decision committees in each of the system's schools. Half of each decision committee was composed of teachers, and the other half was composed of the principal and parents. In high schools, a student was added to the principal/parent half of the committee.

The Los Angeles settlement dramatically changed the power relationship within the schools. Instead of the principal being the final authority for making decisions within the school, he or she was faced with a new reality in which the teachers and parents shared in decision making.

The Los Angeles empowerment program was not an isolated phenomenon. Similar school control arrangements were negotiated in other cities across the country. All were based on the assumption that there was a finite amount of power available within the school and the teachers could gain power only at the expense of the principal.

The second version of the empowerment process springs from the participative decision-making tradition. It represents a distinctly different view of power. Power is thought to be an infinite commodity that is available to accomplish the goals and mission of the organization. To expand the amount of power, one involves additional persons in the decisions of the organization. In a school setting, power to accomplish the school's mission is increased when the principal involves teachers, other staff members, and parents in the basic decisions of the school. The saying "the principal gains power by giving it away" appears to sum up the process.

It should come as no surprise that we believe that empowerment is a process of participative decision making. It is, as Scanlon said in describing his plan, a management philosophy. It is a policy of inclusion.

The empowerment study described in this book is based upon the participative philosophy. This study found that empowerment is not a simple process, nor is it one that can be accomplished overnight. Empowerment requires that principals, teachers, staff members, and parents all have mature judgment and the desire to make the school a learning place for all students.

As mentioned earlier, one of the two studies described in this book, The Empowered School District Project (Short, Greer, & Melvin, 1994), was conducted in nine schools scattered throughout the country. Financed by the Danforth Foundation, the school districts, and our universities, the 3-year study sought to document the evolutionary process that leads to a shared governance pattern of decision making.

Participating schools were not required to follow a model of empowerment, although they were told that whatever they did must ultimately benefit the school's students. Each school was encouraged to proceed as conditions dictated. To assist in the effort, an outside consultant and the project directors were available on an on-call basis.

Throughout the 3-year period, representatives from the four high schools and five elementary schools met to discuss their successes, as well as their failures, in bringing about an empowered school. Such exchanges proved to be valuable features of the project and helped the schools establish a communication network that still exists several years after the conclusion of the project.

Even though the schools were invited to participate because of the warm, trusting relationships that existed between their principals and faculty members, it was found that not all of the schools achieved the same level of teacher empowerment in the 3 years of the experiment. Three schools were judged to have made great strides, and their efforts were deemed to be successful. Three schools were slower to implement the process but were rapidly catching up with the successful schools by the end of the 3-year period. The remaining three schools were judged to be unsuccessful in their empowerment efforts. The scenarios in each of the unsuccessful schools appeared to be different, but closer investigation revealed that the principals simply could not yield and share the decision-making responsibilities with their teachers.

Why Empower?

In large part, the answer to the question of "Why empower?" has been answered in the discussion regarding the benefits of participative decision making and the Scanlon Plan. Such participation tends to make the organization more effective and improve employee satisfaction.

As organizations, schools are different from private-sector production companies. The essential difference is that schools are responsible for providing one of the most complex forms of service of any public or private agency. However, in spite of mission differences, the research and understandings gleaned from private-sector companies regarding employee participation do apply to schools.

A second difference between companies and schools is the experience and training of a school's employees. Teachers think and act as professional educators. They have a wealth of insight into the nature of the learning process and are able to apply such understandings to the problems of the school. Empowerment provides them with the avenue to share these understandings and, in so doing, makes the school more effective.

Satisfaction is not always guaranteed with the installation of a teacher empowerment program. In subsequent chapters, several cases from the research are cited in which empowerment did not fulfill the teachers' hopes. However, such cases were few in number, and most teachers in the participating schools became firm supporters over the 3-year course of the project. The heart of the matter is that most adults want to be involved in deciding questions that affect their work or their work environment.

One additional perspective should be added to this discussion of empowerment. Perhaps the most powerful argument for empowerment and other forms of participation was formulated by Douglas McGregor (1960). In what he called the *principle of integration*, McGregor stipulated that the most important work of the manager is to help employees recognize that their best hope of realizing personal goals rests in helping the organization achieve its goals. Empowerment is the process that encourages teachers to help the school achieve its primary goal of improving the learning opportunities of its students.

CONCEPTUAL FRAMEWORK OF THIS BOOK

Linking studies based on a strictly defined concept of empowerment and a narrowly defined perspective of restructuring may appear to be little more than a flight of fancy. As we initiated the second Danforth-sponsored study on multiage, multigrade classrooms, we had not yet made a connection between empowerment and restructuring. As the restructuring work in Arizona evolved, however, it became apparent that the leadership behaviors of principals in schools experimenting successfully with multiage, multigrade classrooms were the same leadership behaviors exhibited by successful principals in the earlier empowerment study.

In the following chapters, the behaviors of principals and teachers in empowered and restructured schools are presented. It should be noted, however, that this volume is not intended as a how-to book; the principals and teachers studied in both projects were unique individuals working in very different educational settings. Their responses to the challenges of empowerment and restructuring were likewise unique. The one common element they all possessed was a belief in the worthiness of their school project, whether it was the empowerment of teachers or the creation of richer educational opportunities for students.

✂ CASE STUDIES

Case Study One: The Restructuring Challenge

Community Background

The community was, until recently, economically strong. However, it has experienced some pockets of aging, or "greying," of its population and the loss of two major industries, which relocated to Mexico under the NAFTA initiative. These events have caused enrollment fluctuations, primarily declines, in the predominantly blue-collar area of the community. The school is located in the area of middle- to upper-middle-class homes in a major greying area. The school survived a school closing program initiated and carried out by the former superintendent, who was terminated after closing two schools in a school consolidation program. The school board had approved the consolidation based on the recommendation of the superintendent. However, because the closings took place in a short period of time—in fact, over a summer—there were some ill feelings throughout the community. Powerful community leaders applied pressure to various school board members, which ultimately led to the termination of that superintendent. In assessing the sense of the community as to the purpose of school, it seems that there is a split between those who take an academic, professional view and those who feel that the primary purpose of schooling is to prepare students for work. The present superintendent has just completed the second year of a 3-year contract.

The Present School Situation

The superintendent believed that a "new broom" would "sweep out the cobwebs" and set in motion a plan to restructure the school. As a result, the present school principal was hired based on her reputation for enabling faculty and staff to operate independently and at high levels of achievement, especially in the areas examined by the mandated state tests. The principal also led the field of applicants because she had no ties to the community or teaching staff and was from another area in the state.

For the past 6 months, the superintendent has been under continual fire by some board members because the state test scores for the school placed it in the "satisfactory" range. There are two levels above this, "recognized" and "exemplary," and there is only one level below it, "needs improvement." The school's overall test scores were at the lower end of the "satisfactory" classification scale. The physical plant, built in 1958, was originally designed to accommodate 900 students. The school has a current enrollment of 752 students. There are 46 teachers, an assistant principal, three counselors, and an in-house library with a librarian and two assistants. Most of the staff have been at the school for at least a decade, and many of the staff have strong local political and community ties.

The principal has been charged by the superintendent to raise overall student performance. The superintendent senses there will be a call for his ouster and a demand for a new superintendent if there is not significant improvement in the state-mandated test scores. To further complicate matters, two of the board members have been raising concerns that, from their reading of the school board magazine, the school appears to be overstaffed. They feel that this should create a learning environment that would enable the school to achieve at least at the "recognized" level on the state tests. Thus, the charge to the newly appointed principal is to present a winning restructuring plan. The superintendent has pledged to support the new school principal, but he awaits the principal's presentation of her restructuring plan.

The principal did not realize the political implications when she accepted the position. Nor did she realize the staff's total commitment to the status quo until her first faculty meeting, when she was assailed with "If it isn't broken, it doesn't need to be fixed" and "You are an outsider, we aren't. You couldn't possibly understand how we do things or what we really need."

The superintendent told the principal that she was hired to make positive changes. He also told her that while he would support her, she needed to realize that restructuring would not be easy and that she would be fighting a difficult battle with some of the older staff who were politically connected. "I know it will be tough to bring this school's test scores up, but we both know it can be accomplished. You do have fine, hardworking students who want to achieve, and you do have a well-qualified and very experienced staff. You just have to provide the necessary leadership and convince them they really want to change for the betterment of the students, the school, and the community."

Conversations About the Case Study

1. Develop a plan of action for the principal to follow.
2. What would you do as the first step?
3. Who would you involve? What would their roles be?
4. What kind of a time frame would the plan need for development? Implementation?
5. How and when would you assess the success of the implementation of the restructuring plan?
6. How would you address the staffing needs of the school?
7. Would site-based decision making work? If yes, what would be the role of the principal? Of the teachers? Of the community? If no, why not?
8. Would it be advisable to use a model of restructuring such as the Scanlon Plan? Theory Z? Total Quality Management?

JAMES K. WALTER

MICHAEL L. SUPLEY

Case Study Two: Empowered to Make Decisions—Not Always Easy

When the superintendent of 18 years announced his retirement at the beginning of the school year, effective the following summer, the district hoped for a smooth transition. The board of education would have time to carefully screen and interview candidates for the position over the next 9 months. However, this period was soon marked with uncertainty, accusations, and mistrust that resulted in the superintendent's leaving with 2 days' notice early in January before the interview process had fully begun. This period of chaos carried over into teacher negotiations in the spring. The result was an impasse.

The new superintendent was facing a demanding start in her first assignment as superintendent. The board of education was anxious for her to fix the working relationships within the faculty, address the grievances of the classified staff in their first year under a union contract, establish a solid financial base, and begin the process of continuous improvement. She appeared to be a "take charge" kind of individual, and there was little doubt that she would soon gain control of the situation.

CHAPTER 1

In August of that first year she called a working meeting for the school board and building administrators to discuss general guidelines in establishing an understanding of the roles and responsibilities of the board, as well as the administration. However, unlike the previous administrator, her method for discussion was to pose a question and expect full participation from all members at this meeting. To many of the board members, this felt "fuzzy" and unclear, with little direction—just one of those "feel good" meetings.

The first administrative meeting resulted in similar hesitancies. In the past there had been a token attempt at site-based management. Schools had been given some control over building budgets, but only in the areas of supplies and professional development. The new superintendent's expectations were for the building administrators to develop a comprehensive fiscal plan for their buildings based upon goals of continuous improvement for the district. The goal of improved student learning was the common thread. How the principals utilized their budgets to reach that goal was left to the creativity and professional understanding of those individuals.

The building administrators reacted to this challenge in different ways. The high school principal struggled with the freedom of decision making. He performed best with controls, parameters, and clear-cut plans of action. Countless hours were spent in isolation trying to develop a building budget and master schedule that met the expectations of the goals for continuous improvement. High school teachers became disillusioned. They also wanted a plan that was clear and gave them specific guidelines. He presented numerous budgets and schedules to the staff and then to the superintendent, and each time there appeared to be gaps. He resigned his position the following summer.

The middle school and elementary principals approached this challenge in a fashion similar to the way in which the superintendent presented the information. A full staff meeting was held in which the staff discussed the goals of the school. They were then presented the budget and were allowed to determine how best to meet the needs of their students through fiscal planning.

Fiscal planning was only part of the plan. A curriculum audit was also held that first winter. Historically, the district had participated with the rest of the county in developing a common course of study for many years. Results from the audit showed that the curriculum was weak in many areas. Most obvious was the lack of local participation and understanding of curriculum. The following year, the district put 4 days of staff development into the school calendar to address curriculum. Instead of bringing in a speaker or a team of curriculum professionals, the entire district identified across-grade-level curriculum teams, integrating elementary and middle school teachers with high school teachers.

The first curriculum meeting was difficult. Teachers were confused and uncertain what they were supposed to do. It appeared that more questions were being addressed than answers given. Administrators acted as facilitators for the teams, but did not chair them. By the end of the second meeting, professional dialogue on curriculum became more evident in staff meetings. Teachers from this district began to question direction from the county course of study. They became vocal at the county meetings. By the end of the year, each teaching member of the district had contributed toward the development of a curriculum map for the entire district.

The entire school district became involved as community stakeholders with a voice. The district was in line to participate in a state program that would allow the district to build a new K–12 building. As the board of education questioned what direction this process would take, they listened to numerous architectural firms give presentations. The district elected to go with a firm that strongly believed in a community process. The board of education would allow community groups to form various committees and not just act as information groups, but present the board with recommendations that best responded to the desires of the community. This process was perceived by many in the community as "passing the buck." As a consolidated district, the question of where this building would be located was a hot topic. Many individuals wanted the board to make the decision. But a firm commitment by those on the committees allowed them to carefully identify potential sites and develop criteria, with the help of the architects, and then rank those sites. The final selection would come through consensus of those attending a large community meeting.

Conversations About the Case Study

1. How was empowering leadership evident in this case?
2. Describe the ways that teachers were empowered?
3. What role did the community play?

AMY MILLER

REFERENCES

Callahan, R. (1962). *Education and the cult of efficiency.* Chicago: University of Chicago Press.

Center for Educational Reform Website: http://edreform.com.

Frost, C. F., Wakely, J. H., & Ruh, R. A. (1974). *The Scanlon plan for organizational development: Identity, participation, and equity.* East Lansing: Michigan State University Press.

Gerth, H., & Mills, C. W. (1946). *Max Weber: Essays in sociology.* Oxford, England: Oxford University Press.

Goldman, P., & Dunlap D. (1990, October). *Reform, restructuring, site-based management, and the new face of power in schools.* Paper presented at the annual meeting of the University Council for Educational Administration, Pittsburgh, PA.

Greer, J. T. (1993, August). *The autonomous school.* Paper presented at the annual meeting of the National Council of Professors of Educational Administration, Indian Wells, CA.

Greer, J. T., Allen, P. M., & Slawson, A. F. (1994). *Final report to the Danforth Foundation of the Arizona Educational Restructuring Project,* Tucson, AZ.

Johnson, P. E., & Scollay, S. J. (1998). *School-based, decision-making councils: Conflict, leader power, and social influence in vertical teams.* Unpublished manuscript.

Kastle, C. (1990). The public schools and the public mood. *American Heritage, 41*(1), 66–81.

Lesieur, F. G., & Puckett, E. (1958). The Scanlon plan: Past, present, and future. *Proceedings of the Twenty-First Annual Meeting of the Industrial Relations Research Association,* 71–80.

McGregor, D. (1960). *The human side of enterprise.* New York: McGraw-Hill.

National Institute on Student Achievement, Curriculum, and Assessment. (1998). *A national study of charter schools: Executive summary.* Washington, DC: U.S. Office of Education.

Ouchi, W. (1980). *Theory Z: How American business can meet the Japanese challenge.* Reading, MA: Addison-Wesley.

Short, P. M., Greer, J. T., & Melvin, W. M. (1994). Creating empowered schools: Lessons in change. *Journal of Educational Administration, 32*(4), 38–52.

Taylor, F. W. (1916). The principles of scientific management. *Bulletin of the Taylor Society.*

Wohlstetter, P. (1995). Getting school-based management right. *Phi Delta Kappan, 77,* 22–26.

𝕊𝕆

Leadership and School Change

Perhaps the most enigmatic term in the organization theory literature is *leadership*. No concept has intrigued students of administration as much as descriptions of the behaviors of great leaders. One of the earliest of such descriptions highlighted the logistical prowess of Alexander's father, Philip of Macedonia.

Beginning in the 19th century, attention centered on founders and entrepreneurs of the companies that were being formed as part of the Industrial Revolution in the United States. One of the earliest writers to describe the work and behaviors of leaders in corporations was Frederick Taylor (1916). Building upon the work of Taylor were other classical theorists such as Henry Fayol, Mary Parker Follett, and Luther Gulick.

The leadership literature of the 19th century chronicles one discarded approach after another. This history and brief descriptions of research approaches are detailed in the following section.

LEADERSHIP

When a field of study lacks knowledge about a certain variable, this often reflects a paucity of research. Such is not the case with the topic of leadership. No other facet of organizational behavior has received as much attention from researchers. Literally hundreds of studies have been conducted over the years, as well as exhaustive reviews (Stogdill, 1948; Mann, 1959).

The Great Man Studies

The earliest of the leadership studies were labeled *great man studies*. The great man methodology consisted of studying biographies and other descriptions of military, political, and industrial leaders. Authors of the studies conceived of leadership as a set of one-way, directive behaviors through which the leader influenced others to behave in accordance with his wishes. (The use here of the masculine pronoun *his* is not sexist; the great man studies were indeed all studies of men in leadership positions.)

It was thought that by studying the personal qualities of men considered great, it would be possible to identify the universal personality qualities that were possessed by leaders and not by followers. Such information would be important, it was thought, in the identification and selection of future leaders. An important point to note is that the researchers believed that great men possessed natural talents and skills. Such qualities were thought to be inborn qualities that could not be acquired by training or experience.

The effort to find universal qualities of leadership in the biographies of great men proved fruitless. Biographers tended to discuss their subjects from a variety of perspectives without regard to any single list of generic qualities. Rather than warn upcoming researchers that the great man approach was flawed, however, the researchers convinced themselves and others that it was the research methods that were lacking rather than their perspective on leadership.

The Trait Approach

The need for more precise measures of leadership characteristics coincided with the measurement movement in psychology. The result was the *trait approach* to leadership. As with the great man methodology, leadership was conceptualized as a one-way, directive process in which the leader obtained the behavior he required from his followers. Such an outcome was possible, it was assumed, because of the personality traits possessed by the leader that set him apart from his followers.

Initially, long lists of desirable leadership traits were obtained from leaders through the use of questionnaires and interviews. However, personality traits that were deemed desirable in one context would be undesirable in another, and reaching consensus about the most desirable traits was impossible.

Attention was then focused on identifying discriminating leadership traits. In this search various procedures were used: interviews, observations, tests, checklists, and rating scales. From this series of studies, certain traits were found to be in greater evidence among the leaders than the followers. According to Stogdill (1948), who reviewed 124 studies, the leader surpasses the average member of the group in the following five categories of leadership traits:

1. *Capacity* (intelligence, alertness, verbal facility, originality, and judgment).
2. *Achievement* (scholarship, knowledge, and athletic achievement).
3. *Responsibility* (dependability, initiative, persistence, aggressiveness, self-confidence, and desire to excel).
4. *Participation* (activity, sociability, cooperation, adaptability, and humor).
5. *Status* (socio-economic, position, and popularity). (p. 55)

Mann (1959) generally agreed, saying that intelligence, adjustment, and extroversion were highly related to leadership and that dominance, masculinity, and interpersonal sensitivity were positively related.

Criticism of the trait approach was not long in coming. Two major criticisms were noted. The first was similar to the criticisms of the great man approach. The traits identified in well-designed studies were not transferable. A leader in one situation, possessing one or a combination of Stogdill's personality traits, would not necessarily be a leader in another situation. Once again, the trait approach, like the great man approach, did not yield universal leadership characteristics.

The second set of criticisms was focused on the researchers and their methodologies. Essentially, these criticisms centered on the lack of consistency between the measurements of the formal and informal group structures, the insensitivity of the outside observer due to a lack of involvement in the group's activities, and the bias that the social scientist held while making the observations. This last criticism reflected the belief that scientists focused on what they wanted to see rather than on what was actually going on within the group.

Thus, the trait approach foundered because it was based on the assumption that leadership was a one-way, directive process that could be transferred from one situation to another. The work on trait identification, however, was not a total loss. It did identify several personality traits that are still thought to be critical to any leader's success: intelligence, responsibility, and participation.

The Situational Approach

The inability of the trait approach to predict who would be an effective leader in every setting led to a rather emphatic rejection of the study of psychological traits. The attention of students of leadership then turned to the *situation*, which often meant the group or social setting in which leadership was practiced. Characteristics such as group size, homogeneity, stability, satisfaction, and cohesion were measured through observation, interviews with leaders and followers, ratings of performances on simulation exercises, analyses of group procedures, and the use of sociometric instruments. The *situational approach* thus viewed leadership as a composite response to the peculiar characteristics of a given group. Labels such as *potential leadership, permissive leadership,* and *emergent leadership* emerged from this body of research.

The situational approach had the same basic flaw as its predecessors: nontransferability to other settings. If each group was unique, its leader probably could not become a leader of another group because of the second group's unique characteristics.

The Behavioral Approach

The last unified approach to the study of leadership is known as the *behavioral approach*. Its focus is on the behavior of the leader as observed by group members. This approach emerged from the efforts of researchers at The Ohio State University in the early 1950s. Their research took place in a variety of settings, ranging from air crews to school faculties. The instrument used to collect observations of group members became known as the Leadership Behavior Description Questionnaire (LBDQ). The LBDQ obtained group members' observations of their leader on two dimensions: consideration and initiating structure. *Consideration* referred to the leader's relationships with group members, the human relations dimension; *initiating structure* referred to the leader's efforts in organizing the work of the organization, the task dimension. The LBDQ, in its original and expanded versions, remains today the primary research instrument available to gather observations of leadership behavior from group members. Its two-factor description of leadership behavior can be found in nearly all current theories of organizational leadership.

The Contingency Approach

The behavioral approach was not abandoned in the same way that the trait and situational approaches were set aside. Rather the interest in leader behavior merged with earlier thoughts about situational properties and personality traits. Current theories are known generally as *contingency theories*. When asked, "What is a leader?" the contingency theorist would reply, "It depends." Then the theorist would go on to explain that leadership depends on variables such as situation favorableness, task specificity, leader–member relations, leader personality, and group maturity (Fiedler, 1969; Hersey, Blanchard, & Natemeyer, 1979; House & Mitchell, 1974; Tannenbaum & Schmidt, 1973).

An interesting question raised by contingency theorists is whether or not a leader can change administrative style to fit the conditions of a new position. The theorists themselves are divided on this issue. Fiedler (1969) stated that it is not possible for the leader to change his or her style, that it is far better to place a person in a situation in which the person's style (or personality) matches the demands of the situation. Hersey and Blanchard (1977), on the other hand, have stated that as a school faculty matures, the leader can change his or her style to fit the human and task needs of the group.

Of the nine principals in the empowerment study, the writers found only one who could be described as changing his administrative style to accommodate shared governance. Four of the remaining principals entered the project as supporters of empowerment, while the remaining four believed that it was the principal's responsibility to make the decisions in the school. These last four never changed their attitudes regarding full teacher empowerment throughout the course of the project. They did increase the amount of teacher input in their schools, but, in the final analysis, they still believed that the principal had to make the final decision because she or he would be held responsible by the central office officials and the community.

AUTHENTIC LEADERSHIP

Authentic leadership has relevance to creating empowered schools. This concept has its roots in the concepts of stewardship and servant leadership (Duignan & Bhindi, 1997). The concept of authentic leadership challenges the traditional notions of leadership that are more narrowly focused on dominance and manipulation—power *over* rather than power *with* (Duignan & Bhindi, 1997). Block (1993) suggested that authentic leadership focuses on worker empowerment through culture building and decision making. Critical to authentic leadership is the ability to build a trusting environment through stewardship, whereby something is held in trust for another and leaders are held accountable for their use of power (Block, 1993). Furthermore, Duignan and Macpherson (1992) suggested that authentic leadership is tightly connected to asking questions about what is significant and what is right. Leaders must fully understand their own values and beliefs and must reflect upon those as they make choices and build relationships with faculty and students.

ASSESSING LEADERSHIP

Research on leadership has led to the development of instruments for assessing the leadership of individuals in organizations. One of the benefits of this assessment is to better understand how certain elements of various types of leadership impact the organization. It is also true that leaders benefit from knowledge about their own leadership through self-assessment as well as the perceptions of those who share leadership within the organization.

Leadership assessment is critical for those who wish to create empowered schools. Feedback from school participants on the principal's leadership provides the principal with important data about how he or she is exercising influence with others in the school. Examples of two excellent leadership assessment instruments are provided in Figures 2.1 and 2.2.

The Leadership Orientation Survey (Bolman & Deal, 1990) is a highly useful instrument based on research the authors have conducted that suggests that leaders' views of their organizations influence the

Directions: Please indicate on the scale below *how often* each of the items below is true of you:

1	2	3	4	5
Never	Occasionally	Sometimes	Often	Always

_____ 1. Think very clearly and logically.

_____ 2. Show high levels of support and concern for others.

_____ 3. Have exceptional ability to mobilize people and resources to get things done.

_____ 4. Inspire others to do their best.

_____ 5. Strongly emphasize careful planning and clear time lines.

_____ 6. Build trust through open and collaborative relationships.

_____ 7. Am a very skilled and shrewd negotiator.

_____ 8. Am highly charismatic.

_____ 9. Approach problems through logical analysis and careful thinking.

Note. Excerpted by permission of the authors from *Leadership Orientations,* © 1990, by Lee G. Bolman and Terrence E. Deal.

Figure 2.1
Excerpt from the leadership orientation survey.

The following statements are descriptions of leadership that may or may not reflect leadership practices in your school. You are asked to indicate the extent to which you agree that each statement describes leadership in your school as you experience it.

Indicate the extent to which you agree with each statement by circling ONE of the codes: SD = Strongly Disagree; D = Disagree; A = Agree; SA = Strongly Agree; NA = Not Applicable. (Try to use NA as infrequently as possible.)

TO WHAT EXTENT DO YOU AGREE THAT THE PRINCIPAL IN YOUR SCHOOL:

1. Excites us with visions of what we may be able to accomplish if we work together to change our practices/programs.   SD   D   A   SA   NA

2. Encourages us to work toward the same goals.   SD   D   A   SA   NA

3. Expects us to be effective innovators.   SD   D   A   SA   NA

4. Leads by "doing" rather than by simply "telling."   SD   D   A   SA   NA

5. Provides for adequate training to develop my knowledge and skills.   SD   D   A   SA   NA

6. Encourages me to reexamine some basic assumptions I have about my work.   SD   D   A   SA   NA

7. Gives high priority to developing within the school a shared set of values, beliefs, and attitudes related to teaching and learning.   SD   D   A   SA   NA

8. Distributes leadership broadly among the staff, representing various viewpoints in leadership positions.   SD   D   A   SA   NA

Note. From *The Nature of Leadership* by K. Leithwood and D. Jantzi, 1994. Ontario Institute for the Study of Education, University of Toronto.

Figure 2.2
Excerpt from the Nature of Leadership questionnaire.

ways they frame problems and issues and the ways they exercise influence. Research by Short, Rinehart, and Eckley (1999) indicates that principals who view their schools from Bolman and Deal's (1990) human relations and symbolic/cultural frames are regarded by their faculties as being more empowering than principals with different perspectives.

The Nature of Leadership questionnaire (Leithwood & Jantzi, 1994) is used to assess teachers' perceptions of their principals' transformational leadership behaviors. This 43-item instrument measures the nine dimensions of transformational leadership: develops a widely shared vision for the school; builds consensus about school goals and priorities; holds high performance expectations; models effective behavior; provides individualized support; provides intellectual stimulation; builds a collaborative culture; provides a structure for participative decision-making; and provides contingent rewards.

ORGANIZATIONAL CHANGE

Historical Perspective

The interest in change is a relatively recent addition to the literature of educational administration. Intense interest can be traced to the enactment of the National Defense Education Act of 1958 (NDEA). NDEA proved nationalism to be alive and well in the United States. It was a reaction to the launching of the first Russian satellite, Sputnik, in October of 1957. The general reaction within the United States was that the reason for the Russian success was that the United States had not produced a sufficient number of high-quality scientists over the years. To rectify the problem, the science and mathematics curricula of the nation's secondary schools needed to be revamped. Study teams consisting of university-based scholars, curriculum specialists in science and mathematics, and classroom teachers met together during much of the late 1950s to produce the revised curricular programs. A sample of these programs reads like acronym heaven: BSCS (biology), PSSC (physics), CHEMS (chemistry), and NMSG (mathematics).

The new programs were widely adopted throughout the nation during the early 1960s. One reason for their instant popularity was the makeup of the study teams. University personnel were working closely with school personnel to produce programs based on the latest knowledge in the subject fields. Furthermore, the newly produced materials were pilot tested and revised over the first years to ensure that the materials and instructional approaches were appropriate for secondary science and mathematics students.

Calls for evaluating the effectiveness of the new programs began shortly after their initiation. A number of post facto studies of the new programs were completed. The data were discouraging in the sense that the new programs did not seem to be living up to the expectations of the developers. The reasons for the lack of success, however, were elusive (Gross, Giacquinta, & Bernstein, 1971). Most studies suggested that change could not be conducted in a school on a piecemeal basis. A dramatic program change in one department had to be supported by the entire school, or the effort would surely fail.

A second major finding of the evaluative studies was that the designers of the new programs had failed to establish a level that would designate when the new program was fully implemented. An example of such a level would be to declare that implementation was complete when the teachers of the department were using the new curriculum materials at least 80% of the time. Without such a preestablished level, program developers could not establish the reason for a program's lack of success. Was it because the program was never fully implemented? Or was it because the program was seriously flawed?

These findings drew students of educational organizations to seek greater understanding of the change process from the work of social scientists (Bennis, Benne, & Chin, 1969). The use of such materials helped educators to enlarge their perspectives of educational change and to see such change as a deliberate process that must be carefully planned (Herriott & Gross, 1979; Schmuck & Runkel, 1972).

A number of generalizations regarding the change process were drawn. There was general agreement that the organization had to be viewed as a system. A change in any part of the system would affect all parts of the system. In addition, educators recognized that for an innovation to be successful, it had to be fully supported by the organization's leadership, and they noted that organizations that had been successful innovators in the past were more likely to be successful innovators in the future.

Another generalization was that successful implementation of an innovation depended on the extent to which individuals changed their behavior. Since attitudes were seen as the basis for a person's behavior, it was thought that if attitudes could first be changed, a person's behavior would readily change and the desired result would be more likely. It was also recognized that people move through the stages of attitudinal change and behavior change at different rates. It could not be assumed that every member of a group would come to support a change at the same time as every other member. Change was seen as painful and stress producing for those involved. Persons are more willing to be involved in a change effort, however, when they see the need for the change and are involved in planning the effort.

Problems in Creating Change

Attempts to create change are replete with problems. Fullen and Miles (1992) suggested the following seven reasons why change may not work:

1. *Faulty maps of change.* Principals have a personal map about how change occurs. Those maps influence the way principals approach change.

2. *Difficult solutions.* A school is a complex system, and attempts at change are more complex.

3. *Symbolic over substantive efforts.* It appears easier to adopt initiatives packaged outside the organization than to work collaboratively within the organization on hard-to-solve issues.

4. *Superficial solutions.* Schools become impatient in change efforts and may opt for surface changes rather than substantive change.

5. *Misunderstanding of resistance.* Change agents may label as "resistance" what is really another issue, such as lack of technical skills, insufficient resources for change, or diffuse objectives.

6. *Failure to institutionalize change.* Schools may fail to support pockets of progress toward actual change in structures, procedures, and culture.

7. *Misuse of knowledge of the change process.* Change agents sometimes use half-truths to implement change.

Change Strategies of the Leader

The interest in organizational change has been accompanied by an interest in leaders' effective change strategies. In many respects, it may be helpful to consider leader change strategies alongside the leader personality traits discussed earlier in the chapter. The major difference, however, is that, unlike personality traits, the leader change strategies identified in the organizational change literature appear to be available to any leader. No single leader is thought to be stuck forever with a single change strategy. Rather, the leader may choose whichever strategy appears to be the most appropriate for the task at hand.

The foremost classification of change strategies was developed by Chin and Benne (1969). They described three types of strategies: empirical-rational, normative-reeducative, and power-coercive. All of the strategies involved some type of change agent and utilized some type of knowledge as a means of modifying practice.

The *empirical-rational strategy* is based on the assumption that persons are rational and they will decide on a course of action that is in their best interest when such a course is justified with objective evidence. Essentially, the role of the change agent/leader is to assemble and present the necessary information to the group, and the members will choose the course of action suggested by the data. No coercion is needed by the leader. The strategy assumes that rational persons will be persuaded by rational knowledge.

The *normative-reeducative strategy* is essentially a group consensus strategy. Although rational knowledge is not rejected within the strategy, it is not as important in changing the behavior of individuals as are the norms of the group, which govern patterns of action and practice. Changes in group norms require changes in attitudes, values, skills, and relationships. Such changes come about through group activity, which may be initiated, but not ruled by, the change agent/leader.

The *power-coercive strategy* is based on the application of power by the change agent/leader. Such power may be available to the change agent/leader for a number of reasons: the person's position in the organization, the knowledge and experience the person possesses, or the person's control of rewards. The essence of the strategy is the influence of those with more power over those with less.

The Chin and Benne topology of change strategies has been used to study the change strategies of leaders. Watson (1975), in studying the implementation of new curriculum programs, found few instances where leaders utilized only one strategy. Far more frequent was the use of two or even all three strategies, depending on the problem to be solved or the behavior to be changed.

In brief, this review reflects the organizational change literature as of the mid-to-late 1970s. Generalizations about how members of organizations responded to change efforts were available, as was information about the strategies that a change agent/leader might use to conduct a change effort. Yet there was also a great suspicion that the available knowledge regarding change was not sufficient to guide a change effort in any particular school. Only generalizations were available, and they might or might not be relevant to a school's change project.

It was at this point that a landmark study was published by Cusick (1973). This study focused on what came to be known as the *culture* of the school. Simultaneously, organizational culture was being rigorously studied by a number of social scientists. As with the earlier interest in organizational change, the perspective of educators was enhanced by the work of scholars in other disciplines.

Fullen and Miles (1992) suggested the following seven propositions for successful change:

1. *Change is learning,* loaded with uncertainty. Even well-developed innovation requires new meaning and new learning.

2. *Change is a journey,* not a blueprint. Change efforts are continually shaped, revisited, and considered.

3. *Problems are our friends.* One cannot build effective solutions to complex situations unless one confronts difficult problems that exist.

4. *Change is resource hungry.* Change efforts require extra time, energy, money, patience, and fortitude.

5. *Change requires power to manage it.* Change efforts require attention to monitoring, linking, communication, problem solving, and taking action.

6. *Change is systemic.* Change efforts must focus on cultural change and the development and interrelationships of curriculum, teaching, and teacher development.

7. *Large-scale change is implemented locally.* Local implementation of change efforts by teachers, principals, parents, and students is the only way change happens.

ORGANIZATIONAL CULTURE

The broad concept of culture has been a topic for behavioral scientists throughout the century. For the most part, the scientists have focused on collectives of people: groups, societies, nations, and so forth. During the 1970s, the scientists' attention turned to organizations and their distinct cultures. They found that no company or business had a culture like that of any other company or business.

Just as companies and businesses do, schools have unique cultures. Following Cusick's (1973) study, literally hundreds of qualitative studies of American schools were completed. Each documented the uniqueness of the subject school even when the school was compared with other schools of the same school district and subject to the same state regulations, board of education policies, and central office mandates. The defining difference was *school culture*, a term borrowed from organization theorists and popularized during the 1980s and 1990s by education writers including Cusick (1987); Deal and Kennedy (1982); Erickson (1987); Kilman, Saxton, and Serpa (1985); and Willower (1984).

Definition of School Culture

Willower (1984) described the school's culture as its essence, composed of its traditions, beliefs, policies, and norms. Schein (1992) defined the culture of an organization as the basic assumptions the organization made as it struggled with internal and external forces—assumptions that had worked well enough to be taught to new members of the organization.

Nurturing the School Culture

The shaping, enhancement, and maintenance of a school's culture are primary responsibilities of the school's leaders. A portion of these responsibilities is fulfilled as the leaders induct new members into the school (Schein, 1992). The induction process is conducted in several ways: formally, in orientation sessions led by the principal and other leaders; informally, through interactions with experienced staff members; and with written documents such as public relations releases, descriptive brochures, and the like.

Benefits to Staff Members

One of the functions of the culture is to provide security to staff members. It protects them from internal and external forces that the members alone could not withstand. As long as the members do not violate the strictures of the culture and accept its standards for personal behavior, they can expect acceptance and support. Some would call such behavior "getting along," as apt a description as any. Essentially, one who is in harmony with the school's culture can expect to always be welcome in the organization. One who chooses to ignore or clash with the culture can expect a lonely and sometimes difficult future.

The all-pervasiveness of the culture is the most important factor to consider. The culture conditions the degrees of freedom for administrators and teachers alike. It is a powerful force that the leader contemplating a change in the school must never forget. The culture can make the change effort a success or a failure.

Modifying the School Culture

Schein (1992) described three levels of an organization's culture. Listed from the most visible to the least visible, they are:

1. *Artifacts* (visible organizational structures and processes).

2. *Espoused values* (strategies, goals, and philosophies).

3. *Basic underlying assumptions* (unconscious, taken-for-granted beliefs, perceptions, thoughts, and feelings).

The first two levels are reasonably easy for the leader to address. The artifacts and espoused values are visible to all. Applying some combination of the Chin and Benne (1969) change strategies will quite likely result in changing these elements of the culture.

Changing the culture can become treacherous, however, when the contemplated change is perceived as a threat to one or more of the underlying assumptions of the culture. The unknowing leader may violate such assumptions and not even be aware of what has been done. Needless to say, when the leader and the proposed change challenge an underlying assumption, it will be difficult to implement it successfully. Teachers and members of the staff will resist the proposal, often not even understanding what prompts their resistance.

A proposed change is even less likely to occur when it is initiated from outside of the school. The literature is filled with reports of reform measures mandated by state or federal officials that have not been successful. It is almost a certainty that such changes would violate at least one of the underlying cultural assumptions of every targeted school. Resistance to change, therefore, would be inevitable.

∞ CASE STUDY

Murray High School: Changing a School's Culture

Murray, Utah, is located in the middle of the Salt Lake valley. When it was founded, it was several miles from Salt Lake City, but the city has grown to surround Murray. Nevertheless, Murray retains its identity as an incorporated community with its own city government and school system. There is a single high school serving all of Murray's students. A middle school and several elementary schools complete the inventory of school buildings serving the district.

The principal of Murray High School is Richard Tranter. Richard was raised in Murray and attended the district schools, including the high school. Following graduation from college, Richard began his education career as a teacher at Murray High School. After several years in the classroom, Richard was appointed as an elementary school principal in the district. From this position, he was appointed as principal of the high school upon the retirement of his predecessor, a veteran principal for 17 years.

Richard had many positive attributes as principal. He was young, energetic, and absolutely dedicated to the future of Murray High School. Having been both a student and a teacher at the high school, Richard was well acquainted with the school's culture and its basic assumptions. He also had served under his predecessor as a teacher and was familiar with the man's approach to the principalship and his administrative style. Outside of the school, Richard was well acquainted with the community and its members. He was highly regarded as an educational leader throughout the community.

However, Richard also carried some heavy baggage as he assumed the principalship of the high school. It had not been many years since he had been a student at the school, and many of the faculty had been his teachers. An even shorter period of time had elapsed since Richard was a member of the faculty.

Shortly after Richard began his principalship of the high school, the school was invited to participate in the empowerment study described in this book. Richard welcomed this invitation, for his natural administrative style differed dramatically from his predecessor's traditional style. In conversations during the 3 years of the project, Richard explained that empowerment was a part of his basic beliefs. He was first exposed to empowerment when he served as the assistant to the mission president during his 2-year mission. Richard explained that the mission president was the most empowering person he ever knew.

Later, as a teacher, he encountered a number of nonempowering principals and couldn't understand why principals had difficulty understanding that they were on the same side as teachers. From the positive model of the president and the negative models of former principals, Richard began his principalship as a believer in teacher empowerment.

As a part of the national empowerment study and because he held positive beliefs about empowerment, Richard's major problem was to change the culture of the school from one created by an autocrat who made the governance decisions to one that supported participation and collaborative decision making. All of this would be a gigantic task even for a principal who had no earlier ties to the school. For Richard, a former student and peer, the task was even greater. There would always be some teachers who would think of Richard as their student rather than the leader. Others would see him as a colleague and resist his leadership initiatives.

Following several faculty meetings in which the empowerment effort was explained and discussed, the faculty warmly endorsed the effort. A steering committee of influential faculty members was established to set the direction of the project. In addition to being a member of the steering committee, Richard embarked on a series of private individual meetings with the faculty members. The purposes of the meetings were to help the faculty members better understand empowerment and to identify which issues and projects needed to be addressed first by the school staff. Interestingly, the first project was a general cleanup of the school. It seems that the community portions of the building (the auditorium, sports facilities, and so forth) had received a great deal of attention over the years, but the academic classrooms, halls, and laboratories in the back of the school were sadly neglected. Over the summer, these areas were refurbished.

From nearly the beginning of the project, Richard adopted a pattern of working with faculty members that demonstrated his willingness to share the decision-making responsibility with the staff. He used the simple device of throwing a question asked by a faculty member back to the faculty member. After a faculty member would ask a question, Richard's response would be, "What do you think we should do?" When the teacher outlined a course of action, Richard would put the suggestion into action if the suggestion was legally and educationally defensible. It did not take long for the word to spread throughout the faculty that Richard was serious about empowerment and that he believed teachers' opinions did make a difference.

A note regarding teacher participation in empowerment is necessary at this point. Recall that, during the initial empowerment meetings, the idea of empowerment was warmly endorsed by the faculty. Following this burst of enthusiasm, the actual number of faculty members who participated in planning the school's future and making decisions dropped until the number of true believers in empowerment included only the original steering committee and a few others. Over the 3-year course of the project, however, the number of participants grew steadily. Somewhere toward the end of the second year, Richard indicated that the number of faculty members participating in the empowerment committee had grown to the extent that the empowerment effort had established its own momentum. The school had acquired the "critical mass" necessary in all school-wide change efforts.

Following the cleanup of the school, the faculty indicated that academic achievement should be celebrated within the school just as athletic achievement was honored. Trophy cases were set aside to recognize outstanding scholars, lists of high achievers were prominently displayed on bulletin boards in the community portions of the building, weekly luncheons with the principal honored other high-achieving students, and those identified by their teachers received congratulatory notes from Richard.

The empowered teachers quickly initiated other programs that focused on improving the academic program. The graduation requirements of the State of Utah included one and one-half credits in art, three credits in history and two credits in other academic areas. Program planning was made difficult by the extra one-half credit in art and the third credit in history. The Murray faculty proposed that the requirements be changed to one credit in art and two in history. The remaining one and one-half credits would then be earned in courses related to the students' career objectives or college entrance requirements. The single requirement for the one and one-half units was that they must be earned in academic disciplines.

Richard and the faculty discussed the changes with the district superintendent, who then took the request to state department officials. The state superintendent granted a waiver, and the change advocated by the faculty became official for Murray students. Members of the accrediting association visiting committee expressed criticism of the change, but the faculty was able to defend the decision to the committee's satisfaction.

Another change advocated by the faculty was a change in the school schedule. The teachers studied almost every high school schedule available and found none to their liking. They decided to construct a schedule of their own. The schedule that emerged consists of regular seven-period days on Monday, Thursday, and Friday. On Tuesday and Wednesday, the schedule consists of four 90-minute periods. The last 90-minute period on Wednesday is a "student's choice" period. All of the teachers are in their classrooms during this period to help whoever comes in. Some teachers announce beforehand that they will be focusing on specific topics during the period (for example, if a major test is scheduled in the near future); others might invite lower-achieving students to come in for extra help (and give extra credit); and still others will simply be available to provide whatever assistance a student requests. Students may go to as many classrooms as they wish during the 90-minute period, or they may leave the campus. The faculty and students have been very satisfied with the new schedule. It provides for longer laboratory periods and responds to individual student needs.

In the years following the official end to the empowerment project, Richard and the faculty have continued to work on improving students' academic opportunities. The most recent effort is called "Renaissance Vision." This program was begun with a retreat organized by Richard and the faculty and included teachers, parents, and business leaders. They addressed the question of what to do to help students academically. The program that resulted targeted students, teachers, programs, the school building, and the citizen boosters of the school.

Renaissance Vision at Murray High School is an effort to improve the school by improving its image in the eyes of those in the school and others throughout the community. Academically, the recognition programs for high achievers have been expanded, and new programs have been initiated for underserved students. Recognition programs and other perks make the faculty's work more visible and enjoyable. The building and grounds continue to be upgraded and made more comfortable. Most important, all of the constituencies of the school (alumni, parents, other citizens, and business leaders) are drawn into the program and invited to participate.

The empowerment program at Murray High School is finished. Richard and the faculty, however, see Renaissance Vision as the second generation of the empowerment effort, and shared governance is alive and well at the school. When asked retrospectively how difficult it was for him to accept the decisions made by the teachers, Richard replied that early in the project it was difficult for him to accept a shaky decision and one that he would not make himself. But he forced himself to go along with such decisions and to trust that things would work out. Now he believes that those shaky faculty decisions were probably better than those he would have made by himself.

∞ VOICES FROM THE FIELD

Teacher Empowerment at Weller Elementary School

At Weller Elementary School in Springfield, Missouri, teacher empowerment is seen through the Accelerated Schools cadre process. Teachers meet regularly in cadres that focus on improving student achievement in reading, writing, and math. The cadres conduct needs assessments, establish priorities to determine the most urgent needs, and form and evaluate action plans. The cadres report to a steering committee made up of teachers, parents, community members, and the principal. As a result, there is a constant conversation occurring at school about the instructional and curricular processes in place.

When teachers attended a literacy conference and returned with new ideas for individualized instruction in reading and language arts, support was given to develop their new knowledge. Books were purchased, and time was given to code the books according to reading levels. Teachers used their own time to create a checkout system so all books could be shared.

The collaborative process continued as the cadres met and looked at data. Continued collaboration with Title I and classroom teachers extended the professional development, and as a result a common language was developed to use when teaching reading. Significant gains in reading levels of first graders were an indication that this process enhanced learning.

When a new textbook adoption was implemented, the teachers collaborated on ways to maintain their integrity as professionals while they met district guidelines of accountability. It was a difficult year, and a challenge to teacher empowerment, because regulations imposed on them threatened their professionalism and autonomy. However, they were able to find areas where they agreed with the district, and they focused on the strategies they knew worked with students. The teachers reported that they felt ahead of the game because they had already implemented many of the strategies being promoted by the new adoption.

A culture of empowerment exists at Weller Elementary School as teachers' ideas are incorporated into the school's everyday life. The teachers and the librarian implemented a new program for using the library as a resource for research, rather than just as a library class. After several meetings, teachers agreed to schedule flexible times with the librarian, giving up their weekly one-half hour of scheduled library time. The flexible time would be used to develop research projects, which would be team-taught by the classroom teacher and the librarian. Although the teachers were willing to give up their one-half hour of release time, it was unnecessary to do so because the computer instructor was able to provide a half hour of classroom computer time to compensate.

The teachers wanted to redecorate the library to signal the changes that were occurring. The librarian and principal discussed the fact that this was a nonessential part of the new approach to the use of the library, but they agreed that teacher input was an important part of the process. The staff spent part of 2 days, with some substitutes provided and some time being volunteered during teachers' normal release time, moving furniture, bookshelves, and computers. In a true collaborative spirit, the custodian jumped in and did the major moving of large furniture pieces, and the principal helped to unload shelves and move books to their new home. The end result was a library that provided more spaces for individual reading and small-group work and a feeling of pride in accomplishment by all the staff.

Although the redecoration of the library was not a part of the philosophy of the library program, it provided a common cause to help initiate a successful program. The librarian was able to give up ownership of the library, and the results were seen in increased collaboration and teaming. Students benefited from this effort and produced written, verbal, and media-generated reports.

NANCY COLBAUGH

Leadership, Autonomy, and Trust

With the beginning of the 1999–2000 school year, I started in a new position. I had been named the new assistant principal for the middle school building where I had spent the previous 2 years as a sixth-grade teacher. Prior to that, I had taught in the district for 8 years. The least of my concerns at this point was gaining the trust of the teaching staff. In my opinion, I had already earned their trust by being one of them. I knew their concerns and frustrations because I had lived those same concerns and frustrations right alongside my colleagues. This was a mistaken belief, however. What became apparent very quickly was that I was no longer viewed as "one of them." It was as though I had changed teams in the middle of the game. To have the trust and respect of the teaching staff, I would have to earn it.

Leadership style became very important. I had to prove that I valued the input, decision-making ability, and commitment of the staff in my new capacity as an educational leader, just as I had as their colleague. The first year was difficult. I felt as though I was being viewed with suspicion and distrust. I had to prove that my belief in teamwork and cooperative leadership was sincere. In other words, I had to demonstrate that my exposed beliefs were my true beliefs. I had to prove that I was not an "office" principal. To do this, I made a sincere effort to be in the classrooms and hallways as much as possible. Teachers were asked to form teams to revise scheduling, curriculum, student discipline codes, and other issues important to the staff. I acted as a liaison to the central office. Trust and autonomy are being developed through a relationship of professional respect and an understanding of the importance of team building. We still have a long way to go to achieve the level of trust and autonomy I had hoped for; however, we are making progress.

DEBORAH A. MYRACLE

REFERENCES

Bennis, W. G., Benne, K. D., & Chin, R. (Eds.). (1969). *The planning of change* (2nd ed.). New York: Holt, Rinehart, and Winston.

Bolman, L. G., & Deal, T. E. (1990). *Leadership orientations.*

Block, P. (1993). *Stewardship: Choosing service over self-interest.* San Francisco: Berrett-Koehler.

Chin, R., & Benne, K. D. (1969). General strategies for effecting changes in human systems. In W. G. Bennis, K. D. Benne, & R. Chin (Eds.), *The planning of change* (2nd ed., pp. 85–110). New York: Holt, Rinehart, and Winston.

Cusick, P. A. (1973). *Inside high school: The student's world.* New York: Holt, Rinehart and Winston.

Cusick, P. A. (Ed.). (1987). Organizational culture and schools. *Educational Administration Quarterly, 23*(4), 486–499.

Deal, T. A., & Kennedy, A. A. (1982). *Corporate cultures.* Reading, MA: Addison-Wesley.

Duignan, P. A., & Bhindi, N. (1997). Authenticity in leadership: An emerging perspective. *Journal of Educational Administration, 35,* 195–209.

Duignan, P. A., & Macpherson, R. J. S. (1992). *Educative leadership: A practical theory for new administrators and managers.* London: Falmer.

Erickson, F. (1987). Conceptions of school culture: An overview. In P. A. Cusick (Ed.), Organizational culture and schools. *Educational Administration Quarterly, 23*(4), 11–24.

Fiedler, F. E. (1969). Style or circumstance: The leadership enigma. *Psychology Today, 3*(4), 38–43.

Fullen, M. G., & Miles, M. B. (1992). Getting reform right: What works and what doesn't. *Phi Delta Kappan, 74,* 745–752.

Gross, N., Giacquinta, J. B., & Bernstein, M. (1971). *Implementing educational innovations: A sociological analysis of planned educational change.* New York: Basic Books.

Herriott, R. E., & Gross, N. (Eds). (1979). *The dynamics of planned educational change.* Berkeley, CA: McCutchan.

Hersey, P., & Blanchard, K. H. (1977). *Management of organizational behavior: Utilizing human resources.* Upper Saddle River, NJ: Prentice-Hall.

Hersey, P., Blanchard, K. H., & Natemeyer, W. E. (1979). Situational leadership, perception, and the impact of power. *Group and Organization Studies, 4,* 418–428.

House, R. J., & Mitchell, T. R. (1974). Path-goal theory of leadership. *Journal of Contemporary Business, 10*(3), 81–97.

Kilman, R. H., Saxton, M. J., & Serpa, R. (1985). *Gaining control of the corporate culture.* San Francisco: Jossey-Bass.

Leithwood, K., & Jantzi, D. (1994). *The nature of leadership.* Toronto: University of Toronto, Ontario Institute for the Study of Education.

Mann, R. D. (1959). A review of the relationships between personality and performance in small groups. *Psychological Bulletin, 56,* 241–268.

Schein, E. H. (1992). *Organizational culture and leadership* (2nd ed.). San Francisco: Jossey-Bass.

Schmuck, R. A., & Runkel, P. J. (1972). *Handbook of organizational development in schools.* Washington, DC: National Press Books.

Short, P. M., Rinehart, J. R., & Eckley, M. (1999). The relationship of teacher empowerment and principal leadership. *Educational Research Quarterly, 22*(4), 45–52.

Stogdill, R. M. (1948). Personal factors associated with leadership: A survey of the literature. *The Journal of Psychology, 25,* 35–71.

Tannenbaum, R., & Schmidt, W. H. (1973). How to choose a leadership pattern. *Harvard Business Review, 51*(3), 162–180.

Taylor, F. W. (1916). The principles of scientific management. *Bulletin of the Taylor Society.*

Watson, L. R. (1975). *The relationship between perceived change strategy and the successful implementation of an innovation.* Unpublished doctoral dissertation, Georgia State University, Atlanta.

Willower, D. J. (1984). School principals, school cultures, and school improvement. *Educational Horizons, 63*(1), 35–38.

CHAPTER 3

℘

Focusing and Structuring Processes

In the two national studies featured in this book, the overriding issue became the importance of a school's freedom to make the decisions necessary to best serve that school's students. The Empowered School District Project required participating districts to issue letters—signed by the superintendent and the president of the board of education—giving the project schools freedom to plan their own staff development activities, make scheduling and curricular decisions, reorganize programs, and operate with a great deal of autonomy in approaching change. For the most part, these original agreements were honored throughout the 3 years of the project. Exceptions were noted when dramatic changes in school board membership occurred or when the superintendent left the district.

No such agreements were made with the districts participating in the Arizona Restructuring Project. The differences in the autonomy given to individual schools were, therefore, marked. In one Arizona district, the superintendent who participated in the project's organizing conference and gave public support to the school's participation withdrew her support midway through the first year of the project. She took this startling action after the school had planned its initial multiage, multigrade classroom. The reason given was that an outside curriculum consultant to the district had indicated that not one of the district's schools was ready for multiage, multigrade classrooms.

Other schools in the Arizona project experienced a variety of problems; superintendents and other central office personnel either showed indifference to the efforts being made in the experimental schools or erected barriers to the schools' autonomy. Of the two problems caused by central office administrators, indifference was the most damaging. The usual scenario was that the experimental school was given no flexibility or room to maneuver. It was expected to follow the district regulations and conduct the district-wide programs just like any other school in the district. The central office simply ignored the unique requirements of the project school; its staff behaved as though nothing special was happening in the school.

Fortunately, such conditions did not prevail in most of the districts. Superintendents and board members were impressed with the aims of the project and supported the experiment insofar as resources allowed. Nevertheless, complete building autonomy was a rarity among the 26 schools included in the two projects. It occurred naturally only when a particular school was the only high school in the district. Then the school could make the decisions and establish the programs it felt were needed.

The other condition that allowed a school to have autonomy was when the school was so completely supported by its community that the superintendent and central office dared not interfere with its operations. The best example of such a situation was Abraham Lincoln High School in Denver. The school is highlighted several times in this chapter.

The essential fact learned in the two studies was that a school that wishes to experiment must be allowed freedom to do so. If the project is teacher empowerment, the school must have control over the basic budget, personnel, and program decisions, or shared governance becomes an exercise in futility that will destroy the morale of the principal and staff alike. If the project is restructuring, the benchmarks and standards established for the district's graded schools serve to confound the effort. New structures require measures and standards that reflect the school's new reality.

VISION AND GOALS

Vision is a word that has become popular in the literature since the publication of *Leaders: The Strategies for Taking Charge* (Bennis & Nanus, 1985). In it the authors argued forcefully that an important characteristic of leaders is that they have a vision for their organizations.

In our two national studies the emphasis was on developing a shared vision, one that was common to teachers, members of the school community, and the school leader. As described in the case study in Chapter 2, Richard Tranter was able to share the governance responsibility with the staff of Murray High School. Once the staff accepted its role in establishing the school's direction, a vision began to take shape of a school in which the scholar would be celebrated in the same way as the athlete, musician, or actor. For nearly 5 years, this vision has served as a kind of Rosetta Stone for the school. It has established the programs and activities that will be given the highest priority and necessary resources.

Abraham Lincoln High School in Denver provides another, even more vivid, example of the process that leads to a shared vision for a school. Prior to being selected for the empowerment study, the school had begun to look at itself. The principal during this period was Christine Johnson, who earlier had served as an assistant principal at the school and then as a middle school principal in the district. Upon the retirement of Lincoln's veteran principal of 14 years, Christine applied and was appointed as the school's new principal. Abraham Lincoln served a multiethnic community located in a low socioeconomic section of the city. The neighborhood was not an inner-city ghetto but was a community of very modest homes and apartments. In most families, one or both parents worked at service-oriented, low-paying jobs. Others were employed in light industries in Denver, usually holding blue-collar jobs.

Reflecting on the number of ethnic groups represented in the student body, Christine and the staff described the school as the United Nations School of the district. It was a well-run school, orderly, and without any major drug or discipline problems. But Christine observed that there was little interaction between the school and its community. The school lacked energy and vitality; there was no sense of mission.

As Christine began her tenure as principal, she did so knowing the school was okay but could be better. Dropout rates were high, and graduation rates were low. The school was organized much like any other high school and offered programs found in all the district's schools.

In Christine's mind, Abraham Lincoln needed to develop a sense of mission that was shared by all of its constituencies. Her approach was to appoint a task force named the "Think Tank." The Think Tank consisted of 16 carefully selected teachers and 2 businesspeople from the community. One of the businesspeople was an executive of Gates Rubber Company, which was located in the school's attendance area. The other was the president of a small liberal arts college also located in the school community. The Think Tank's 18 members met regularly throughout the first year. Their single topic was school improvement, and numerous readings were distributed and discussed at their meetings.

At the end of the first year, the think tank had a 1-week retreat at a nearby ski resort and invited additional businesspeople to attend. The purposes of the retreat were to create a mission or shared vision for the school and to design strategies for involving the rest of the faculty and parents from the school community. Both tasks were addressed in numerous brainstorming sessions throughout the week. The shared vision that emerged focused on students. The participants recognized that the school was not doing all that it could do to serve the learning needs of all of its students. Forcing them to enroll in the same diploma programs offered in high schools throughout the district created "sink or swim" conditions for Abraham Lincoln's students, and, unfortunately, too many were sinking.

Murray and Abraham Lincoln High Schools were not the only schools in the empowerment project to have developed a shared vision. They are used here because they are good examples of how important a shared vision is in building a consensus among a school's constituencies and in illuminating the pathway to the school's future.

Underlying Values and Beliefs

Embedded in a school's vision is a collection of values and beliefs. Often these remain unspoken and unexamined unless a skillful group facilitator helps the group to explore the subtleties of a particular set of values. The process of revealing the beliefs undergirding a proposed course of action helps participants to build a high level of commitment to the new program or effort, even though this process may be personally painful.

The Arizona study of multiage, multigrade classrooms began with a presentation of our beliefs about learning and classroom learning strategies. How each school designed its multiage, multigrade classrooms, however, was a choice made within each school. For example, the school could use teams of teachers or individual teachers in its experimental classrooms. It could also choose which grades would be included and the instructional materials that would be used.

The beliefs that structured the entire project were based on a rejection of the traditional model of American schools in which the graded school system is like a factory, wherein a group of students arrive at a classroom to receive a teacher's ministrations for a 9-month period. At the conclusion of the period, the group is moved along to another teacher and the ministration cycle is repeated. Students who fall off the assembly line and fail to measure up are simply recycled through the 9-month cycle, and no further organizational response is required.

FOCUSING AND STRUCTURING PROCESSES

The Arizona Restructuring Project used a different model. The project's metaphor was the family. In a family, an adult guides, leads, teaches, and nurtures the children over a period of years. Young children enter the family and leave it, years later, more mature and better able to face life's exigencies. During the time a child is in the family, he or she learns from the older children and, in turn, teaches the younger children. Above all, there are always people who look out for one another, protect each other, and make certain that no family member becomes lost or forgotten.

The classrooms in the Arizona Project schools were designed to have the following family attributes: (a) An adult works with a child for 3 years or longer; (b) younger students enter in the fall of the school year and older students typically leave in the spring; and (c) students learn academic, leadership, and other skills from other students as well as from the teacher. Also, in these classrooms (a) traditional promotion and failure processes are eliminated; (b) carefully designed programs that maximize individual student progress are utilized; and (c) a vast array of technology enhances the instructional program.

The specific project beliefs were as follows:

1. The multiage, multigrade classroom provides a setting in which the learning and growth needs of the individual child take precedence over teaching groups of students.

2. The relationships between teacher and students and the quality of time spent together in the classroom are central to each student's success.

3. Technology enables the teacher to serve as a facilitator of learning and allows each student to become actively involved in managing his or her own learning.

4. The role of the teacher changes in project classrooms from a disseminator of knowledge to that of a facilitator of learning.

5. Each student in the project has the obligation to be more responsible for his or her own learning.

6. The most time-consuming task of the project is the development of curricula that enable students to progress independently.

7. The success of the project rests with teachers who have complete support and assurance of their administrators.

8. Students educated in project classrooms will stay in school longer and be more likely to graduate from high school than their counterparts in traditional settings.

Communicating the Vision

Communicating a school's vision is vital to the school's future success. However, there is a danger of turning off stakeholders such as parents, faculty, or board members if a careful information strategy is not chosen. For example, a public announcement of a new vision statement in news outlets and PTA meetings might well serve to reduce the amount of public support for the school rather than build support for the school's new initiatives. The surprise factor alone will engender suspicion among those who already are skeptical of the school. Others will be turned off by the new terminology normally found in vision statements. Finally, there will be those who simply do not follow the reasoning behind a new vision statement. A vision statement that indicates that the primary focus of the school will be on the learner might not be understood by many members of the community. The typical response might be, "Well, of course, isn't that where the emphasis has always been?" Such a response would indicate two realities. The first is that any simple statement of a school's vision probably will fail to communicate the full meaning of the vision. The second is that the beliefs and values undergirding the vision statement will not be stated and therefore will not be communicated to those who would provide vital support for the new vision.

The following phrase, used in the Arizona project, probably is good advice when thinking about how to communicate a vision: "Think big, but start small." This strategy would guide the school to begin discussing the vision in small groups, in which the beliefs and values of the vision could be explained and discussed. The changes necessary to realize the vision also could be explored. From such meetings, a consensus supporting the new vision could emerge. At the very least, the members of the school staff would become aware of the community's fears or objections to the course of action represented by the new vision. The school might then wish to modify the vision in order to build the support base necessary for a successful change effort.

PARTICIPANT INVOLVEMENT

The Need for Involvement

In Chapter 2 it was noted that changes featuring participant involvement were more likely to succeed than those without such involvement. Changes planned outside of the school, or even within the school by the principal, take on the air of imposition. They are planned elsewhere and given to the teachers to implement regardless of what programs the teachers are currently using. It is not difficult to see that such an event is likely to be resented by the targeted teachers. If they comply at all, it is only grudgingly, and there will be many who delay or sabotage critical elements of the program simply because they feel they are being coerced. In such cases, it makes little difference if the change is good or bad; it is the *intrusion* that makes teachers angry.

The researchers in the empowerment and restructuring projects recognized this phenomenon. In the empowerment project, the teams of teachers and administrators from the invited schools attended the organizing meeting in Chicago. They spent 3 days discussing the concept of empowerment and designing a plan of action each school would pursue initially, should it agree to participate. The only value imposed on the teams was that their empowerment efforts had to benefit the students attending their schools. Following the Chicago conference, the teams returned to their schools to discuss the project with the schools' other teachers and administrators. The decision to participate was a voluntary one. No school was pushed into being a member of the consortium of schools working in the project, and no individual teacher was forced to be a member of the empowerment committee in his or her school.

In the Arizona project, the project's overall philosophy, beliefs, and classroom characteristics were set out for the invited school teams during the first organizing conference. The task of the conference participants, therefore, was to learn about the proposed project and, if they wished to experiment with multiage, multigrade classrooms, to volunteer to be a member of the consortium. As volunteer schools, they knew that all of the implementation decisions would be their own. The project directors would be available if the schools asked for suggestions, but decisions regarding single-teacher or teaching-team classrooms, primary or intermediate experimental classrooms, and so forth were left strictly to the individual schools.

Thus, the initial meetings were quite different for the two projects. In the empowerment project, the participants helped to define the concept of teacher empowerment. In their schools, they could begin to work at empowering teachers from any perspective they chose. If they wished to begin with some sort of change project planned by the teachers, that was acceptable. If they wished to study the process as described in the literature and then establish procedures to be used for many purposes (e.g., governance issues, curriculum innovations, school improvements), that also was acceptable.

The result of the empowerment project approach was that all teachers in a school were made aware of the empowerment effort. In most schools, this general awareness of empowerment encouraged the active participation of an ever-increasing number of teachers. The inclusion of teachers in the project's Chicago meeting, where the concept of empowerment was discussed and at least partially defined, led to high levels of commitment among faculties of participating schools.

In the initial meeting of the Arizona project, the participants were presented with a rather detailed model of multiage, multigrade classrooms. Although implementation was left to each school, the basic definition of the classroom was foreordained. The result of this approach was an intense effort among the teachers who participated in the initial conference but not a lot of interest among the other teachers in their schools. Several schools proved to be exceptions to this rule, but, for the most part, the experimenting teachers were viewed with some suspicion and even resentment by fellow faculty members. These situations were characteristic of the so-called rate-buster phenomenon so often discussed in the management literature (Hare, 1976). The rate buster is the person who deviates from the performance norms of the other workers. His or her behavior is always viewed with resentment by those who conform to the norms.

For the most part, the multiage, multigrade experimenters were not supported by other faculty members, nor were the other faculty members encouraged to begin their own experiments with such classrooms. Most faculty members were content with their judgment that multiage, multigrade classrooms were just a fad that would soon disappear.

Thus, it seems clear that participant involvement in the earliest stages of the two programs ensured faculty participation in the empowerment schools and thwarted such participation in the multiage, multigrade Arizona schools. It should be added, however, that some of the Arizona schools did have high participation rates because of the efforts of their leaders. Gilbert Elementary School is one such example; the work of its principal and staff is highlighted in the case study at the end of this chapter.

Structures and Strategies for Involvement

Much has been said so far about the need to involve participants in planning the change effort to ensure their commitment. Several structures such as empowerment committees have also been mentioned. There is more to be said, however, regarding strategies and structures that can be used to further the change effort over the long term.

In the Murray High School case study in Chapter 2, the formal empowerment effort ended after 4 years. There was no formal burial ceremony, because the end of the project did not signal the end of the school's interest in empowerment. Rather, the project ended because it was no longer needed. The staff and members of the community were empowered; they fully participated in making the school's basic governance decisions. Renaissance Vision, the school's current improvement effort, would not have been possible without the empowerment project, for the perspectives and hard work of all the school's stakeholders (which had been mobilized first during the empowerment project) were critical to the success of the new program.

At Abraham Lincoln High School in Denver, the initial school improvement efforts of the Think Tank resulted in the establishment of two new governance structures. Teachers, parents, and businesspeople were formed into 11 committees to focus on topics of vital importance to the school operation such as values, personnel, curriculum, school building, and support staff. Each committee was headed by a parent, teacher, or business leader. The chair of each committee also served as a member of the school's steering board, the body that set the direction for the school.

The only administrator on the steering board was the principal, Christine Johnson. All the others were faculty members, parents, and businesspeople. Orientation to the work of the steering board was Christine's responsibility, and she focused on determining the topics the board could address and which were not appropriate because of federal statutes, state mandates, or local board of education policies. By defining the boundaries, Christine was able to help the steering board realize the limits of its power. Many aspects of the school operation were nonnegotiable because of outside constraints.

It should be noted that Abraham Lincoln had a principal and four assistant principals at the time of the project. It was the assistant principals' responsibility to manage the school's operation. Since none of the assistant principals were chairs of the teacher-parent-businessperson committees, they were not on the steering board.

Abraham Lincoln's steering board was given credence a year or so later when the governor of Colorado, Roy Romer, mandated that such bodies be established in each of Denver's schools. This action was taken as part of the governor's efforts to avoid a city-wide teacher strike in 1990. The governor was well acquainted with Abraham Lincoln's governance structure, because he had visited the school and held discussions with Christine several times in the months prior to the threatened teacher strike.

The important fact to note in both Murray High School and Abraham Lincoln is that the effort to empower teachers was not allowed to die when the project was completed. Structures had to be constructed and put in place to ensure that teachers and others would continue to have voices in school governance. It is important to establish new structures that will ensure maximum empowerment. At Abraham

Lincoln, Christine established the steering board with only one administrator, herself, as a member. Other administrators served on the committees, but not as committee chairs. Consequently, they were not eligible for steering board membership, and the responsibility for setting the direction for the school lay with the teachers, parents, and businesspeople.

When asked whether being the only administrator on the steering board, and without veto power, made her nervous, Christine replied that it did not, for she felt secure in her role as a board member. She knew that the other members would listen to her and that her knowledge and experience would always be a part of the board's decisions.

These two examples show that the principals carefully designed structures that would serve their schools well in the future. The voices of all their constituents would be heard, and all would influence the schools' basic decisions.

RESISTANCE TO AUTONOMY

The primary conceptual issue of this book is the degree of autonomy that highly bureaucratic school systems can give to their schools. In our experience, the answer is very little. Greer (1993) explored the issue by analyzing school districts, from the board of education, to the central office, to school principals and teachers. Districts used in the analysis were, in part, those found in the Arizona and empowerment studies.

In analyzing the board of education, Greer's conclusion was that, even with very good board members, there is a sense of stewardship that prompts the board members to insist on equity in all district schools. Equity normally means equal resources, ranging from financial, to physical, to human. To ensure equity throughout the district, therefore, critical decisions about these resources can be made only at the central office level. Board members who ran and were elected to support a particular point of view (i.e., single-issue board members) are even less likely to support individual building autonomy than non-single issue board members. If decisions about the instructional program were given to individual schools, the reason for being a board member (i.e., to push a particular point of view) would no longer exist. Board members are supported in their love for bureaucracy by their written board policies. Policies rarely consider the vast differences in the students attending a district's schools. In effect, the policies seem to be based on the assumption that all students are similar in their learning needs, experiential backgrounds, ethnicity, and economic circumstances.

Superintendents, for the most part, are also deeply committed to the central coordination offered by the bureaucracy. Many will support site-based management, but, when such plans are examined closely, site-based management is revealed to mean little more than control of the school's petty cash fund. It often seems that superintendents embrace site-based management in order to maneuver schools into believing they have power to make meaningful decisions. Superintendents serve at the pleasure of the board, and thus they must support the board's thinking regarding central office direction.

Central office staff members also resist building-level autonomy. Their reasons are more easily understood than are the reasons of other members of the bureaucracy. If schools are awarded the autonomy to make their own basic decisions, what is the need for the central office staff? There would no longer be a central-office-approved curriculum to enforce.

At the building level, the principals presently serve as middle managers. Their responsibility is to carry out the programs and organizational decisions made by central office personnel. It is unlikely, therefore, that they would be enthusiastic about serving as leaders of schools that were not bound to centrally established programs and procedures.

Finally, teachers by and large do not wish to spend the time and effort required to participate in the governance of their schools. Time and time again in the empowerment projects, teachers would blurt out, "Just tell us what you want us to do." Making decisions—considering alternative solutions as well as the consequences of their decisions—is difficult and time-consuming work. Until teachers become accustomed to the lengthy discussions and meetings required in shared-governance schools, their frustration levels will lie close to the surface and exclamations such as the one just quoted will be common.

These observations led Greer (1993) to express grave doubts about the possibility of building autonomy. None of the major players in the school district seemed anxious for schools to have meaningful independence.

ஐ CASE STUDY

Leadership Issues in Innovative Schools

The success of an innovation should not be measured in terms of whether or not the experiment is a success with the targeted students and teachers. For a number of years, students of organizational change have argued that the success of an innovation is determined by the dissemination of that innovation (Bennis, Benne, & Chin, 1969).

CHAPTER 3

The following case study addresses a number of leadership issues: building a collaborative school vision, using teams and cross-group structures, and communication. It also documents the success of the multiage, multigrade experiment as judged by the dissemination of the effort.

Gilbert Elementary School

Gilbert Elementary School is a kindergarten through sixth grade school located in the community of Gilbert, Arizona, a suburb of Phoenix. It has approximately 750 students, of whom 72% are Anglo and 28% are from different racial and ethnic groups. Of the students attending, 37% are on a free or reduced-price lunch program. There are 37 faculty members.

The principal is Sheila Rogers. Sheila had been an elementary school teacher in the district for 17 years before going to the central office for 1 year as the acting personnel director. She then was given the principalship of Gilbert Elementary and had been serving in that capacity for 3 years before the restructuring project began.

After being at the school for a short period of time, Sheila realized that the primary program needed improvement. In discussions with her primary grade teachers, she expressed her dissatisfaction with the program but did not suggest what action needed to be taken. Three of the teachers came to her later and expressed interest in organizing multiage, multigrade classrooms. The classrooms would be single-teacher classrooms with students aged 6, 7, and 8 (grades 1, 2, and 3). The teachers were interested in forming a three-person team, even though they would each have their multiage, multigrade classroom. Sheila supported the idea and added herself, the school's special education coordinator, and the school's media specialist to the team.

The first year was spent in planning the multigrade effort and identifying the students who would participate. Many of the students were those who had been in the three teachers' classrooms the year before. All of the students, however, participated because their parents wanted them to be in the multiage, multigrade classroom. No student was assigned to an experimental group.

Shortly before the beginning of the experiment, the school was invited to join the Arizona Educational Restructuring Project, and they accepted the invitation. The year of planning that had been completed at the time helped the other project schools, which were just beginning their efforts.

The effort at Gilbert was successful from many points of view. The parents were immediately impressed with the dynamics of the classrooms and how younger students were interacting and learning from the older members. They were also impressed with the caring atmosphere of the classrooms and the enjoyment their children were having as members of the groups.

After 2 years with the three classrooms, the parents began to be concerned with having a similar experience for their children after they had left the primary classrooms. During the third year, an intermediate multiage, multigrade classroom was organized to receive the children leaving the primary unit. Other primary teachers became interested in forming classrooms of their own. All were volunteers, and those who wished to keep their traditional classrooms did so without any prejudice on the part of the principal.

In one of our last interviews with the principal, Sheila said that Gilbert was a multiage, multigrade classroom school. Students were doing well, there were practically no discipline problems, and the multiage experiences were well suited for meeting the learning needs of students with disabilities.

Although the school did not broadcast its experiment, word about the Gilbert project became known throughout the area. Two factors contributed to this informal dissemination: Gilbert's membership in the Arizona Educational Restructuring Project and informal discussion among the Gilbert teachers and among their friends in graduate classes and at conferences. It was not long before parents new to the district were searching for homes in the Gilbert attendance area. Faculty members from other schools in the district also became interested in having their children attend the school.

As the project ended, 5 of the 11 elementary schools in the district had established multiage, multigrade classrooms. As was mentioned earlier, the experiment had spread both vertically and horizontally within the school. Parents of older children who were leaving the school even inquired about the possibility of establishing multiage, multigrade classes in the district's junior high school.

In reviewing the Gilbert story, it can be seen that a number of leadership issues were addressed. Although Sheila initially planted seeds for change, the faculty members responded with the new approach to instruction. From the beginning, they had ownership of the experiment, and, through their daily lunchtime planning meetings, they developed and polished the concept.

Although all teachers volunteered to participate, Sheila, through her participation on the team, demonstrated her total support for the project. Those who might have thought that the experiment would go away quickly got the message that the multiage, multigrade classroom was the Gilbert plan for the future. If they wished to participate, they were more than welcome, but the experiment was not going to go away.

The Gilbert approach was a team approach for planning purposes, but the classroom work was carried on by individuals. Sharing experiences from their classrooms was an important aspect of the daily planning meetings, particularly in the first 2 years.

Finally, the communication pattern that carried the news of the experiment was almost exclusively informal. The original group of three teachers did not go out of their way to share their experiences with other faculty members. They did, however, invite other teachers to visit if they expressed an interest. Sheila also did not mention the project in faculty meetings, because she did not wish nonparticipating teachers to feel pressured. Outside of the school, the word of the experiment was carried largely by nonstaff members. The only exceptions were a presentation by the teachers at one board of education meeting and several presentations at state and regional teacher meetings and workshops. Otherwise, news of the experiment was disseminated by those who had come to know about the effort through visiting the school or by listening to parents and friends of the school. Dissemination occurred just like the organizational change experts said it should.

༄ VOICES FROM THE FIELD

Planting the Seeds at Hollister Elementary School

To effect change, teacher empowerment must be nurtured at the grassroots level. School leaders at Hollister Elementary School in Hollister, Missouri, planted the seeds for such empowerment through the school's advisory council.

Representatives serving on the advisory council were encouraged to lead study groups, researching educational topics of personal interest. The groups were open to all staff to join as desired. Study topics included brain-based research, looping, multiage classrooms, and year-round school calendars, to name a few. Study groups encouraged staff to expand their own parameters of educational trends and research. Moreover, the study groups became local experts for colleagues' reference.

The results were a more knowledgeable staff and one that became more open to change. Teachers began to better understand that empowerment is not something that is granted to teachers by administrators; rather, teachers practice empowerment for their own benefit.

BARBARA J. CROSSLAND

REFERENCES

Bennis, W. G., Benne, K. D., & Chin, R. (Eds.). (1969). *The planning of change* (2nd ed.). New York: Holt, Rinehart, and Winston.

Bennis, W. G., & Nanus, B. (1985). *Leaders: The strategies for taking charge.* New York: Harper and Row.

Greer, J. T. (1993, August). *The autonomous school.* Paper presented at the annual meeting of the National Council of Professors of Educational Administration, Palm Springs, CA.

Hare, A. P. (1976). *Handbook of small group research* (2nd ed.). New York: The Free Press.

CHAPTER 4

𝔰𝔬

Building a Trusting Environment

This chapter highlights the numerous issues of power and the trust relationships found in schools that want to become more empowered. Most educators, when they think of trust in the schools, focus on the trust between teachers and principal or between teachers and students. We found that many other trust relationships existed and contributed to the success or failure of the empowerment and restructuring experiments.

POWER

Power is defined as the "ability of one party to change or control the behavior, attitudes, opinions, objectives, needs, and values of another party" (Rahim, 1989, p. 545). Power is determined by the extent to which the leader can influence subordinates (French & Raven, 1959; Krausz, 1986). The source of power that leaders use is critical to the influence they acquire. French and Raven (1959) created a typology to identify the following five power bases:

1. Referent power—the subordinate's desire to identify with the leader.

2. Legitimate power—the legitimate right of the leader, usually by virtue of the position that the leader holds, to prescribe or control behavior.

3. Coercive power—the leader's control over punishment.

4. Reward power—the leader's control over reward.

5. Expert power—special knowledge or expertise.

Leaders influence through use of one or more of these power bases. However, the persons being influenced must perceive that the leader's particular power bases are important and necessary to them. In other words, reward power is influential to others only to the extent that others desire and need that reward and believe that the leader has the reward to give.

FACILITATIVE POWER

Facilitative power is rooted in interaction, negotiation, and mutuality (Goldman & Dunlap, 1990). It reduces the tight links between power and status, minimizing claims to legitimacy based primarily on either organizational position or professional expertise. Facilitative power appears to be required for the success of restructuring and site-based management, and it differs acutely from the more commonly understood conceptualization of power as an exercise of dominance or control. Facilitative power is most appropriate in circumstances that favor decentralization and in which educational problems appear to demand individualized solutions (Goldman & Dunlap, 1990). Facilitative power reflects a process that, by creating or sustaining favorable conditions, allows subordinates to enhance their individual and collective performance. It is especially helpful when staff members must work together on new or complex tasks. Four distinct activities characterize facilitative leadership:

1. Providing for resources that support educational activities.

2. Selecting and matching people who can work together effectively, paying attention to both the skills and the personalities that comprise the mix. (This type of leadership can also include modeling collaborative behaviors.)

3. Monitoring activities, providing feedback, providing reinforcement, and offering suggestions. (This can include symbolic support, especially when the activities and relationships are new and threatening, and it is the leader who must manage and resolve conflict.)

4. Providing networks for activities, helping groups go "public" with activities, and diffusing new ideas.

THE PRINCIPAL IS THE KEY

The principal is the key to building a trusting environment. Trust begins with the principal. If the principal presents herself or himself as the authority in the school, then a trusting environment is not possible. One of the principals in the empowerment study, for example, declared before representatives of the entire consortium, "I've spent 4 years studying for my doctorate just so I could make the decisions in this school."

Another phrase that identifies a principal as one who will have a difficult time building an atmosphere of trust is "but if anything goes wrong, I'm the one who will be held responsible." Such principals in the empowerment study were identified as those who had trouble relinquishing control. Our studies found that some principals, regardless of their verbal support for empowering teachers and their ready support for shared governance, just could not bring themselves to give up any of their power to control. The saying "The principal gains power by giving it away" had no meaning for them.

One might speculate about the gender, age, or experience of these principals. The studies found that none of these three variables predicted which principals were capable of sharing power, nor did the type of school in which they served. Elementary school principals had just as much trouble letting go as did secondary school principals.

The problem appears to rest more with the image of the principalship that people carry than with anything else. It may be that the best predictor of how a person will administer a school is how the schools where he or she was a student or teacher were administered. Perhaps administrators carry some picture of the principal and the principal's behavior and attitudes that serves as a constant reminder of how they themselves should think and behave. Be that as it may, the principal's behavior is what conditions the levels of trust that can occur in the building. Perhaps the biblical-sounding expression "Trust begets trust" illustrates the phenomenon.

In the empowerment study, we found that when a principal placed himself or herself on some higher plane, reserving veto power over the decisions being made by the teachers, there was little trust in the school. This was the ultimate form of disdain for teachers found in the study. Essentially, these principals were giving teachers the message that their efforts at empowerment would be indulged, but the principal would still reject any decision he or she did not like.

There was a second group of principals who played the empowerment game but didn't really mean it. These principals gave lip service to empowerment in working with staff, in public meetings, and in meetings of the entire consortium. The examples of empowerment activities that would be shared in their schools included new programs for at-risk students, new discipline programs, teacher participation in the hiring of new teachers, teacher advisory committees, and programs for parents. Such activities may well have been suggested by the teachers, thus making it appear that the schools were well along the road to shared governance. However, visits to the schools by the project directors revealed that decisions were still being made exclusively by the principal, although perhaps with some teacher input. This is not to say that the new programs and activities did not help the school. They did not, however, result in greater shared governance, and the school environment was not filled with greater amounts of trust than before the project began. Such a pretense was manufactured by several schools. They gave the appearance of great activity but, in the end, nothing changed. Teachers were not more empowered, nor had trusting relationships been established.

Fortunately, there was a third group of schools and principals who truly believed in the concepts of trust and, from there, empowerment. A quick picture of these principals at work would show principals who were right down there in the trenches working along with everyone else, who were never afraid of getting their hands dirty. They would do everything anyone else did and then go even further. These were the principals who, through personal behavior and example, inspired trust from all. They trusted others and earned reciprocal trust.

It is from this third group of schools that the following discussions related to trust relationships are drawn. Some of the relationships are obvious; anyone would identify them. Other relationships, however, are not obvious, and it was only as participants identified them that we became sensitive to their relevance in the empowerment and restructuring processes.

TRUST BETWEEN THE PRINCIPAL AND TEACHERS

Principals Trusting Teachers

The studies found that a principal's trust of teachers resulted from many factors that varied from principal to principal. In the case study in Chapter 2, Richard Tranter spoke of the "shaky decisions" his faculty members had made. In the end, however, he acknowledged that things had worked out all right and, retrospectively, he had come to believe that the decisions the faculty made were better than those he would have made himself. Thus, in Richard's case, even though he had believed for many years that the faculty should be actively involved in the decisions of the school, it was his actual positive experiences that cemented his belief in the process. Furthermore, having had success, he was encouraged to use the process with ever-increasing frequency on even more important issues. His trust in the faculty and their decisions was strengthened through experience with the process.

Other principals developed high levels of trust with the faculty for other reasons. Charlie Blanton, at Newman Smith High School in Carrollton, Texas, exhibited a high level of trust in his teachers from the beginning of the empowerment project. He demonstrated his trust by advancing a series of strategies whereby faculty and students who were closest to a problem made the decisions. If he ever had any doubt about the success of the strategy, it was not apparent to his teachers and students, his facilitator, or the project directors.

Building upon the strategy of giving the decision to those closest to the problem, Charlie turned the staff development program over to the faculty for them to develop and conduct. Preschool workshops were designed and conducted by the faculty with the help of the school's facilitator. Other sessions were similarly planned and conducted throughout the year. The strategy ensured that the topics were always of vital interest to the faculty.

Charlie trusted the faculty to conduct the staff development program because it was an inherent part of him as a leader; he trusted others because it was a natural thing for him to do. His overall empowerment strategy flowed out of this trust and was applied to other groups in the school, including students.

At Gilbert Elementary School (discussed in the case study in Chapter 3), Sheila Rogers was a fully contributing member of the school's first multiage, multigrade team. From the beginning, she took her cues from the experimenting teachers, helping in every way possible. Besides her contributions, based on many years of teaching experience, she provided human and material resources to the effort. Because she was a viable team member involved in the give-and-take of the team, Sheila experienced all the successes and failures of the initial effort. Through such tempering, a bond was formed among the team members that reflected trust and support at the highest level.

Sheila's participation was not lost on other members of the faculty. Seeing her in warm and personal relationships with the members of the team helped other faculty members realize the trustworthiness of their principal and encouraged them to explore the possibility of their own participation as members of other teams.

Teachers Trusting Principals

In general, teachers were slow to become convinced that the principals truly meant to share the governance of the schools with them. Such a strategy was, after all, a radical departure from the principal-centered schools they had experienced in the past. The teachers had to be persuaded of the principals' sincerity, and even then there were many skeptics. What convinced most teachers was the principals' unwavering support of teacher empowerment. Probably, if any of the successful principals had reverted to an earlier pattern of authoritarian behavior, the teachers' trust would have dissolved.

In addition to teachers being slow to accept their principals' empowerment efforts, they also began to trust their principals' words and behaviors at varying rates. The typical group of those who truly believed in the possibility of shared governance was no more than a handful. Slowly, the handful attracted others, and the effort began to flourish. The lesson to be learned from the study, however, is that moving to a shared-governance school is a long, slow process. In none of the schools did the process take less than 3 years, and in many schools it took 5 years or more. Thus, it is important not to expect empowerment to occur overnight. It is an evolutionary process that is totally dependent upon principals trusting teachers and teachers trusting their principals.

TRUST BETWEEN THE PRINCIPAL AND THE DISTRICT OFFICE

A trusting relationship between a principal and the district office personnel must be addressed from at least two perspectives: that of a bureaucratic structure and that of an autonomous school. A trusting relationship in a bureaucracy is very different from a trusting relationship between the district office and an autonomous school.

Trust in a Bureaucracy

In the bureaucratic pattern that characterizes most school systems throughout the country, the principal is viewed as a middle manager whose responsibilities are to run the school in a manner acceptable to the central office. Actions of middle-manager principals reflect a bedrock belief that if something goes wrong they will be held responsible.

According to the school effectiveness literature, 80% of the typical principal's day consists of conversations of 2 minutes or less (Hallinger,

Murphy, Weil, Mesa, & Mitman, 1983). Such conversations are spent responding to teachers' requests for decisions, such as "How should we do . . .?" or "What do you want us to do about . . .?" Although this sounds like a hectic life-style, it is not as difficult as it appears to be. Most of the decisions being requested are decisions the principal has made repeatedly, or they are decisions that have already been made by the central office and the principal is merely passing them along to the teachers. In addition, it can be very gratifying to have everyone come to you for answers. It is a concrete manifestation of your importance to the school.

To be successful in such a setting, the principal dares not make decisions that are outside of the expectations of the central office. Such actions label the principal as a "loner" or a "loose cannon." The situation is worsened immeasurably should the principal make an independent decision that is wrong or that does not produce the expected result. Then the combined condemnation of the central office, the superintendent, and even the board of education is likely to fall on the principal. The result of being wrong is a black mark on the principal's personnel record that makes promotions and other rewards nearly unobtainable. Even worse, the principal is labeled as untrustworthy, and his or her effectiveness in obtaining special programs and other favors for the school and its students is jeopardized.

These bureaucratic realities make the life of the successful middle-manager principal fairly routine and colorless. But in the eyes of central office officials who are in charge of selecting principals, "good" principals can be trusted to carry out the central office directions, explain and sell the central office point of view, and always ask for directions from their supervisors when facing a new situation.

Trust between principals and central office personnel results from stable conditions. When conditions are steady, no surprises are generated in the school that are sprung unexpectedly on the central office. Reciprocally, central office personnel look out for their favored schools. These bureaucrats can be counted on to alert the school of upcoming district-wide changes, they will patiently remind the school if it is tardy in completing certain tasks, and they will provide individual consultative assistance to the school and principal whenever necessary.

Much of this chapter describes the dehumanizing effects of a bureaucracy. School systems, like all bureaucracies, are ruled from the top down, with the work being done by those on the bottom. Participation or feedback from those doing the work is rarely solicited by the decision makers, even though the workers are professionally trained, with years of experience, and the decision makers are largely lay persons. One is reminded of the famous quote attributed to Frederick Taylor: "Don't think! Others are paid to do the thinking around here" (1916).

This is overstating the case to illustrate how dreary school systems can be. Up and down the bureaucracy, it seems that persons are expected to do as they are told. They should not question the central office and the board of education. Above all, they are not permitted to depart far from the system-approved programs. Individual initiative is permitted, but only within the context of the teacher's classroom, and it is best if the teacher first checks out such initiatives with the building principal.

Trust Between an Autonomous School Principal and the District Office

An entirely different arrangement exists when a principal and the school are given a high degree of autonomy by the central office. In effect, in such an arrangement the central office is giving up its authority over the school. Typically, such autonomy results from an understanding between the superintendent and the principal. In the empowerment study, for example, the superintendents in the first project meeting pledged that the experimental schools would be given a high degree of autonomy so that major decisions could be made at the building level by the entire staff. These pledges were confirmed in writing by the superintendents and the board of education presidents in the period immediately following the initial conference.

Part of the reason that superintendents were willing to make the autonomy commitment was that they had themselves selected the principals and schools that would participate in the project. The project directors had asked the superintendents to select schools in which warm and trusting relationships existed between the principals and the staff and also where the superintendents believed there was enough initiative and energy to conduct the experiment for 3 years.

Because the superintendents had great confidence in the principals at the beginning of the project, trust between them did not have to be established, only maintained. With few exceptions, the superintendents honored their initial pledges. About the only times when the trust level between superintendent and principal was imperiled were when superintendents left their districts. Then the high level of trust between the principal and central office became problematic. In only one of the four districts that experienced superintendent turnover did the trust level remain high; when the superintendent left, a new superintendent was appointed from within the district who had been a strong supporter of the project while in his former position of assistant superintendent. In the other three schools, support and trust for the school's efforts deteriorated.

In the five schools that retained their superintendents throughout the project, the superintendents maintained a high level of trust and support throughout the project. The following observations were made regarding the behaviors of the principals and their superintendents throughout the 3-year period:

- Most superintendents did not hover around the experimental school throughout the project. In fact, they were rarely seen by the project directors and other visitors to the school.

- The principals enjoyed a warm and personal relationship with their superintendents. These relationships, in nearly every case, were nurtured by frequent discussions between the two persons. Most such discussions served to keep the superintendents informed of project developments and also enabled the principals to seek advice as needed.

These warm and trusting relationships were a far cry from those in one of the districts considered for the Arizona study. In anticipation of going to a fully implemented multiage, multigrade classroom format in grades 1 through 3, all the teachers of the three grades spent the year before the initiation of the ungraded classrooms teaching in either a grade level they had never taught or one they had not taught for some time. This voluntary effort to prepare for ungraded classroom teaching brought the school and its principal to the attention of the project directors. After a site visit, the directors invited the school to join the consortium of schools experimenting with the ungraded classroom. The school did not join the network, which seemed surprising until one of the directors happened to discuss the school with the district's superintendent at a meeting several weeks later. In the conversation it became apparent that the superintendent was not pleased with all the attention the school, but more particularly the principal, was receiving. The superintendent's comments revealed a lack of support for the school's efforts and resentment toward the principal.

This example from the Arizona study represents a superintendent who wanted the principal to be a middle-level manager and not an autonomous school principal. The independence of the principal and school violated the superintendent's perception of good principal behavior. It was a shame to see such a problem arise, for the school had designed a truly creative approach to establishing its ungraded classrooms. In addition, the school served a population of students largely from one-parent families in which the parent was working much of the time the child was out of school. If ever there was a need for the nurturing environment of the ungraded classroom, it was at this school.

CHAPTER 4

TRUST BETWEEN TEACHERS AND
THE BOARD OF EDUCATION

Except for those in small school districts, most teachers do not know the members of their board of education. They think of the board as a far-removed force that passes restrictive measures that are largely resented by the teachers. Likewise, the board members do not know the district's teachers, other than perhaps those who teach the board members' children. The classic bureaucratic model prevails in most school districts. The direction-setting board sits far above the workers who must carry out their decisions. Located between the board and teachers are several layers of administrators and central office staff members.

Communication between the board and teachers is almost exclusively in writing. Policies adopted by the board and implementing regulations prepared by administrators are usually the only messages a teacher receives from the board. If any trust is to develop between the board and teachers, the board's policies must show a willingness to share governance. Yet, as mentioned earlier, boards do not often believe in noncentralized, autonomous schools. Rather, they support their own supremacy by establishing policies that restrict teachers and schools and force both into a common mold of programs, textbooks, and instruction.

TRUST AMONG TEACHERS

In the typical elementary and secondary school, teachers carry on their work largely in isolation. Even among members of the same department or grade level, teachers rarely observe other teachers at work in their classrooms. Team-taught classrooms offer about the only opportunity for teachers to work together, to observe the teaching strengths of one another, and to share the common experiences that generate reciprocal trust.

This description might make it seem that schools are friendless places for teachers, but nothing could be further from the truth. Teachers do indeed form lasting friendships with their fellow teachers in all schools, but such friendships are based on personal qualities rather than professional experiences. Rarely, as schools are presently organized, do friendships develop because of shared professional values. In the 26 schools that participated in the empowerment and restructuring projects, shared professional experiences were the norm rather than the exception. Shared governance makes it possible for teachers to have more shared professional experiences, as does collective planning.

One critical observation made by the researchers in the empower-ment experiment is that there is a danger that the increasing familiarity that occurs as teachers work through the process leading to empower-ment can be divisive, rather than unifying. Occasionally, the work un-covers value conflicts regarding professional issues that had never be-fore surfaced. Usually discussions of such value differences are healthy and result in closer relationships between faculty members. But coming together is not always guaranteed in value conflict discussions. In one school, the faculty divided according to their views of certain profes-sional values, and the wounds never healed. In follow-up discussions af-ter the project was completed, faculty members and the principal con-cluded that empowerment was not for everyone. Since the phenomenon was observed at only one of the nine schools in the study, no generaliza-tions were made. The one thing the researchers did conclude, however, was that empowerment is a growth-producing process. Trust results from teachers working with one another on issues critical to the school and the education of its students. Sometimes efforts to coalesce a faculty and to develop a consensus on professional issues fail. More often than not, however, they unify the faculty and help the school move forward.

TRUST BETWEEN TEACHERS AND STUDENTS

The trust relationship between teachers and students was one of the most intriguing topics of the empowerment study. It was assumed from the beginning of the project that teachers, like workers found in all or-ganizations, would like to be involved in making the decisions that have an impact on the quality of their working lives, as well as those that are essential to the success of the organization. This assumption proved to be correct; teachers in the project schools readily accepted the premises of the empowerment project and volunteered to be involved.

After the project had been under way for about a year, the teachers were asked about sharing their decision-making authority with students. While no complete canvass of all faculty was made, it was surprising to see how many of the teacher representatives firmly rejected including students in the decision structure of the school. Several hypotheses were put forth for this surprising teacher response: The problem is a genera-tional problem; adults do not wish to share their decision authority with the younger generation. Empowering students is a refutation of tradi-tional student and teacher roles. In schools, teachers teach and students learn; it is not expected that learners will be able to participate in deter-mining what they are to learn. Since the teachers had only recently acquired the status attendant with being decision makers, they did not want to dilute their status by expanding the number of decision makers.

All of the hypotheses appeared to have some validity, but the evidence was too thin to conclude that one was more predictive than the others. Perhaps the readers of this book will have better insight about why sharing decision authority with students is anathema to so many teachers.

TRUST IN THE SCHOOL CULTURE

One would not normally expect to find high levels of trust in the schools discussed here or norms supporting trust relationships in the schools' cultures. Exceptions in the 26 experimental schools were found, however, and those schools were effective in implementing the empowerment process and ungraded classrooms. Schools with high-trust cultures were always schools with long-term principals who worked hard to maintain and strengthen the trust relationships throughout their schools. They actively participated with the teachers as the teachers undertook new programs or activities, they were nonjudgmental in their work with faculty members, and they modeled high-trust attitudes toward all staff members.

With their principals setting the tone, trusting others gradually became a norm of the schools' cultures. It was a long, slow process, according to teacher and administrator observers, but gradually the school culture would swing away from competition, suspicion, and distrust to a culture in which every individual was valued and appreciated. In accordance with Schein's (1992) definition of the culture as being those things that have worked well in the past and are taught to new members of the organization, the new members in the high-trust schools were made aware of the trusting environment of the school. Initially, trust was discussed by the principals in orientation sessions, but the reality was made known by fellow teachers through informal discussions related to "how things work around here."

TRUST IN A HEALTHY ORGANIZATION

An organization in which critical processes are well developed and effective is known as a *healthy organization* (Miles, 1965). Among the critical processes are communication, goal setting, decision making, conflict management, and problem solving (Schmuck & Runkel, 1972). In the healthy organization, challenges are addressed, solutions to problems are found, and new methods and innovations are initiated.

It scarcely needs to be said that trust among members of the school organization is essential to improving its critical processes. A culture that features a high level of trust among the its members does not guarantee that the basic processes of the organization are effective. What high trust does for a school is to permit members to disagree and be authentic without worry, to not "play games." Two staff members working together on school goals, for example, should not have to worry that their words will be misunderstood and taken as personal affronts by one another. With high trust present, work can proceed more quickly and without rancor. Thus, a healthy organization not only has effective processes, but it also is likely to have a high-trust culture. Certainly the successful schools in the empowerment and restructuring studies had both characteristics.

LEADERSHIP ISSUES AND TRUST

Building Trust

In the two studies, it was found that the most successful principals were trusting individuals. This certainly does not mean that they had no guiding principles or visions of their schools' future. All of the principals were strong leaders. They had a good understanding of where they wanted their schools to go, what objectives needed to be achieved, and the strategies most likely to achieve the objectives. Having said this, it also needs to be said that they all had great trust in the abilities of their staff members. To a person, they would be classified as Theory Y principals (McGregor, 1960). (In contrast, Theory X principals' attitudes stem from the belief that people basically do not like to work and are therefore not to be trusted to do their jobs without close supervision.) The successful principals believed that:

- Work is as natural as play or rest.
- Individuals will exercise self-direction when working toward meaningful objectives.
- Commitment is related to the rewards associated with achievement.
- Individuals learn to accept and seek responsibility.
- The capacity to help the organization solve its problems is widely distributed among the members of the organization.
- In most organizations the intellectual potential is only partially utilized.

Holding Theory Y attitudes encourages a principal to trust others. As has been stated throughout the chapter, the successful principals who empowered their teachers to the greatest extent, and those who worked with the most successful ungraded classroom experiments, trusted their staff members.

The issue, then, is how to determine what sort of person is most suited for a principalship when empowering teachers is an objective of a school. A person holding Theory Y attitudes toward others would certainly seem well suited, but the question is whether a person holding Theory X attitudes could also empower teachers. The findings of this study suggest that a person holding Theory X attitudes could not be expected to empower the staff.

This is a difficult issue because it is so easy to give lip service to Theory Y attitudes. When faced with creating a true shared-governance school, however, the person who pretends to hold Theory Y attitudes will revert to his or her true self and say, "Yes, but if anything goes wrong, I'm the one who will be held responsible."

Resisting Hierarchical Barriers

It should come as no surprise that many principals enjoy their status in their schools. It is deeply satisfying to occupy the pinnacle position of the hierarchy. Members of the staff, the students, and the parents pay deference to the leader of the school through their questions and requests. Furthermore, many principals feel that such respect is their due for many years of successful teaching and serving in lesser administrative positions.

The problem is that such haughtiness is a luxury that few schools can afford. Without question, a remote principal distracts from and perhaps makes impossible the teacher empowerment process. Such behavior also discourages those who might wish to experiment with different instructional delivery systems.

The question is, How does the principal divest herself or himself from the trappings of the office? The answer, in part, is to be found in the advice of McGregor (1960), who indicated that successful leaders work alongside their staffs "in the trenches." For principals, this means being out in the building instead of hidden away in the office, constantly conferring with teachers who are working on new projects, lending a helping hand to all staff members, being a cheerleader whenever possible, and not allowing one's status as principal to get in the way of personal relationships with the staff.

Communication Networks

Another way a principal can throw off the trappings of the office is through communication patterns that diverge from the stereotypical vertical and horizontal patterns found in the bureaucracy. Certainly there is a need in every organization to send out memos and announcements occasionally, but such one-way devices are kept to a minimum in schools experimenting with empowerment and restructuring.

In the schools included in the empowerment and restructuring studies, communication abounded. Perhaps the person most heavily involved was the principal, because so many of the messages were either initiated by or directed to him or her. But others were heavily involved as well, and many messages did not involve the principal at all. This was perhaps the most outstanding feature of the communication networks in the experimental schools. People communicated with one another whenever it was necessary to communicate. There was no waiting around for the principal's permission; the message was sent, usually informally, by one staff member to another. If the principal needed to be aware of the content of the message, he or she would be included. Otherwise, the staff members were comfortable simply communicating with one another.

Perhaps the best and yet most extreme communication action came in an elementary school that was working on empowerment. There was a need for a faculty meeting to discuss various aspects of the empowerment effort, and so one of the faculty called the meeting without first checking with the principal. This episode was shared with other representatives of the consortium schools at a meeting shortly after the event occurred. The principal acknowledged that indeed the teacher had called the faculty meeting, and that he was startled but not angered by her initiative. This example serves to reflect the "let's get on with it" attitudes found in the shared-governance schools. The communication networks served to forward the effort instead of blocking it, as is so often the case in the traditional school setting.

Authenticity and Disclosure

The final quality found among principals of the experimental schools that served to remove the hierarchical barriers between themselves and their staff members was the principals' willingness to be open and authentic. Deception was not a characteristic of these principals as they worked with staff members, parents, community members, and students. It was almost as though they had learned the wisdom of the old bit of advice that if you always tell the truth, you don't have to remember what you said.

This principal behavior paid off in three ways, according to reports of observers in the schools:

1. It portrayed the principal as an open, honest, and sincere person who wanted to make the experiment a success. He or she was not interested in secretive practices, such as disclosing information only to a certain few or providing only partial information.

2. The behavior of the authentic principal encouraged the staff members to respond in kind. The result was a school in which all were able to disclose information without fear. Relationships improved, and the work of the school was enhanced.

3. The school culture began to reflect authenticity and openness as norms.

TRUST AS THE FOUNDATION OF SHARED GOVERNANCE

It is rare to find a school filled with trust and respect; when one is found, it is cause to rejoice. Such were our feelings as we visited several of the schools in the two projects. Not all of the schools could be so described, but those that did were wonderful schools to visit. The warmth of the school, the constant interaction between students and teachers, even in informal settings, and the positive feelings that existed between staff members and the principal all created the impression of a school that truly knew its role and purpose. As we discussed various elements of the program with faculty members, it was evident that each person was proud of the work he or she was doing and proud of the school's accomplishments.

Throughout our study of empowerment and restructuring, we became increasingly convinced of the power of shared-governance schools. Trust is the foundation of shared governance.

℘ CASE STUDIES

Case Study One: Johnson Elementary School— A Changing of the Guard

Johnson Elementary is a small school in a rural setting in the Midwest. Approximately 300 students attend grades K through 8. The school is situated in a traditional farming community with some light industry. Until the recent expansion of a factory in the area, immigrants typically were not drawn to the area. The majority of the students and their families are English-speaking Caucasians, with a small, but increasing, minority of Spanish-speaking immigrants.

The school had been led for 15 years by the same principal, Mr. Miller. A native of the area, Mr. Miller had worked for the district for a total of 26 years, making his way through the ranks to his position as principal. A sudden deterioration in his wife's health precipitated his hasty decision to retire from this position. His leadership style was authoritarian; he typically made unilateral decisions that were generally accepted by the staff and parents. He was not without his critics, however, some calling him "old-fashioned" and "closed-minded." Mr. Miller saw no need to relinquish control to the teachers and reserved veto power over any teacher recommendations. He spent a great deal of time in his office and communicated with the teachers via memos or by making announcements at staff meetings. His authority was followed primarily because he was so well known in the community, because of his long-term tenure with the school, and because the all-male school board was largely made up of his long-term friends, prominent business owners and leaders in the local church.

After such a long and stable history, the school has recently undergone several changes. Within the year prior to Mr. Miller's retirement, three of the eight members on the school board died of various age-related causes. They were quickly replaced, significantly changing the dynamics of the board. On the average, the new members are 25 years younger than the other members, and two of the three are women. The third is a young man of Hispanic background employed in a management position at one of the larger factories in the region.

Ms. Burns, the new principal, was promoted from within the teaching ranks. She had been teaching at the school for 10 years, having originally moved to the area with her husband, who is currently president of the newly expanded factory in the region. Ms. Burns's style of leadership is very different from that of her predecessor. She spends a great deal of time in the building, visiting classrooms, helping with classes, and eating lunch with the teachers. At staff meetings she asks the teachers to make recommendations for various problems, and she has implemented several of their ideas. A younger group of teachers is particularly excited about the changes in the school, having been given authority to implement a new program on improving attitudes about cultural diversity. A group of veteran teachers is uncomfortable with the recent changes, and they have been heard expressing the desire for things to go back to the way they used to be. There have been gatherings away from the school involving various subgroups of the teaching staff. The gatherings are informal, but the major topic of discussion is the situation at the school and the recent changes in the school board and the building administration. Ms. Burns is unaware that there are dissenting opinions among the teaching staff.

The school board has been watching the situation closely, with mixed opinions. Some of the longer-term members have been questioning the recent changes, while others are reserving judgment. The newer members are intrigued by the changes while becoming oriented to the roles and responsibilities of the school board. No attempts have been made yet to push for changes in the principal, but her behavior is being monitored carefully. There are rumors that the more powerful members of the school board have discussed replacing Ms. Burns as principal, but they are concerned about adverse consequences due to the prominent position her husband holds in the community.

Conversations About the Case Study

1. What characteristics of each principal's leadership style encouraged trust? Discouraged it?
2. What characteristics describing the school board are evidence of trust? Evidence of a lack of trust?
3. Did the teachers in this case behave in a manner that encouraged the principal's trust? Why or why not?
4. How would you describe the level of trust among the teachers?
5. What characteristics of the community might help or hinder trust?
6. What other factors appear to have affected the level of trust in this school?
7. Overall, what conclusions would you make regarding the level of trust within this school?
8. What recommendations would you make to Ms. Burns in order to improve the level of trust in this school? To the school board? To the teachers?

CYNTHIA MACGREGOR

Case Study Two: Trusting Empowerment to Work

You have been in the school district for 9 years and have just completed your third year as a successful principal in a school where you have supported and practiced empowerment. The staff and teachers at this school are both highly motivated and highly professional. These educators have responded well and have grown enormously under your empowering philosophy of leadership. You are proud of the great strides your staff has made during your 3-year tenure. Your empowering style of leadership has helped to increase test scores, parent groups are active in your school, teachers in the district seek to teach at your school, and you are beginning to involve local area businesses in partnerships with your school to benefit the students.

Your superintendent of 1 year has just named you principal of another school, where you are replacing the principal, a local man who has gone through the ranks, left the district for a year to be a principal elsewhere, and is well connected politically in the community. Upon his return to the district he was named principal, a position he held for the past 15 years. You have heard that the former principal ran the school in an extremely authoritarian manner and that the teachers and staff knew what the word "jump" meant. Furthermore, they knew that they were to say "Everything is great" at all times. As you assume your position you begin to understand the climate and the culture of the school. You find that the former principal held weekly faculty meetings, and once a month announced all the birthdays of the faculty members and led the entire faculty in singing "Happy Birthday." The principal had many committees that generated volumes of reports under his name, but none of the recommendations were ever implemented. On staff development days, the former principal expected the teachers to be in their rooms until 4:30 even though the district-sanctioned workshops ended at 3:30.

The superintendent complimented you on the way you worked with faculty and staff and asked you to take this new principalship and "breathe life" into the school. You examine the personnel records to discern the preparation levels of the faculty and staff and are impressed with the quality of many of the personnel. On your first day at the school you are further impressed with the highly professional way the teachers and staff dress. You note that there doesn't appear to be much informal conversation among the faculty and staff, but you attribute it to the business of beginning the school year under an unknown leader. At the first general faculty meeting, the level of attentiveness is very high, and you notice that there is no talking among any of the teachers during the presentations.

You decide to gain some further insights regarding the faculty and staff. In checking with the personnel office, you find that about 15% of the teachers left the school each year under the former principal. You also notice a number of memoranda in many of the files that you find to be essentially meaningless nonsense. There are also some memoranda that (based on your coursework in school law) appear to violate basic constitutional rights, and this alarms you. There had been gossip about such matters, but not being a gossip monger, you summarily dismissed it, as you always do with gossip.

Back at your new school, in your beginning conversations with the teachers and staff, you sense a high reluctance to discuss anything other than the weather. When you make a suggestion and ask for input, the staff members just nod their heads in agreement. To test the waters, you make a suggestion that is really outrageous and ask for input before working to implement it. Again, everybody just nods in agreement. You are disheartened by the apparent lack of caring about what is done. It seems everyone is just standing around waiting to be told what to do, how to think, and what to say.

At the second general faculty meeting, you introduce some new ideas about the concept of empowerment and the scope of empowerment in a school setting. You explain that you believe in collegiality and that you see your role as that of facilitator and resource gatherer. Once again, you are met with nods of agreement and no substantive discussions. Puzzled, you think about some of your coursework in informal group processes. This leads you to examine your faculty interactions. You note a trio of faculty members who, once they speak or act, everyone appears to follow. In meetings, these three teachers tend to speak positively about the former principal.

Back at the personnel office, you find that these teachers came to this school with the former principal. Furthermore, they don't seem to have the memoranda in their files that are prevalent in the other teachers' files. In examining these three teachers' credentials, you find that their qualifications are lackluster. You realize that your answers to the issues of breathing life into the school through empowerment lie outside the available documents. However, the available documents do give some clues as to the psychological posture of the school's faculty and staff.

Conversations About the Case Study

As principal with a mandate to vitalize the school, you realize, as always, that there is much work to be done to bring the faculty and staff into the realm of empowerment. You ask yourself the following questions:

1. What are the obvious issues with which you need to deal?
2. What are some of the latent issues, and how will you deal with them?

3. What kind of plan can you devise to discover what other issues need to be addressed to bring about empowerment?

4. What is your model of empowerment for this school?

5. How will you determine reality versus perception versus gossip?

6. How will you evaluate the information you gather throughout the entire process?

7. How will you implement empowerment for the school?

8. How will you evaluate your plan and its implementation?

9. Do you think it will be possible to "breathe life" into this school? Why or why not?

JAMES K. WALTER
MICHAEL L. SUPLEY

℘ VOICES FROM THE FIELD

Trust Between the Principal and Teachers

The tradition of the high school allowed only graduating seniors to participate in commencement exercises. When the board of education made the decision to allow students who lacked 1 credit hour toward graduation to walk across the stage at graduation, the principal exercised his right to retire early and terminated his employment 6 weeks before school ended in May. The faculty and community also were outraged that the tradition had been changed. The community soundly defeated the bond issue/tax levy that followed in June because they felt betrayed.

A new principal was hired in July for the coming school year. The change to restore trust and credibility was given to that principal, who immediately opened communication channels through an open-door policy and participatory decision-making procedures. Staff and community stakeholders had access to the new principal. Teacher, student, and parent advisory committees were formed to address critical issues, and thus, the revival process was activated.

The new principal fostered a shared vision within the organization to provide guidance, encourage motivation, and create favorable working conditions for staff members. The aim was to ensure that the entire staff was functioning as a cohesive unit to maintain the vision. He reinforced the importance of teacher support of school reform by including teachers in key positions at every level of planning. The teachers also worked hand in hand with parents and students to provide the necessary input in the newly proposed school improvement plan.

When asked to give a synopsis of his anticipated effect on the organization, the new principal stated that people feel more a part of an organization when they are given the liberty to do their job the way they want to do it. His attitude about risk taking encouraged his staff to try new ideas. He believed that if mistakes occur people should correct them and go on. As a result of his philosophy, the school initiated the Renaissance Program, which recognized student achievement in academics, athletics, attendance, and other areas. More students were motivated to be successful in their own individual areas. Curricular departments were given more autonomy to make curricular and budget decisions that directly affected them. Teachers were fully involved in building-level decisions.

One of the teachers' recommendations was the initiation of a monitor–protégé support program for beginning teachers. Noting that new teachers often leave the field within their first 5 years, the experienced teachers wanted to provide guidance and support. The teachers were given the professional days and budget to develop their own mentoring protocol.

Teachers placed a high priority on making technology accessible to staff and students. Recognizing that few staff members possessed the skills to use the technological equipment effectively, the teachers recommended that staff members be given the opportunity to attend a training academy. Monies were allocated to support the technological training for the teachers in this shared decision-making process.

The principal initiated featuring teachers in "Highlights of Education" at each monthly board meeting. Teachers were recognized for their instructional competency and creativity in the teaching–learning process. This afforded board members opportunities to see first hand what outstanding teachers were accomplishing in their district, as well as building a positive rapport between teachers and board members. When the principal requested stipends for departmental chairs, the board wholeheartedly supported this effort at recognizing the teachers' professional expertise.

When presented with proposals, the principal considered their relevance to the articulated mission of the school's improvement plan. Sharing governance with the teachers, parents, and students was the key to the principal's efforts to foster a trusting climate. Within 3 years, teachers were accepting empowerment to frame their own accountability and responsibility.

BETTY CHONG
ROSE TALENT

Trust Between the Principal and the District Office

The vision, mission, and goals of the entire school district are the responsibility of the district office. A principal dedicated to the empowerment of teachers realizes the importance of becoming a link between building needs and these planning cornerstones. By gaining the trust of the district office, the principal can become a voice for the teachers he or she represents.

The school districts I have served have a committee represented by various teachers, administrators, parents, and students to develop the school district vision, mission, and goals. Principals taking the time to inform and educate the district office regarding building needs were many times placed in leadership roles on this planning committee. Those principals who led through the empowerment of teachers seemed well prepared to represent what building needs existed. The time the empowered principal takes to build trust with district office administrators reaps dividends for teachers through an increased voice in district planning.

BRUCE JOHNSON

REFERENCES

French, J. R. P. Jr., & Raven, B. (1959). The bases of social power. In D. Cartwright (Ed.), *Studies in social power* (pp. 150–157). Ann Arbor: University of Michigan, Research Center for Group Dynamics, Institute for Social Research.

Goldman, P., & Dunlap D. (1990, October). *Reform, restructuring, site-based management, and the new face of power in schools.* Paper presented at the annual meeting of the University Council for Educational Administration, Pittsburgh, PA.

Hallinger, P., Murphy, J., Weil, M., Mesa, R., & Mitman, A. (1983). School effectiveness: Identifying the specific practices, behaviors for principals. *NASSP Bulletin, 67,* 83–91.

Krausz, R. R. (1986). Power and leadership in organizations. *Transactional Analysis Journal, 16,* 85–94.

McGregor, D. (1960). *The human side of enterprise.* New York: McGraw-Hill.

Miles, M. (1965). Planned change and organizational health: Figure and ground. In R. Carlson (Ed.), *Change processes in public schools* (pp. 58–69). Eugene, OR: Center for the Advanced Study of Education Administration.

Rahim, M. S. (1989). Relationships of leader power to compliance and satisfaction with supervisors; Evidence from a national sample of managers. *Journal of Management, 15,* 545–556.

Schein, E. H. (1992). *Organizational culture and leadership* (2nd ed.). San Francisco: Jossey-Bass.

Schmuck, R. A., & Runkel, P. J. (1972). *Handbook of organizational development in schools.* Washington, DC: National Press Books.

Taylor, F. W. (1916). The principles of scientific management. *Bulletin of the Taylor Society.*

Stimulating Risk Taking and Innovation

Schools have long been entrenched as bureaucratic organizations, offering teachers and students little say in their work life. This type of organizational structure impedes the development of a professional organization. There are several reasons why school bureaucracies hinder teacher efforts to be innovative and take risks. Most of those reasons result from the basic characteristics of the bureaucratic structure: (a) its hierarchy of decision making and (b) its centralization and standardization with bureaucratic rules that govern decision making and activities in the organization.

SCHOOLS AS BUREAUCRATIC ORGANIZATIONS

Hierarchy of Decision Making

One of the central requirements in developing innovative ideas and activities within an organization is for participants to be involved in the central decision making that affects their work and life in the organization. In a bureaucracy, decision making is reserved for those at the top of the hierarchy. In schools, this means that teachers and students have little voice in decisions that directly affect them. Teachers perceive that many things are imposed upon them without their input. Schedules, curriculum, job assignments, and discipline are just a few of the decisions that bypass teacher input in the typical bureaucratic organization. Teachers teach in isolation from other adults, with little opportunity for collaboration and collegiality. Involvement in decision making and collaborative and collegial opportunities are important practices that are at stake in the conflict between the bureaucratic and professional orientations (Hoy & Miskel, 1991).

Bureaucratic Rules

Rules, not professional judgment or innovative thinking, govern decision making within the bureaucratic organization. Rules provide little flexibility in actions and problem solving. Rules, codified and made explicit, leave teachers few opportunities to frame problems in alternative ways. Rules narrow their choices for problem solution and inhibit creative problem solving. Most important, rules prohibit experimentation with new ideas that run up against existing rules and regulations. One of the most troublesome issues perceived by teachers is that bureaucratic rules, meant to facilitate efficiency, do not allow for the mistakes and the back-to-the-drawing-board mentality that are essential for organizations that support and cultivate innovative thinking and action. Teachers may fear retaliation for mistakes or wrong decisions.

The bottom line is that standardization of procedures ensures that things will be done the same way they have always been done. Bureaucracies cannot tolerate changes in procedures, a characteristic that is directly in conflict with experimentation with new ideas and risk taking.

ORGANIZATIONAL ISSUES AND INNOVATION AND RISK TAKING

Organizational Health and Risk Taking

Any effort at change and innovation in an organization is predicated upon the nature and health of the system in which the innovation occurs. Firth and Kimptson (1973) stated that innovation is an essential element in organizational change. They reported that some common conditions that encourage change include the community and its acceptance of change, district support, and the role of the principal in helping to create an organizational climate that is open to and supportive of change. The principal can set the tone for professional educational discourse as a part of meetings and daily teacher contact (Lippitt, 1967). When principals show greater support for innovation (Lippitt, 1967), teachers tend to be more innovative and creative in their teaching.

For some time, Miles (1965) has suggested that the condition of an organization deeply affects attempts to change and implement innovation. In essence, for change to occur, the organization must be healthy. According to Miles (1965), efforts to innovate must target improvement of the organization's health if real change is to happen.

Miles (1965) identified the following 10 characteristics of a healthy organization:

1. Clear goals accepted by the participants.
2. Adequate communication that flows in all directions and is distortion free.
3. Equalized influence among all players in the organization.
4. Human resources used effectively.
5. Clear vision concerning what the organization is about.
6. High morale.
7. Innovativeness.
8. Autonomy.
9. Adaptability.
10. Problem-solving strategies and procedures.

Having clear goals entails having people and groups who are able to understand and accept the goals. The type of communication that characterizes a healthy organization is relatively distortion free and travels up, down, and across the organization. In a healthy organization, there is relatively equitable distribution of power and influence among all players. Resources can be maintained and coordinated with little strain on the organization. In addition, people and groups have a clear sense of identity and feel a great sense of membership in the organization. Morale is high. People have a sense of well-being and satisfaction with being members of the organization, and they believe that they can innovate and be supported in endeavors that may harbor some risk. A healthy organization remains autonomous from its larger outside environment, able to make decisions and develop ideas free from outside constraints. It can tolerate the stress placed on it from the outside while coping and maintaining stability. A healthy organization has the problem-solving processes it needs to function while coping, changing, and growing (Miles, 1971).

Role of Risk Taking and Innovation in School Change and Problem Solving

Amabile (1983) studied the impact of social factors in the creative or innovative work of people in organizations. Her research suggests that people who work in environments that have strong extrinsic constraints generally produce work that is less innovative or new. However, Amabile found that people placed in conditions that provide intrinsic motivation—specifically, free choice—generally produce more innovative work.

Getzels and Csikszentmihalyi (1976) conducted further research, looking at the interaction between person and environment in innovative work. Their longitudinal study of 179 art students at the Art Institute of Chicago identified the critical nature of problem finding in innovative work. In essence, their findings suggest that environments that support innovation provide many opportunities for people to engage in problem-finding exercises. Getzels and Csikszentmihalyi (1976) suggested that the type of problem-finding activity that should occur in organizations can be characterized as open and exploratory. They noted that integrating these dimensions in practice may be central to innovative leadership. However, Mink, Rogers, and Watkins (1989) found, in a study of school superintendents, that leaders experience dilemmas and binds in the more open, problem-finding orientation. Rather, they are better able to analyze problems in retrospect than in the immediacy of the activity.

Hennecke (1991) indicated that organizations should be more sensitive to change. For schools to support change, Hennecke (1991) suggested that encouraging constructive dissent and innovation, posing "what if" scenarios, establishing informal and unstructured groups, and gaining participant involvement must be the work of leaders. House's (1977) research extended this idea further by suggesting that leaders must hold high expectations of participants in the organization while avoiding the temptation to program their work and delimit their authority and discretion. Both dimensions support innovative practice and risk taking by participants.

Research by Leithwood and Montgomery (1982) indicated that a climate of experimentation and risk taking has a positive impact on school staff trying out new practices. It is interesting to note that Hall and Griffin (1982) suggested that school climates that encourage innovative thinking and openness among members of the organization provide a positive context for increased member involvement. Therefore, risk taking and trying new approaches and ideas may be necessary ingredients for change to occur, particularly change that involves restructuring the way people work, the school culture, and roles that people assume in school organizations. Lightfoot (1986) noted that a climate of experimentation and risk taking provides empowering opportunities for teachers to shape the educational environment. Some researchers (Berman & McLaughlin, 1977; Little, 1982) believe that teachers engage in greater innovative effort and change their classroom practices when they perceive that experimentation is encouraged and expected. According to Barth (1990), "Considerable research suggests that risk taking is strongly associated with learning . . ." (p. 513), and a climate of experimentation involves risk taking. Risk taking is critical if new ideas are to emerge in schools.

However, change is difficult. The principal's involvement in and support of efforts to bring about change in the school setting are critical factors in creating a risk-taking environment where change occurs. Lippitt (1967) viewed the principal's support for innovation as crucial in two ways: making visible the rewards for teacher innovation and encouraging conversations and dialogue that focus on trying new ideas.

Some researchers (Hall, 1988) have suggested that school principals should have the attributes of professional internal change agents. They should have knowledge of the change process; the phases of change; their role in the change; and skills relevant to the techniques, processes, and roles involved in the change. Wolcott (1973) pointed out that school principals often are in the position to assess the need for changes in the school because of the time they spend talking with small groups or individuals throughout the school building.

Hall (1988) noted that principals involved in a change facilitating team can provide leadership for change. Research on change facilitating teams suggests that these teams have a greater impact on change in schools when the principal is highly and effectively involved with the other outside change facilitators.

Teacher participation is critical. Schriesheim and Neider (1988) suggested that participants may perceive their involvement in organizational decision making in two ways. First, their perceptions are based on the belief that they have the authority to make final decisions. Second, their perceptions are influenced by the manner in which their input into decisions is solicited. Short, Miller-Wood, and Johnson (1991) found that efforts to create a more change-oriented environment in schools, capable of supporting innovation and risk taking, should consider strategies used to involve teachers in decision making. Teachers perceive a more change-oriented environment when they work collaboratively with their administrators and have the authority to make final decisions

(Short et al., 1991). These researchers found that, conversely, simply contacting teachers to solicit their opinions and information but failing to involve them in the final decision undermines teachers' perceptions that they work in an innovative, risk-taking environment. In addition, they found that failure to give teachers authority to make final decisions appears less critical when teacher input was not solicited than when input was solicited but teachers were not given authority or opportunity to make decisions.

Sivage (1982) suggested that there are certain characteristics of those who support innovation, including the following:

- Understanding of the change effort.
- Acceptance of the common vision about the innovation.
- Commitment.
- Negotiation so that outside forces do not erode the effort.
- Clarity of roles and responsibilities.
- Resources.
- Encouragement of involvement.
- Social support.
- Feedback.
- Evaluation.

Teacher Concerns About Innovation

When faced with new strategies for teaching or school organization, teachers understandably approach the adoption of these new strategies with some level of concern. Hall (1979) identified a number of stages of concern in which teachers may find themselves when undertaking an innovation. Hall's model, the Concerns-Based Adoption Model, provides some insight into the types of issues teachers face when exploring innovative ideas. Teachers initially may not have any information or knowledge about the innovation. At another level, they may have some knowledge but want to know how it works and how it will force them to change habits and practices they already use and know. Eventually, they may totally adopt the innovation and begin to change it, reconstructing it to be more effective.

Hall (1979) pointed out how teachers vary in their attitudes and anxieties toward new ideas. Understanding where they are in their level of concern can allow for the creation of strategies to help them move to an acceptance stage.

LEADERSHIP ISSUES AND INNOVATION

Organizational Change and Risk Taking and Innovation

Schlechty (1990) argued that "to change an organization's structure . . . one must attend not only to rules, roles and relationships but to a system of belief, values and knowledge as well. Structural changes require cultural change" (p. 38). The term often used is *reculturing* the organization. Creating an environment supportive of teacher risk taking and innovation will often require a large change in the culture of the school.

Rewarding Innovation

Only when innovation is rewarded does it become seen as valued in an organization. Participants who observe innovative efforts being acknowledged and having some impact on the organization will be more likely to engage in risk-taking, innovative behavior. The exercise of leadership, which facilitates greater innovative effort in a school, openly and frequently rewards such effort through verbal recognition, public display, and other forms of acknowledgment. Principals who reward innovation find resources to support innovations in their school, whether it be through writing grant proposals or soliciting funds from other outside sources. They see no barriers to trying new ideas. A typical strategy for rewarding innovation is to advocate for the teachers and their ideas to the public.

Supporting Innovation Through Systematic Processes

Innovation must be seen as a value that permeates the school organization. One of the many ways a principal can facilitate the development of such a value is by establishing systematic processes for cultivating innovative thought. Structures such as problem-solving teams can engage teachers and students in thought processes that render new ideas and alternative solutions to possible problems. Processes that bring groups of teachers together in some systematic way to provide direction and new ideas for a school can help the school grow in its ability to become adaptive and innovative.

The principal in Case Study One at the end of this chapter implemented two distinct processes that helped the school begin to think creatively and see things in a new light. She developed a "think tank" as a means of garnering the best thinking about the direction of the school and its mission. She used eight miniteams developed around eight "We believe" statements to create positions regarding what the school would look like if the school were to practice each statement. In addition, she solicited the help of a large corporation to conduct an environmental audit of the school to gain information about its health. These data would help to guide future decision making and to formulate new ideas for creating a more empowering environment for teachers and students. In Case Study Two, in contrast, little movement to empower occurred; the principal found it difficult to involve the teachers in shared decision making, much less any other processes to encourage innovative action.

Developing Teacher Problem-Solving Skills

Training in creative problem solving is important if teachers are to gain skills in problem framing, solution development, and evaluation. The untrained problem solver typically jumps to problem solution without spending much time framing and defining the problem. Also, these problem solvers develop few alternative solutions. Thus, principals who want to facilitate creative problem solving in their schools should provide training in the process. Training also promotes the value of problem-solving teams and the process itself. Once the training has occurred, it is important to develop structures within the school that involve teachers and students in problem-solving activities. These activities will be much more productive if participants are involved in issues of importance to them and their work life.

The principal in Case Study Three formed seven problem-solving teams around common planning periods for teachers. The very large school had 175 faculty members, so the communication required for problem solving was difficult. Each of the seven teams met and identified problems within the school. A representative from each team formed an eighth team, which then presented these problems to the entire faculty. The faculty then agreed about problem priorities. The seven teams met again to work on solutions, which were brought back to the eighth team. They prioritized the solutions and shared them with the seven teams. Finally, the faculty voted on the top solutions, and a faculty implementation team was established to oversee the problem solutions.

∞ CASE STUDIES

The following case studies are presented to illustrate how three schools approached the creation of an environment that fostered and facilitated teacher risk taking and innovation. Two were successful; the other was not. The questions that follow the case studies are provided to provoke stimulating conversations about issues in developing a risk-taking environment and culture in a school setting.

Case Study One: Leadership for Change

How do you create a more empowering environment in a large high school in an urban setting that enjoys great student diversity? We found great innovation and experimentation at work in this school.

Prior to attending the Chicago conference and being selected for participation in the empowerment project, the principal, a young Hispanic woman, organized a "think tank" consisting of 16 school personnel who had begun meeting during the previous summer. The purpose of this group was to generate goal statements and innovative ideas for helping the school to become a better place for students. After the principal attended the Chicago conference, the think tank became a vehicle for dialogue about empowerment and what that would mean for the school.

One decision made by the think tank was to establish action committees around the 11 goals or value statements developed by the think tank over the summer. Those values related to valuing each other; literacy; interpersonal communication; academic skills; purposeful direction; critical thinking; creativity; self-discipline; life readiness; social conscience; and open, nurturing, safe environments. Parents, teachers, students, and administrators were placed on the action committees. These committees addressed the question, "If this is one of our beliefs about our school, what should we be able to see happening in the school that would illustrate that we act on that belief?" The committees worked throughout the first year. Another committee that developed out of the work of the think tank attempted to restructure the school's management.

In the first year, the principal realized that they had not conducted any type of assessment of the school. Through the principal's initiative, a private engineering company agreed to conduct an environmental audit. Results of the audit were to be used in planning new programs for the school.

It became evident during the first year that the principal believed in networking with the community, business, and industry in order to find resources to support initiatives within the school. She worked hard to build links and dissolve boundaries between the school and community resources. A prolific grant proposal writer, she secured funds from a statewide business alliance, the governor's office, and many businesses in the state.

In February of the first year of the project, the state's governor visited the school to view the innovative activities being developed. He had heard about the school after its selection for the empowerment project and said that he wanted to visit schools that were doing creative things. While visiting the school, he held a meeting with faculty to talk about empowerment. At that session, a number of the teachers credited the principal for her vision and initiative in bringing about a greater focus on teacher empowerment in the school.

The facilitator for the school, a professor from an area university, attended faculty meetings during the spring months to get to know the faculty better. In these meetings he would discuss empowerment, invite the faculty's questions, and express support for all that the faculty was trying to accomplish. He had been a teacher and principal and related well to the faculty. Unfortunately, he moved out of the state by the end of the summer of the first year, but he became a confidant to the principal and provided a link to the university. In addition, his analytical skills, knowledge of organizations, and prior experience in schools helped him provide the principal and faculty with helpful insight in problem solving. The new facilitator for the school also was a professor at the university. It was hoped that she would bring these same skills and abilities to the facilitative role.

It should be noted that the teacher in the school who served as president of the local teachers union was supportive of the empowerment project. In fact, he was the initial lead teacher in the project, attending the Chicago conference. This seemed to lend some credibility to the empowerment efforts in the school. However, it was evident during the first year that the faculty achieved only about 50% acceptance of the empowerment idea.

The third year of the project was a tumultuous time for the school. The school implemented the new block scheduling developed the previous year, and this brought with it problems to be solved in terms of student and teacher concerns. In addition, the school district faced a teacher strike that threatened to close down all schools. Contract negotiations broke down, and teachers threatened to strike. It is interesting to note that teachers, on an individual basis, made a point of coming to the principal and telling her that she should not take the strike personally as an administrator. They told her that they respected her and appreciated all she was doing to empower them. They also told her that they were experiencing some conflict in striking because, although the strike was against administrators in the district, they appreciated her as their administrator.

This became a critical point for the principal. However, the state governor took over the strike situation as allowed by law. He conducted

STIMULATING RISK TAKING AND INNOVATION

2 to 3 weeks of hearings and put forth a contract that ultimately was accepted by the district teachers. Interestingly, the new contract called for collaborative decision-making teams in all 110 schools in the district. Because of its participation in the empowerment project, decision-making teams already were established at the school.

One of the action committees established by the think tank was the Interaction Group Team; in the third year, it was renamed the Collaboration Decision-Making Team. Originally made up of representatives from all of the action committees, by the third year it consisted of teachers, students, and business and community members. The team was functioning very well during year 3.

Everyone at the school felt that morale was good after the settlement of the teacher contract problem. The level of teacher involvement in decision making was very high at this point. The principal was encouraging the faculty to assume a large share of the leadership of the school. She assumed a stronger role of facilitator and resource person. Her ties with business, industry, and government brought several grants and much recognition to the school.

The third year of the project was an exciting year for the school, which had implemented many ideas that had been developed and tried out during the first two years. However, one decision brought an interesting reaction from the empowered faculty. The principal decided that the school would move to block scheduling. When this was announced to the faculty, they were upset. Their response was that they were an empowered faculty and they wanted to know why the principal had made the decision independently. Consequently, the faculty developed seven different proposals for the block scheduling. They held three public hearings, and the faculty voted at one. They decided on three 88-minute blocks and three 45-minute blocks for each day. It is interesting to note that when the principal made the decision about the block schedule, the faculty felt unempowered. Fortunately, the principal understood their concerns and empowered them to take leadership in designing the schedule. At issue was the fact that the principal had been urging the faculty for several years to think about moving to block scheduling. The faculty would not move on it, so the principal decided to take the initiative. However, the faculty did not want to be unempowered and responded by assuming leadership in the development process.

The primary goal of block scheduling was to improve instruction by increasing time on task, thereby enabling the teacher to fully utilize effective scientific teaching strategies and techniques that would enhance learning, comprehension, and achievement. It was during year 2 of the project that the faculty began to accept the notion of student as worker and teacher as facilitator.

During year 3, the principal decided to move to another district as head of the elementary and secondary programs. The Collaboration Decision-Making Team interviewed candidates for the principalship and ranked their choices. Their recommendations were sent to the board of education for the district. Unfortunately, the board of education appointed an individual who had not been on the school committee's list. This upset the faculty, who saw this as the traditional way of treating teachers. The individual who had been principal during the 3-year project responded, "They do not realize that not having a voice in a decision can give people, particularly in urban areas, permission to be cynical."

This principal called the empowerment project experience "3 years full of paradoxes." In those 3 years, the school experienced four superintendents, three assistant superintendents, a board recall, a teacher walkout, and a call for a teacher strike. Despite all of the instability at the district level and the tremendous changes within the school, the principal and faculty felt that meaningful involvement was a key accomplishment. They also indicated that intra-agency collaboration brought many resources to the school that aided in the successful implementation of many new ideas. The school attendance records, reviewed at the end of the third year, indicated that attendance was up. Records also showed that college-bound students rose from 25% to 69% of the school population. In addition, drop-out rates were down and test scores were up.

The faculty felt that the quality of relationships and the level of trust with honest communication had increased over the 3 years. Also, they felt that the honesty allowed disagreements that were free of rancor, with an increasing respect for diversity among faculty and students. Students felt real pride in being part of the school. Faculty and students expressed a sense of ownership in the school. The recognition coming to the school was especially appreciated by the faculty and students. A local business journal recognized the teachers' work in an article published in year 3. The *MacNeil-Lehrer Report* on PBS featured the school on a special program on education.

The principal and teachers have described the efforts at the end of the third year as transcending the process. They believe that it is an unfinished and complex story. The faculty identified three paradoxes involved in the empowerment effort. First, improvement is as real as the disruptions that it brings. Second, support for empowerment must be from the top down and from the bottom up simultaneously. Third, changing the norms of collegiality creates greater conflict among peers than when they do not interact in a collegial manner. The faculty at the school believe that they are modeling "respectful interaction."

Case Study Two: What Went Wrong?

What happened in this rural school? While the faculty of this school with 944 students in grades 3 through 5 felt great loyalty to the principal and believed that they had a strong school, little was accomplished in creating an empowering environment for teachers or students.

The interest of the superintendent precipitated the school's involvement in the project. At the beginning of the empowerment effort, the principal stated that he felt that his school already was empowered and he saw involvement in a formal effort to create an empowered school as an opportunity for professional growth. However, the idea of empowering students was met with less enthusiasm. The relationship of teacher empowerment to student empowerment was unclear to him. He described the school's first attempt to hold a retreat to discuss empowerment as mandatory, stating, "We are committed to the project, so all must attend."

During the first year of the empowerment effort, much confusion reigned. Teachers expressed concern about what the principal wanted them to do. They were looking for specific directives from him regarding how to proceed. It is important to note that the teachers had little involvement in decision making in the school with the prior principal. The new principal had allowed some teacher input, but the teachers expressed great insecurity about their ability to make decisions. One teacher said, "It is very scary to be turned loose." Another said, "Some teachers are satisfied with being told what to do and may not want to decide. Suppose our decisions are not good?"

During the first year of the effort, the school struggled due to the faculty's limited decision-making ability and confidence. The contrast between the former principal and the new principal created the illusion of empowerment; they were being asked for their input but experiencing little involvement. However, teachers expressed even greater concern about the barriers created by the central office and the board of education. The school's notion about the definition of empowerment proved to inhibit risk taking. The focus on empowerment as being only shared decision making created such a narrow definition that all effort began to center on that as a problem. At one meeting, the principal commented, "How much am I willing to give up? Will the superintendent be willing to give up power?" One teacher stated, "I may have been empowered too much. I once would sit back; empowerment will force me to speak out for what I believe."

In a faculty discussion about an upcoming retreat, the entire time was spent debating the location of the meeting. At the end, and after a few minutes of discussion, it was determined that the content of the retreat would focus on decision making. At a subsequent meeting to plan the retreat, teachers expressed confusion about "what the principal expected them to do." The teachers continued to see the empowerment effort as a project "to do" for the principal.

At the retreat there was mixed interest and involvement in the activities. Each grade level attended 1 whole day of the 3-day retreat. A consultant presented ideas on risk taking, decision making, group dynamics, and problem solving. Some teachers expressed negative reactions to the activities.

At an end-of-the-year meeting, results of teacher surveys were used to discuss concerns of importance to the teaching staff. They discussed areas of satisfaction and dissatisfaction and selected both long- and short-term goals on which to focus the next year. However, comments such as "If we plan it, can we do it?" and "How can we make decisions in areas in which the state has tight control?" were typical at this meeting.

During the summer prior to the second year of the effort, teachers met in committees they had selected to formulate directions for the long- and short-term goals. The major target goal centered on student self-discipline. A "Positive Action" curriculum was to be implemented in each classroom during the year. It is important to note that the goals did not focus on teacher decision making. Instead, they focused on the curriculum, implementing team teaching in the fifth grades, and a new media center schedule. However, ability grouping, a predominant activity in this school, was left unchallenged and unchanged in the goal-setting activities.

Much of the second year was spent on implementing the Positive Action program and team teaching. In a set of interviews during that year, teachers made the following comments:

"I wonder if we are on the right track."

"We have not made as much progress as we did last year."

"I understand the term [*empowerment*] better, but I am unsure of the direction we are heading."

"I don't fully understand the project even at this point."

"I am confused, I don't understand what it really is now, but last year I thought I did."

At the end-of-the-year retreat, the faculty discussed the development of class discipline plans, cooperative learning consistency in academic goals, the school dress code, and the compilation of a list of school supplies that needed to be mailed to parents.

Little happened during year 3. The principal found it difficult to involve teachers in decision-making activities. He was comfortable with their input regarding classroom curricular issues, an area in which teachers normally have control, but he hesitated to build involvement in any other school decision areas. The paternal "my teachers" response characterized the relationship between the principal and teachers. The teachers appeared to be very concerned about pleasing the principal. One said, "He takes care of us." By the end of the third year, little difference in school culture, roles, and norms could be seen from those observed 3 years earlier, prior to the empowerment effort.

Case Study Three: The Power to Change

This large suburban high school of nearly 3,000 students is considered one of the best high schools in the area. The faculty have demonstrated that they consider themselves to be good. They dress in a professional manner, and a stroll through the school indicates that quality and nice appearance are important to the faculty.

The principal had been at the school for 5 years when it entered the empowerment project. He is innovative, resourceful, and well connected with business and community leaders in the larger metropolitan area. He has skills in planning, evaluation, and group process. He had established a collaborative relationship with professional team effectiveness trainers from a local industry as well as with university faculty in order to share their expertise. He encouraged professionals to get involved in the school and regularly sent his faculty to visit places where innovative programs were under way. He had sent the guidance counselor to another state to observe and learn more about an innovative dropout prevention program. This openness to resources, new ideas, and change is characteristic of the principal.

It is important to note that the principal provided the impetus to become involved in the project. He had worked previously with one of the national project directors and greeted the school's selection with much enthusiasm. Upon his return from the Chicago conference, he immediately selected a team effectiveness trainer at a major area corporation to become the facilitator for the school. This choice was based on his desire to see the team concept implemented in his school and to provide appropriate training for these changes. He had also had prior experience with a national association for total quality management and had begun to incorporate into his management approach some of the concepts from Deming's work in that area.

In late fall, the facilitator and small groups of faculty began sessions to develop the teachers' abilities in creative problem solving. She worked with the faculty to create a collective vision for the school. Individual classroom teachers held discussion sessions within classes to look at problems, successes, and ways to make the school better in the future. Results of these sessions were conveyed to the department heads, who brought them to the Advisory Council. The results eventually led to the decision to develop leadership retreats for students.

During year 2, groups of teachers and students began participating in group process training. Teachers began to take responsibility for planning and coordinating all professional development days held in the school. The principal created the Common Planning Time Teams, which were seven teams composed of teachers with common planning periods who met to frame problems. On a monthly basis, a representative from each of the seven teams came together with the administration and the Advisory Council to discuss problems identified. Problems were prioritized and taken back to the Planning Time Teams for generation of alternative solutions. Those solutions were brought back to the larger group, and ideas were explored and initiated on a trial basis. One such problem, chronic lateness to class, was solved through the identification and solution generated by the Common Planning Time Teams.

The principal in this school was an "idea" person. He had tireless energy and was never satisfied with the status quo. He planted ideas and gave people resources to move forward with them. The Common Planning Time Team structure ensured that a faculty of over 175 persons had a voice in framing and solving problems. When the chronic lateness problem was solved, the faculty were elated that their idea had worked.

By year 3, all teachers had participated in the team effectiveness training. The focus shifted to training the students at a leadership retreat developed by the faculty. The principal was resourceful in finding potential supporters in the business community for activities under way in the school.

Case Study Four: Taking Risks

This suburban school district has six elementary schools. The district is divided into attendance areas that determine the assignment of students to the elementary schools. Those attendance areas had not been adjusted since they were established in 1983. During that same year the board of education adopted a policy that set limits for classroom enrollment in elementary schools. The limit set for kindergarten classrooms was 30 students per classroom. To address enrollment increases, the district established an administrative policy that assigned a sequential number to each kindergartner as he or she enrolled. Students whose numbers exceeded the building capacity were transferred to another elementary attendance center in the district. As the years passed, the demographics of the district changed. There was a shift in housing patterns in the district as the white population moved from the southeast to the northeast part of the city. The significance of this shift was twofold. One important result was that the percentage of the minority population of the schools in the southeast part of the city increased as the overall student population decreased in these schools. The second significant effect was that the student population in the predominantly white upper middle class attendance center increased to the point that there were more kindergarten students enrolled than could be accommodated. Although parents and teachers had voiced objection to transferring kindergartners in the past, these had generally been individual sets of parents expressing their personal opinions and concerns about the transfers.

Early enrollment projections indicated that there were 18 more kindergartners enrolled at Jefferson Elementary than could be accommodated. Concerned teachers and parents attended the regular board meeting conducted on June 30, 1997, to publicly express their opposition to the transfer of kindergarten students and requested the board members to consider other options. Many parents opposed the transfer because they had purchased their homes based primarily on the elementary school assignment boundaries. Others who had children currently enrolled at the neighborhood school felt it added an extra burden on parents who would have to attend conferences and meetings at two different elementary buildings. Teachers agreed with these concerns and expressed a third concern about students missing valuable instructional time while they were riding the bus from their neighborhood school to the assigned building. The superintendent suggested to the board they were being forced to make a decision on policy because a small group of constituents was applying pressure by publicly misrepresenting the board's motives. He contended that the board was being asked to ignore the issues of the quality of the educational program and the financial condition of the district. Board members instructed the superintendent to form a committee that included participants from the parent group, teachers, and building administrators to study other options and devise a workable plan for the approaching school year.

On July 6, committee members met to discuss viable options. The committee consisted of three elementary principals, kindergarten teachers from each of the six attendance areas, a parent representative from each of the attendance areas, the Community Teachers Association president, and the director of elementary education. Although the cost to transfer students to other buildings was estimated at $358 per student for the school year, the committee voted to present the option of adding a third section of kindergarten to the overcrowded attendance center by placing a trailer to accommodate the students and adding a teacher. This required an expenditure of $55,800. The committee presented this option to the board members at the next board meeting. It was approved unanimously. The superintendent and director of elementary education were instructed to begin the process of hiring a teacher and getting the trailer in place before August 21, the first day of school.

ROSE TALENT

Conversations About the Case Studies

This section is intended to foster a "conversation" regarding risk taking and innovation in schools. As you discuss and explore the leadership issues related to this topic, use the following questions to focus your thinking and exploration.

1. How would you characterize the leadership strategies of the principals in Cases One and Three? How do they compare with those of the principal in Case Two?

2. How would you characterize the organizational health of each of the schools in the cases?

3. Could you identify the goals for each of the schools?

4. How would you explain the confusion expressed by the teachers in Case Two?

5. Describe the problem-solving skills of teachers in the cases. Compare and contrast.

6. How was the valuing of innovation communicated by the principals in Cases One and Three? Compare this with Cases Two and Four.

℘ VOICES FROM THE FIELD

Role of Risk Taking and Innovation in School Change and Problem Solving

Students in our district who face severe emotional, social, and/or environmental problems are at risk of academic failure. Parents blame teachers, and teachers blame parents. Negativity dominates the teachers' room, and struggling students either give up or act up. The spiraling effects of academic failure frustrate the community, administrators, teachers, parents, and students alike.

It is my experience and conviction that the ability to reverse the tide of academic failure lies in empowering parents and members of the community to be actively involved in the educational process. In 1997, a community and parent volunteer program was implemented in my school district to foster healthy self-esteem and academic success at the fourth and fifth grade levels. Community members and parents became aware of their power to make a positive impact upon the lives of our students. Volunteers contributed their skills, talents, encouragement, and spirit of commitment to education. Programs were designed in collaboration with the teachers to combat student histories of poor social adjustment, stressful home lives, and academic failure.

Three years later, results of these programs were evident in the reduction of referrals of students for special education services, increased communication and trust between teachers and volunteers, and the creation of a cooperative family atmosphere throughout the school. When barriers that separated our school from the community came tumbling down and parents and members of our community were empowered to play a vital role in the educational process, all students benefited, including those who were at risk of academic failure.

JUDY K. STATLER

REFERENCES

Amabile, T. M. (1983). *The social psychology of creativity.* New York: Springer-Verlag.

Barth, R. S. (1990). A personal vision of a good school. *Phi Delta Kappan, 71,* 512–516.

Berman, P., & McLaughlin, M. W. (1977). *Federal programs supporting educational change: Volume VII. Factors affecting implementation and continuation.* Santa Monica, CA: Rand.

Firth, G. R., & Kimptson, R. D. (1973). *The curricular continuum in perspective.* Itasca, IL: Peacock.

Getzels, J. W., & Csikszentmihalyi, M. (1976). *The creative vision: A longitudinal study of problem finding in art.* New York: Wiley.

Hall, G. E. (1979). Assessing and facilitating the concerns-based approach to facilitating change. *Educational Horizons, 57*(4), 202–208.

Hall, G. E. (1988). The principal as leader of the change facilitation team. *Journal of Research and Development in Education, 22*(1), 49–59.

Hall, G. E., & Griffin, T. (1982, March). *Analyzing context/climate in school settings: Which is which?* Paper presented at the annual meeting of the American Educational Research Association, New York.

Hennecke, M. (1991). Toward the change-sensitive organization. *Training, 28*(5), 54–59.

House, R. H. (1977). A 1976 theory of charismatic leadership. In J. G. Hunt & L. Larson (Eds.), *Leadership: The cutting edge* (pp. 125–151). Carbondale: Southern Illinois University Press.

Hoy, W., & Miskel, C. (1991). *Educational administration: Theory, research and practice.* New York: Random House.

Leithwood, K. A., & Montgomery, D. J. (1982). The role of the elementary school principal in program improvement. *Review of Educational Research, 52,* 309–339.

Lightfoot, S. L. (1986). On the goodness of schools: Themes of empowerment. *Peabody Journal of Education, 63*(3), 9–28.

Lippitt, R. (1967). The teacher as innovator, seeker, and sharer of new practices. In R. Lippitt (Ed.), *Perspectives on educational change* (pp. 77–99). New York: Meredith.

Little, J. W. (1982). Norms of collegiality and experimentation: Workplace conditions of school success. *American Educational Research Journal, 19,* 325–340.

Miles, M. B. (1965). Planned change and organizational health: Figure and ground. In R. Carlson (Ed.), *Change processes in the public schools* (p. 96). Eugene, OR: Center for the Advanced Study of Educational Administration.

Miles, M. B. (1971). Planned change and organizational health: Figure and ground. In F. M. Trusty (Ed.), *Administering human resources* (pp. 38–50). Berkeley, CA: McCutchan.

Mink, O., Rogers, R., & Watkins, K. (1989). Creative leadership: Discovering paradoxes of innovation and risk. *Contemporary Educational Psychology, 14*, 228–240.

Schlechty, P. (1990). *Schools for the 21st century.* San Francisco: Jossey-Bass

Schriesheim, C. A., & Neider, L. N. (1988, August). *Distinctions among subtypes of perceived delegation and leadership decision making.* Paper presented at the annual meeting of the American Psychological Association, Atlanta, GA.

Short, P. M., Miller-Wood, D., & Johnson, P. E. (1991). Risk taking and teacher involvement in decision making. *Education, 112*, 84–89.

Sivage, C. R. (1982). Oiling the gears: How the principal helps or hinders change. *Principal, 61*(4), 20–23.

Wolcott, H. F. (1973). *The man in the principal's office: An ethnography.* New York: Holt, Rinehart, and Winston.

Using Critical Events to Frame New Opportunities

Schools can be characterized as social organizations that experience ongoing events, some predictable and others unanticipated. These events revolve around the players in the school setting in rather complex ways. The predictability of some events seems to reduce the level of anxiety within the organization and allows for planning to deal with them. However, many incidents in schools are unexpected and unplanned for, creating chaos, conflict, and retreat from risk taking.

THE EBB AND FLOW OF EVENTS IN SCHOOLS

Predictable Events

Many school events characteristically occur around the opening and closing of school, school holidays, report card grading periods, and annual special school observances, making them cyclical and predictable. For instance, it is well documented that discipline problems are fewer at the beginning of the school year, usually during the first 3 weeks. During this period, expectations are high for a good year. Teachers and students are in a "honeymoon" period with each other, and norms are being negotiated for each classroom. Everyone is taking the measure of everyone else.

It also is a characteristic of schools that there is a "let-down," or relaxed, period following holidays. This can be a difficult time for students at risk for failure, who lose the momentum of school attendance while on break and are thus more likely to drop out of school following holidays. Holiday periods also bring about the predictable behavior problems that occur just prior to the break; discipline problems increase just before Christmas holidays and spring break. Teachers indicate that sometimes they are just persevering until the break.

Unpredictable Events

While predictable events allow for planning and some amount of readiness, unanticipated events can be a source of crisis for schools. Events such as the death of a student, a tornado that tears apart the school facility, the sudden departure of the principal, revelations regarding unethical behavior on the part of a faculty member, and parent anger over a student–teacher episode can trigger chaos and conflict if no mechanism is in place to deal with unpredictable events. Conflict can grow over the perceived negative consequences of a critical event, and laying blame becomes the primary activity of the school participants. Over time, conflict can erode the creative, professional environment of a school and render a faculty unable to recognize opportunities and collaborate together.

THE TRADITIONAL VIEW OF CONFLICT AS A NEGATIVE PHENOMENON

March and Simon (1958) defined *conflict* as a breakdown in the standard mechanisms of decision making, so that an individual or group experiences difficulty in selecting an alternative. This negative view is supported by many other researchers and writers. Associated with conflict are such issues as incompatibility of groups and individuals, frustration over lack of control and autonomy, and struggles over scarce resources. Conflict in schools has been viewed as interfering with teaching and learning. Things are supposed to run smoothly in schools, and conflict has been seen as departure from the norm of peaceful cooperation.

REDESIGNING HOW PROBLEMS AND CONFLICTS ARE MANAGED

Conflict exists whenever people interact. Some conflict is desirable in organizations, because an organization can use it to accomplish certain goals. The appropriate use of conflict can actually have the effect of creating an instability that allows change to occur. Organizations have come to realize that conflict should be managed rather than avoided or thwarted. To stifle conflict is to squelch vitality and the capacity for growth and change. Conflict management has become a dominant theme in organizational effectiveness. Conflict management means purposeful intervention in order to foster and stimulate positive conflict or to prevent or resolve harmful conflict. The concept of conflict management as an approach to dealing with conflict in organizations suggests that conflict can be both good and bad. However, the bottom line is that conflict in organizations is inevitable.

Using Problems to Assess Current Status

The major sources of conflict in schools appear to be values, beliefs, and goal agreement. In other words, conflict can be traced to the frustration people in schools feel about those things about which they care deeply.

Conflict Management Theory

Conflict management styles can be grouped into five categories: *obliging, avoiding, integrating, dominating,* and *compromising* (Thomas, 1976; Rahim, 1983). These five categories can represent two dimensions: a concern for people and a concern for tasks, or, as we learned from Thomas (1976), a concern for others (cooperative) and a concern for self (competitive). Thomas and Kilmann (1974) have developed an instrument, the Thomas-Kilmann Conflict Mode Instrument, to measure conflict management styles. Figure 6.1 provides sample items from that instrument.

One may ask, "Which conflict management style is most effective?" There is some agreement that a combination of integrating and obliging styles (Burke, 1970; Renwick, 1977) can be the most effective conflict management style. However, some (Lawrence & Lorsch, 1967) have suggested that the obliging style may hinder goal attainment. It appears that the avoiding style may be the most ineffective conflict management style used in organizations.

One writer (Labovitz, 1980) has listed strategies that relate to the integrating style. These include

- Accepting the goals of the other person.
- Engaging in problem analysis to identify the issues underlying the problem.
- Framing the problem as a goal or obstacle rather than jumping immediately to the solution.

Figure 6.1
Sample items.

Sample Items for the

Thomas-Kilmann Conflict Mode Instrument

By Kenneth W. Thomas & Ralph H. Kilmann

Instructions: Consider situations in which you find your wishes differing from those of another person. How do you usually respond to such situations? On the following pages are several pairs of statements describing possible behavioral responses. For each pair, please circle the "A" or "B" statement that may be very typical of your behavior, but please select the response which you would be more likely to use.

8. A. I am usually firm in pursuing my goals.
   B. I attempt to get all concerns and issues immediately out in the open.

15. A. I might try to soothe the other's feelings and preserve our relationship.
    B. I try to do what is necessary to avoid tensions.

26. A. I propose a middle ground.
    B. I am nearly always concerned with satisfying all our wishes.

NOTE. Reproduced by special permission of the Publisher, Consulting Psychologists Press, Inc., Palo Alto, CA 94303 from **Thomas-Kilmann Conflict Mode Instrument** by Kenneth W. Thomas and Ralph H. Kilmann. Copyright 1974 by Consulting Psychologists Press, Inc. All rights reserved. Further reproduction is prohibited without the Publisher's written consent.

A discussion of these five conflict management styles may be helpful.

1. *Dominating:* Relies on force and competition, using force and power to solve the conflict. Some examples of this style include physical force, threats, use of authority and expertise, and argumentative dialogue.

2. *Obliging:* Is characterized by an accommodating manner. It is non-assertive in nature with individuals ignoring or covering differences in order to solve the conflict issue.

3. *Avoiding:* Tends to ignore the conflict issues altogether. This style is characterized by withdrawal, refusal to discuss the conflict at all, and general uncooperativeness. As with the obliging conflict management style, individuals are non-assertive with others.

4. *Integrating:* Is assertive yet cooperative in nature. The needs of both parties in the conflict are considered and attempts are made to satisfy both sides in resolving the conflict.

5. *Compromising:* Attempts to make each party to the conflict "give" or sacrifice a little in order to resolve the conflict issue. Both parties win and both parties lose.

- Placing the problem away from a personal frame.
- Considering solutions and evaluations of the solutions apart from the problem statement.

Problem-Solving Processes

When a school faculty has experience in problem solving, it will be more willing and able to deal with unexpected events as they occur during the school year. Chenoweth and Everhart (1994) suggested that the "essence of school change is about learning to work collaboratively on an actual school problem" (p. 423). There are a number of approaches to problem solving in the literature. However, problem-solving models that promote creativity offer the greatest opportunity for critical events to be framed and used to move the school forward. Parnes, Noller, and Biondi (1977) developed a creative problem-solving model that consists of the following five steps:

1. Fact finding (gathering information about the situation).
2. Problem finding (identifying the many problems or subproblems).
3. Idea finding (using many techniques to create new ideas or combinations of new ideas).
4. Solution finding (using criteria to evaluate ideas systematically).
5. Acceptance finding (developing a plan of action for idea implementation).

Within this model, it appears that the activity of brainstorming leads to more creative ideas. It may be that the deferred judgment associated with brainstorming opens the door to alternative ideas and permits participants to explore ideas without risk.

Brainstorming requires that a group generate as many ideas as possible in a short period of time. The process demands that participants withhold any evaluation or judgment regarding the ideas being generated. A recorder keeps a log of the ideas for reference when the team moves to the next stage in the problem-framing, problem-solving process. Rules for brainstorming are as follows:

1. Discourage negative evaluation in order to encourage freedom of thinking.
2. Build on each other's ideas by encouraging and accepting.
3. Accept even wild ideas.
4. Try for quality of ideas.
5. Record every idea generated and set a time limit.

Changing Attitudes

Attitudes that provide resiliency and openness to new challenges are what could be characterized as "can do" attitudes. Teachers who view most problems as an opportunity to learn and make the school a better place for children have the greatest chance of contributing to a school's ability to turn critical, unanticipated events into positive growth. Teachers who believe there is always something that can be learned, who see themselves as professionals with an obligation to improve the school's teaching and learning process, are likely to see themselves as competent and skilled and to believe that creativity and perseverance can overcome all boundaries or obstacles in a situation. Schools that use unanticipated events as challenges to grow have a tendency to view things as neither black nor white and prefer to look at alternatives.

The reality of change is that teachers' and administrators' problems and anxieties may prevent them from embracing the challenges inherent in unforeseen situations. These problems and anxieties (Barell, 1991) may stem from a number of causes:

- Lack of knowledge about one's own way of thinking.
- Lack of experience with problem-solving experiences.
- Rigidities in one's own way of thinking, such as being unable to see multiple perspectives on or possibilities in a problem.
- Fear of losing control in expressing multiple perspectives among peers.
- Fear of loss with new ways of approaching issues within the school organization.

However, it is important to understand that a person can be capable of overcoming these fears and becoming a "thoughtful" participant in the problem-solving process. Barell (1991) suggested that thoughtful people are necessary for effective, collaborative, creative problem solving in the school. He describes the thoughtful person as one who is

- Confident in his or her own problem-solving abilities.
- Persistent.
- Able to control impulsivity.
- Open to other's ideas.
- Cooperative.
- A good listener.
- Empathic.
- Tolerant of ambiguity.

- Able to research problems.
- Able to have multiple perspectives.
- Able to relate prior experiences to the problem.
- Able to pose what-if questions.
- Curious.
- Able to transfer concepts and skills from situation to situation.
- Able to ask good questions.

LEADERSHIP ISSUES AND PROBLEM SOLVING

Using an Outside Facilitator in Problem Framing

Schools involved in any change effort need objective feedback about the meaning of events and help in framing problems that may arise as part of the change effort. A central finding in the Empowered School District Project is that creating empowered schools, where teachers believe that they can treat all events as opportunities, is an evolutionary process. Roles, behaviors, and ways of doing the work of the organization are being restructured. The change effort is enhanced by the support of the outside facilitator, who has expertise in organizational consultation (Schein, 1969). The facilitator can assist the school in processing what is happening and learning how to deal effectively with conflict and problems that arise. Facilitators are critical in helping schools overcome barriers in problem framing and problem solving. In addition, they can act as confidants to the principals, who often are struggling against great odds in the change effort. They also can help principals understand the changing role of the administrator in the process.

Developing Creative Problem-Solving Skills in Teachers

Training in creative problem solving starts with giving teachers the time and opportunity to engage in problem-framing activities. If little time is allowed for brainstorming about possibilities, problems will be defined in the customary way with the usual solutions. A typical response to an unanticipated event within a school is to rush to define and solve the problem. Exploration of the opportunities that might reside within the event is lost, and, thus, the school may not grow from the experience. Conflict may ensue and retrenchment follow.

To enhance teachers' creative problem-solving skills, Barell (1991) suggested using the "Seven R Strategy" to generate alternative views on issues and to advance reflective thinking. The seven steps are as follows:

1. *Recognize* the feelings one has in the situation.

2. *Research* the information needed to understand what is going on.

3. *Represent* the situation internally through visual thinking.

4. *Relate* the situation to others, both similar and dissimilar.

5. *Reduce* the situation to a number of parts.

6. *Reflect* on the assumptions, definitions, and biases that should be questioned.

7. Consult *resources* who can help.

While training in various problem-solving models complements the problem framing, it is important that faculty know how to work in effective groups and performing teams (Katzenback & Smith, 1993). Creative problem solving is a collaborative venture in which those who are untrained in group processes will struggle.

Developing Structures for Collaborative Work on Issues

Teachers need to be given the opportunity to come together to talk about school issues and find ways to improve the school. Structures can be developed that bring them into contact with each other over concerns that are meaningful to them. Working groups (Katzenback & Smith, 1993), or groups that interact primarily to share information, best practices, or perceptions, can provide a forum and structure to begin the collaboration process. These groups simply provide ways for teachers to give each other support and feedback. Working groups can cultivate a more collaborative working environment, which can reduce conflict.

Team structures (Katzenback & Smith, 1993), in which a small number of people are equally committed to a common purpose, goals, and accountability, can provide the problem-framing and problem-solving structures and processes that allow a school to respond to unanticipated critical events as opportunities.

Developing Communication Skills Among Faculty

Information sharing and problem solving occur in empowered organizations in complex ways. The level of communication that must occur if teachers are to engage in collaborative efforts to help them understand unexpected, critical events in school requires (a) listening skills, (b) the ability to use clarifying and probing statements in their interactions in the problem-solving mode, and (c) the ability to check for understanding so that participants have a common perception of what is being discussed. Faculty must learn how to accept and give constructive feedback and share knowledge and skills. In turn, new ideas and suggestions must be encouraged, and structures that bring teachers together to interact must be developed.

⁊ CASE STUDIES

Some schools seize opportunities and build substantially better learning situations for all participants in the organization. Other schools stumble and allow problems to impede efforts at growth, innovativeness, and increased participation of teachers and students in the life of the school. How does that happen? The following cases should provide some insight into how five schools framed critical events in ways that increased or reduced their chances to find opportunities for growth.

Case Study One: A Stunning Blow

This comprehensive high school of 1,400 students faced many challenging critical events during the 3 years it was involved in creating an empowered school. These included the resignation of the principal, who was involved, with other school personnel, in a scandal; the subsequent hiring of an acting principal for a year; the suicide of a student; and other events. In some cases, the faculty took the critical events and used them as opportunities to change; in other cases, the event forced the school into a stalemate.

The faculty began the empowerment effort with the anticipation that their involvement would help them address the needs of students who were at risk. They expressed the feeling that they were already empowered since they were involved, to some extent, in various decisions made in the school. They also became part of the Public Professional Demonstration School Project, although some faculty were concerned about involvement in two major change efforts.

During the first year, the focus of the school's change efforts was on strategies for helping students at risk. These efforts included the development of (a) a parent support team with informal gatherings and seminars, (b) a GED class to enable students who were behind in their studies to take the exam and graduate with their class, (c) a GED class for parents of the students as a means of empowering these parents as role models and student supporters, and (d) a mentorship program with an area elementary school in which high school students met weekly with the younger students who had been identified as being at risk. All faculty were proud of these accomplishments.

Also during the first year, the faculty used the tragic suicide of a student to engage in increased activity focused on empowering students, teachers, and parents to deal with adolescent crises. The school provided mental health professionals to help in counseling students on both an individual and a group basis. Follow-up programs were provided both at home and in the school. A staff development program on suicide was presented, and a community forum was held to address the prevention of teenage suicide. The teachers gathered follow-up data to determine teacher and student perceptions of how things were going in the school and what areas needed attention. Departmental faculty met with the administration to discuss the year and to provide feedback on directions that the school should take in creating a more empowering environment for all participants.

During the June retreat, the faculty focused on creating a vision for the school. They specifically wanted to create a supportive environment in which praise and encouragement were dominant themes. Small groups worked on the vision statement, and participants left the retreat expressing good feelings and enthusiasm for the new year. The accomplishments of the previous year provided a springboard for action during the coming year.

The principal was well liked. The faculty felt that he was someone who would take care of them. People were forgiving of certain characteristics because they liked him so much. During September of that year, the principal urged the faculty to make more of their own decisions without checking with him first. In a faculty meeting he said, "You do not need to check with me first on every decision you make." Teachers were concerned about the growing number of programs in which they had become involved: The Empowered School District Project, 21st Century Schools, and the Public Professional Demonstration School Project. After some discussion, the faculty decided that since each project focused on empowerment, they should proceed with involvement in all of them. They perceived that each would provide a vehicle for shared governance.

During a meeting of the principal, lead teacher, and other administrators in October of the second year, the lead teacher suggested that the teachers did not want to become involved in additional decision making.

USING CRITICAL EVENTS TO FRAME NEW OPPORTUNITIES

The first resistance to change became evident during this session. The lead teacher believed that teachers were realizing that they were being pushed toward being more involved and were balking at the attempts. The principal decided to soften his approach and let teachers who were interested in the process assume the leadership. This collection of persons present at the October meeting, known as the Leadership Team for the past year, changed its name to the Administrative Team, with the lead teacher assuming primary leadership responsibilities.

During November, numerous meetings were called only to be canceled at the last minute. In one meeting, it became obvious that there was concern about the purpose of the meetings. The lead teacher lacked the skills to bring about effective group discussion and decision making, and there was frustration among the members of the Administrative Team regarding the quality of discussion and the lack of productivity of the group. As the team met in late November, it became obvious that teachers were uncomfortable with the principal's decision to leave decision making up to the faculty. There was open hostility at one meeting regarding the role of the lead teacher. Was she to lead, facilitate discussion, or simply coordinate the efforts of the team?

In December, the principal announced his resignation. It had been made public that he had allowed a grade change for an athlete to make him eligible to play football. The grade change incident created much turmoil in the school and community. The football team, which had eight wins and no losses, was forced to forfeit all of its games and became ineligible to compete in the state playoffs. The incident also resulted in the reassignment of the teachers who were involved in the grade change. The superintendent and an assistant superintendent were given letters of reprimand by the school board because of their handling of the incident; both had known of the grade change.

This critical incident created a leadership void. The faculty were at a loss as to how to proceed. They did not seem able to comprehend what was happening to them or how they would be able to overcome the turmoil. The acting principal met with the faculty in December and found an angry group of teachers who had difficulty making any decisions. Within this climate, the Administrative Team began to meet weekly and to request longer meeting times. They decided to focus the faculty on shared decision making and finding answers to the following questions: "Who are we? What do we stand for? How are decisions made? How can we as a faculty be involved in those decisions? Are we autonomous? Is there support from the superintendent for shared governance? What information should be shared? How? With whom? How does the acting principal need to change? What do we need to take on first in goal setting?" It was during this series of meetings that the Administrative Team decided that the faculty must be deeply involved in the selection of the new principal. It was during these months of meetings, also, that the Administrative Team began to address the lack of trust, communication, commitment, and innovation evident in the school. During a February board of education meeting, the athletic director, the school counselor, and all coaches who were involved in the grade-change incident were relieved of their duties and given teaching positions for the fall.

During the spring, the faculty became involved in the selection process for the new principal. The individual chosen expressed great commitment to empowerment and its importance in the school. In the third year, the faculty were involved in the construction of a new budget. They became much more involved in curricular issues. However, it was felt that confusion and frustration carried over from the previous year. Through great upheaval and a leadership void created by the resignation of the principal, the school was given an opportunity to unfreeze and begin to change, although the change was difficult and small. However, the faculty did begin to recognize areas of weakness while addressing specific student needs.

Case Study Two: Empowerment Works

This case describes how one elementary school faced a critical event and used it to move toward greater commitment to the empowerment concept. It appeared that the event might erode all efforts to empower that had occurred in the school. However, the event was framed as an opportunity, and positive results ensued.

During the second year of the Empowered School District Project, this elementary school was faced with a problem. In a faculty meeting, the principal had announced that a district-wide committee had been formed to make a recommendation to the superintendent regarding the program for the federally funded Chapter Two program. He stated that the committee, on which he and a teacher in the school served, might agree to use as a model for all the schools a program that was housed in another elementary school in the district. The teachers were very upset and stated that the program in the other school used ability grouping, a plan fully opposed by this school's faculty. In fact, one teacher stated, "This faculty has the philosophy that ability grouping is detrimental to learning for students. We do not use ability grouping in this school." Many of the teachers perceived that the principal would bow to district pressure and not support their philosophy in the decision process.

In desperation, a faculty representative from the school's Problem-Solving Team contacted the project facilitator and expressed grave concern that "everything we have worked for so far is about to be compromised. We are an empowered faculty, and this should not happen." With the advice of the facilitator, the teachers began a process of gathering literature reporting empirical studies that illustrated the detrimental effects of ability grouping on students. The facilitator assisted them as they conducted literature searches and constructed a logical argument against the use of ability grouping. The facilitator contacted the principal to find out his position on ability grouping and the events surrounding the faculty meeting. She learned that the principal had not seen himself as succumbing to district pressure. He voiced concern that the teachers had perceived him as doing so in his statements. He was functioning on the belief that there was no need to act until the committee had made its recommendation. Upon that step, he felt that the school could present an argument to the superintendent to use an approach to teaching that meshed with the teaching and learning philosophy adopted by the entire faculty.

His discussions with the facilitator caused him to change his view and support an effort to build a case for the school to retain its current Chapter Two model. He contacted the superintendent and learned that they could make a presentation to the board the night the committee recommendation came before the board of education. Armed with a powerful document outlining their argument for their program, based on research, the teachers were successful in getting both superintendent and board approval to retain their current program model even though the other elementary schools were directed to implement the program model using ability grouping.

What is significant about this critical event and its outcome is that a new group of teachers in the school began to see, firsthand, the impact of coming from an empowering environment. Reluctant teachers began to talk about being empowered, for they now had seen the results of responding to a critical event in an empowering manner.

Case Study Three:
When a Principal Does Not Want Things to Change

This large primary school of nearly 800 first and second graders appeared to have a faculty that worked hard at teaching. The principal expressed enthusiasm for the school's participation in the Empowered School District Project while she was attending the Chicago meeting. The school had become involved through the efforts of one of the project

CHAPTER 6

directors in concert with the district superintendent. The district super-intendent expressed great support for the endeavor. The principal seemed to identify with the central administration and wished to partic-ipate in activities that the superintendent felt were important.

During the first year of the project, several retreats were held for faculty to work on ideas for school improvement. The school enjoyed a large staff development budget and could afford well-subsidized profes-sional development activities for the faculty. Their budget for profes-sional activities was much larger than that of any other school in the project. During the first year the school became focused on empower-ing parents. The faculty believed that parents needed to be active in the educational growth and school experiences of their children. They planned several activities to begin their work on parent empowerment. Specific activities were to begin the second year. The school facilitator visited the school on several occasions but found that, many times, the principal had definite ideas regarding the extent to which teachers should be making decisions. This became a central problem during the second and third years of the project effort.

In year 2, it became evident that the principal was removing her-self from any activities related to the empowerment effort. She would have conflicts with the times that teachers wanted to meet. She essen-tially abdicated involvement with and ownership of the empowerment work of the teachers. During year 2, the teachers began to react to the principal's withdrawal as a show of no support. Conflict between the teachers and the principal developed on many occasions. The lead teacher struggled to keep the project going and hold the waning inter-est of the faculty.

By year 3, little work on empowerment was occurring in the school. Teachers were afraid to confront the principal, who was, by now, ruling in an autocratic manner. In a survey conducted during the fall, teachers were asked to respond to questions such as, "I feel that the biggest de-terrent(s) to open communication with administrators is (are) as follows." Some of the responses were:

- Administrators' lack of genuine desire to establish a decision-making partnership with the faculty.
- Teachers' fear of negative reaction by the principal.
- Teachers' reluctance to approach administrators for fear of get-ting a bad reputation, losing their position, and lack of support.
- Too much talk, not enough action.
- Teachers' feeling that their suggestions are not valued.

At the end of the year, when the faculty met in a retreat, everyone cried and questioned how the situation had gotten so bad. The lead teacher saw the effort as a failure, and the principal blamed the project directors and facilitators for not teaching her faculty conflict-management skills. In essence, by the third year of the project, the school was full of problems. At the retreat, the faculty agreed that they lacked skills in the following areas:

- Group process.
- Conflict management.
- Handling divisiveness.
- Establishing priorities.
- Establishing a vision for the school.

The third year could be called one of introspection. As one teacher said, "Why did we move no further?" The lead teacher stated that "this school needed to face how to help people see the need to grow and improve. We could not even express what we felt. We could not handle the conflict. We never came together." The lead teacher summed it up when she said, "The process went as far as the principal would let it go. The principal did not allow teachers a voice in the decision-making process if she did not agree with the decisions. If the principal agreed with the decisions, she would allow it to happen. The principal blocked the teachers from becoming empowered." Eventually, the facilitator stopped visiting the school because his presence just made the situation worse.

Case Study Four: Positive Approaches to Dealing with Conflict

This private school of 800 students in kindergarten through eighth grade had a very professional faculty with an energetic principal. He had been principal for some time and was an enthusiastic proponent of teacher and student empowerment. In many ways, the organization of the curriculum and open structure of the school created an air of excitement and active student learning throughout the school. Free of state-mandated rules and regulations, the private school experimented with both curriculum and instructional strategies. On a single day, a small group of first graders were using the dialogue method to teach each other spelling and to learn how to make informed decisions. The dialogue method teaches children to state the problem, look for alternative solutions, test theories, and make informed decisions. In another area, two children were rocking in the "Red Rockers." The Red Rockers were red rocking chairs that children who were in conflict were sent to sit in to talk with each other in order to resolve the conflict themselves. A group of older children had just returned from spending 3 days in the wilderness and staying overnight in a cave as part of an Outward Bound kind of experience in which emphasis is placed on personal growth and teamwork. Conversations with teachers indicated an intense focus on children, innovative teaching, and the family atmosphere of the school. The intensity they felt about finding new and innovative ways to teach was almost overwhelming in discussions with the teachers. They talked with great passion about their work.

The facilitator for the school was a former teacher the principal invited to serve in the facilitative role. The facilitator spent most of her time gathering data, because she also assumed the role of chronicler for the school. (The chronicler for each of the project schools was to be a teacher who would have some release time to gather data regarding the school's empowerment effort.) She conducted many interviews and observations, and she and the principal shared much information. However, it did not appear that she engaged in any problem-solving role with the faculty directly. Because she was a former teacher in the school, she did not bring an objective, outsider view. Teachers saw her as one of them.

Things seemed to move well for the school; the faculty agreed that they already had done a great deal of work in empowering the students. They wanted to focus on empowering the school's board so that the board would understand what the school was about and become even more supportive of the effort. In a private school, most of the board members are paying parents, so board attitude and support were a primary concern of the principal and teachers. However, during the second year of the project, interviews with the facilitator/chronicler began to indicate that the newest teachers in the school felt a great deal of pressure from the experienced faculty to do as they were told. While the school characterized itself as being empowering for teachers, newest faculty felt that their voices were not heard. In addition, they believed that the school's norm dictated tacit acceptance of new teacher deference to the more experienced teachers even in decision making regarding the curriculum and other issues.

Also during this time, the faculty became involved in a policy issue that would make the school a smoke-free environment. One of the teachers who had been at the school for 18 years resigned because of the proposed policy. The faculty were distressed over the resignation of the teacher, even though they supported the policy. As one teacher said, "It's another one of those experiences that tips the balance for the individual. In this case, the tip toward the institution rather than the individual makes us look insensitive to the needs of the individual."

USING CRITICAL EVENTS TO FRAME NEW OPPORTUNITIES

This feeling came to a head in several faculty meetings. New teachers expressed fear in speaking out. However, one new teacher was very outspoken in her rage about never being heard. For several weeks, the faculty struggled with which reality existed in the school. The facilitator began to talk with small groups of faculty from her interview notes and from her own experience as a teacher in the school. Slowly, the more experienced faculty came to realize that, in their eagerness to uphold the excellent reputation of the school for innovation and quality, they were indeed forcing decisions on new faculty and not listening to their ideas. The faculty's ability to solve problems, listen, and acknowledge different viewpoints appeared to open the way for new solutions to the issue. The faculty decided to reconsider the structures used to make curricular decisions so that new faculty could be placed on those teams immediately upon arrival.

The faculty developed a format for resolution of controversial issues following these events. This model involved the following:

1. An input session, with a time limit, observers, and information gathered put in writing.

2. A clarification session following the input session, with a time limit and observers, to make sure that all parties understood each others' positions and concerns.

3. An observers' session in which the observers summarized and noted patterns discerned during sessions 1 and 2.

4. A brainstorming session in which all involved gave possible solutions.

5. A final session for discussion of input from the brainstorming session.

During year 3, the faculty dealt with a very divisive issue. The Field Day was a day-long program of contests and games in which children competed for ribbons. Some teachers felt that the Field Day presented events that were not developmentally appropriate for many of the children. They were concerned about awarding ribbons when some children would receive none. Feelings ran high over this issue. However, the faculty decided to appoint a committee of observers who were to report back after the Field Day event regarding the developmental appropriateness of the events. It was during the faculty discussion of this event that they decided that they needed training in confrontational skills so that they could learn to remove the personal element in issues that were of a professional nature.

Case Study Five: Change Can Happen

This high school of 1,200 students, located in the western part of the country, enjoys a tight, supportive community. The school has a relatively new principal, himself a former student of the school. Many of the teachers taught him when he attended the high school. The school entered the Empowered School District Project based on the interest of the school district superintendent. The superintendent wanted to give the district schools a greater sense of empowerment through his leadership style. He granted autonomy to the high school, hoping that, in turn, the high school would create a more empowering environment for teachers and students. The superintendent assumed the role of cheerleader, enlightener, and educator in helping the principal and lead teacher embrace the empowerment concepts and practice.

One of the problems that the principal faced was being seen as a former student by some of the teachers. The goal of the first year of the school's empowerment effort was to bring the teachers into the decision-making process. The principal decided to introduce the concept of participative decision making through small groups modeled after a family discussion. In a sense, he was intimidated by his status as a former student and felt that one-on-one interaction with these faculty members would be better than large faculty meetings to discuss the school's involvement. The principal and the lead teacher conducted these discussions, with the principal being careful not to push anyone into a debate. Again, the principal struggled to define himself as principal, not student. The faculty was aware of the superintendent's support for empowerment throughout these discussions.

The former principal in the school had been a traditional top-down manager, often characterized by the faculty as "making teachers beg for equipment on their knees." The new superintendent was moving to site-based management, leaving decisions to principals and teachers in the district.

The lead teacher and principal discovered that the teachers felt very unempowered because they were working in an environment with run-down facilities and equipment. The teachers felt that the physical plant was in disarray. They felt that no one had listened to their complaints about the poor environmental conditions for years. This produced some tension for the principal because he had hoped that faculty would focus the empowerment effort on the students and the curriculum. The lead teacher convinced him that improving the physical plant would improve student and teacher morale. He agreed to give department heads considerable leadership in approaching the changes necessary to improve the school facilities. At this point, however, he struggled to understand that empowerment meant giving teachers a voice, responsibility for their decisions, and autonomy, not just explaining to them why you have to say no.

The change effort was moving very slowly. The principal remained reluctant to confront the faculty with ideas and responded by backing off from any teacher who expressed negative responses to the school's participation in the project. His deference to his former teachers caused the effort to continue at an unusually slow pace. The teachers remained relatively uninvolved, with an attitude of "this too shall pass." However, the lead teacher moved to a position in the central office, and the position of lead teacher opened up. It appeared that no teacher wanted the position. Finally, the principal chose a faculty member who was his former football coach. At the onset this choice appeared to be a mistake, because the teacher was not enthusiastic about the empowerment effort, and, in addition, he interacted with the principal as if the principal were still his student. But an unexpected event occurred that led to a new role for this lead teacher that surprised everyone.

The lead teacher attended one of the project meetings with other principals in the project. He saw firsthand the enthusiasm and intellect of the principals and schools working in the project. He said, "These aren't stupid people. What gets them excited about the empowerment effort? I now realize that what my principal is trying to do is good, and good things are going to happen if we get behind him."

Upon his return to the school, the lead teacher began to discuss the empowerment effort with fellow teachers, urging their support and involvement. With 30 years at the school as a coach and teacher, he had amassed considerable clout with the faculty and now assumed the role of cheerleader, advocate, and spokesperson for the empowerment effort. He became the defender of the effort and the principal, gently suggesting to faculty that it was time to see the principal as principal and not former student. He urged teachers to become part of the committee structure established in the school for building participative decision making among faculty. At one point, he chastised three teachers who said that the project was "just one of those principal things." The shift occurred. Teachers became actively involved in developing the plans for remodeling the science and technology areas. Faculty were given $40,800 to design three computer labs with a writing lab. Teachers actually could hammer nails into the walls, something they had never been allowed to do in the past. The remodeling took place during year 2. At the beginning of year 3 in the project, the faculty decided it was time to look at students and how teachers might better create an environment and program structure that would be empowering for them. Finally, the principal saw the change coming that he had hoped for since year 1.

Conversations About the Case Studies

The following questions about the case studies should provide you with fuel for a conversation about the role of critical events in a school staff's effort to create an empowered school.

1. How would you describe the responses of the schools in terms of leadership roles?

2. How did the nature of the critical events play a role in each school's ability to frame them as opportunities?

3. How did the problem-solving skills of the faculties impact the ultimate outcomes of critical events in the schools?

4. Attitudes play an important role in change. How would you describe that role in the events in the cases?

5. Compare the conflict management styles of the faculties in framing the critical events.

6. What was the role of the outside facilitators in these cases?

7. Describe any structures in the schools that impacted the handling of critical events.

8. How was communication handled in each school?

9. What role did the principals play in the ability of the schools to deal effectively with confrontational issues?

10. How does an empowered organization deal with the tension between organizational and individual issues?

REFERENCES

Barell, J. (1991). *Teaching thoughtfulness: Classroom strategies to enhance intellectual development.* New York: Longman.

Burke, R. J. (1970). Methods of resolving superior-subordinate conflict: The constructive use of subordinate differences and disagreements. *Organizational Behavior and Human Performance, 5,* 393–411.

Chenoweth, R., & Everhart, R. B. (1994). Preparing leaders to understand and facilitate change: A problem-based learning approach. *Journal of School Leadership, 4,* 414–431.

Katzenback, J. R., & Smith, D. K. (1993). *The wisdom of teams: Creating the high-performance organization.* Boston: Harvard Business School Press.

Labovitz, G. H. (1980). Managing conflict. *Business Horizons, 23*(3), 30–37.

Lawrence, P. R., & Lorsch, J. W. (1967). *Organizations and environment: Managing differentiation and integration.* Boston: Harvard Business School Press.

March, J. G., & Simon, H. A. (1958). *Organizations.* New York: Wiley.

Parnes, S. J., Noller, R. B., & Biondi, A. M. (1977). *A guide to creative action.* New York: Scribner's.

Rahim, M. A. (1983). A measure of styles of handling interpersonal conflict. *Academy of Management Journal, 26,* 368–376.

Renwick, P. A. (1977). Effects of sex-differences on the perception and management of conflict: An exploratory study. *Organizational Behavior and Human Performance, 19,* 403–415.

Schein, E. (1969). *Process consultation.* New York: Knopf.

Thomas, K. W. (1976). Conflict and conflict management. In M. D. Diunnette (Ed.), *Handbook of industrial and organizational psychology* (pp. 889–935). Chicago: Rand McNally.

Thomas, K. W., & Kilmann, R. H. (1974). Thomas - Killman Conflict Mode Instrument. Palo Alto, CA: Consulting Psychologists Press.

Reframing School Issues

We became exposed to the practice of reframing during the early stages of the Empowered School District Project. Reframing involves casting an issue in a different light; it encourages unique and creative solutions. We were cognitively aware of the lessons from perceptual psychology and phenomenology regarding how individuals have different views of the same event and how such individualistic views form the basis for subsequent actions. However, even with this background, we were unprepared for the reframing phenomenon we experienced as directors of the empowerment project: A school's ability to recast or reframe an issue had a dramatic impact on the school's capacity to overcome obstacles and seize opportunities.

REFRAMING IN THE PROJECT SCHOOLS

As described in earlier chapters of this book, the empowerment project began with a conference held in Chicago late in 1988. Nine school teams were invited to the conference to learn about the project. Through numerous meetings, discussions, and short workshops, the participants became aware of the major purpose of the empowerment study: to learn about the empowerment process. How they went about empowering their teachers was left up to each school. The only requirement the directors placed on the teams was that the students should directly benefit from whatever occurred under the auspices of the project. The participants learned that the directors believed that empowerment was not an end in itself; it was a process that enabled a school to mobilize its human resources for the sake of helping the school achieve its mission.

During the first year of the project, all nine schools used the reframing process when they were deciding how to become empowered schools. Initially, all of the schools were anxious to learn about empowerment, and materials written by national authorities were sent to them. Following this education process, the schools had to decide how to begin.

Three of the schools saw participation as an avenue to even greater excellence. They immediately began to work on establishing a process that would make them empowered schools. Once the methods for shaping decisions were in place, the schools intended to use the new procedures to raise the quality of all school decisions, with special attention given to the needs of students. These three schools became known to us as the "high-flier" schools. When they agreed to join the project, they saw clearly that their immediate object was to create an empowered school. They wasted little time trying to decide what to do.

The other schools framed the task of creating an empowered school quite differently. They began by deciding on a project for the school. Through joint planning and effort, it was thought that the staff would learn about and become skillful in the subtleties of the empowerment process. (It should be noted that establishing an empowered school through the completion of a school-wide project is a strategy that has been used in other settings. The League of Professional Schools, established by Carl Glickman, is one of the best examples of this approach.)

The first implementation problem the schools encountered was deciding which project to pursue. Endless amounts of time were spent identifying the school project, and several schools spent the rest of the school year on this activity. (The first year was not an entire academic year; the initial project conference occurred in October, and funding authorization and communication with the schools took until the beginning of 1989. Nevertheless, the first 6 months of 1989 were spent deciding what to do for the empowerment project.)

The differences between the high-flier schools and the other schools in the project were marked during this first year. A sense of confidence and direction were the hallmarks of the high fliers; a sense of confusion and frustration characterized the other schools. The difference lay in how each group of schools framed the problem. The high fliers reframed the problem as a challenge and an opportunity to create an even better school. The other schools did not reframe but instead used the tried-and-true method and viewed their involvement as a project to complete.

It cannot be known what would have happened in the other schools if the project directors or the school facilitator had directed and trained them in how to begin. Such a time-saving strategy was rejected for two reasons: (1) The entire purpose of the empowerment project was to learn about the empowerment process. At that time, neither the directors nor any other national authority knew which strategy for getting started would best promote empowerment. (2) The directors were well aware of the history of failure that attended externally imposed change projects. Their decision was to make participation, planning, and execution of the empowerment process a totally voluntary effort on the part of the school; the school's efforts would thus be free of outside interference and direction. In preparing the facilitators for their roles in the schools, the directors even took the no-interference policy a step further. They told the facilitators that if things began to slide and go badly in their schools, they should not engage in heroic measures to save the project. The directors' thinking was that there was much to be learned in a school that was not successful in empowering the teachers. Such information would be a distinct contribution to an understanding of the empowerment process.

Had this not been the posture adopted by the directors, the framing/reframing phenomenon would not have come to light. The remainder of this chapter is devoted to descriptions of other examples of the reframing process found during the course of the empowerment and restructuring projects.

A postscript should be added to this description of the framing/reframing problem that the schools grappled with the first year. During the summer following the first year, a conference of the principals and facilitators was held. Throughout the conference, the participants shared their successes and frustrations of the first year. The following year, two additional schools reframed their approach to empowerment by rejecting their original projects and starting discussions similar to those of the high-flier schools: They focused on the process itself and the new roles people were to play, the structures needed to enhance the process, and so on. They now understood that establishing the process would lead to the inclusion of teachers in the decision process. The school would be better equipped to handle future problems and challenges and thus would be more effective.

In the final count, five schools reframed the problem of creating an empowered school in terms of making the process itself an opportunity for empowerment. The rest of the schools remained with the traditional approach; these were the schools whose faculty had developed new programs and activities by the end of the project yet still had a principal dominating the decision structure.

Thus, the empowerment study showed that there are traditional ways of addressing school problems and also ways to reframe those problems to find fresh and effective solutions. In the next section, three reframing examples are cited to highlight critical features of the reframing process. Two of the examples are taken from the Empowered School District Project and the Arizona Restructuring Project, and the third is an interagency effort being conducted in Atlanta.

HISTORICAL PERSPECTIVE

To set the stage for the discussion of reframing efforts, it is necessary to review briefly the changes that occurred nationally and locally during the second half of the 20th century. Since the nation's founding, the operation of the public schools has been left largely to local boards of education and the professional educators employed by those boards. Arguments would occasionally arise as educators debated the strengths and weaknesses of various instructional approaches, requirements for additional physical education, or the optimum teacher/student ratio. Such problems, however, did not attract a great deal of public attention.

Starting in the 1950s, and with ever-increasing fervor, educational problems have come to the public's attention. The event that first caused a public stir was the Supreme Court's *Brown v. Board of Education* decision of 1954 mandating desegregation of the public schools. The *Brown* decision was followed closely by the launching of Sputnik and the passage of the National Defense Education Act. In 1964, the Elementary and Secondary Education Act brought the spotlight to bear on the needs of individual children. It seemed that almost overnight the general public became aware of schools and schooling. The catalytic event that woke the public to the fact that things were not all rosy in the public schools, however, was the precipitous fall of the Scholastic Aptitude Test (SAT) scores. This was a concrete measure of school effectiveness and truly reflected the fact that schools were not doing as good a job as needed to be done.

Educators responded to the challenges posed by the *Brown* decision, Sputnik, and other events as they always had. Their first response was that the data did not mean what the public thought they meant. The educators argued that there were reasons for the lack of scientists and mathematicians, as well as for declining test scores. Their protestations and explanations, however, did not cool the controversies. Instead the public became more concerned about the problems because it appeared that the educators were being defensive and had something to hide.

Almost overnight, it seemed, the public changed from a rather docile, accepting citizenry to a critical force challenging educators about how the schools were being administered. The battle lines were drawn, and school affairs became contentious matters for communities across the country. With the help of the media, a crisis of confidence in public schools arose that led to proposals for vouchers and other plans of choice, including home schooling.

Into this rather poisonous atmosphere came an entirely new challenge to the public schools in the form of the so-called religious right, a conservative group that insisted that the public schools accept their views on school prayer, sex education, library materials, and so on. Monumental battles between the religious right and educators broke out in community after community. Where the religious right could not have their way, they turned to the ballot box, supporting board of education candidates who shared their points of view.

The latter part of the century found educators being very sensitive to the potential critics in their communities. To be avoided at almost any cost was the establishment of any procedure or program that fundamentally changed the school program, unless such a change focused strictly on academic attainments.

An example of the volatility existing in communities today is the raging conflict over outcome-based education (OBE). In an attempt to measure student progress with instruments other than standardized tests, educators had been exploring instruments that measured students' ability to perform everyday tasks such as balancing a checkbook or filling out an application form. As word of the use of such measurements became known, communities across the nation simply exploded. It seems that the religious right believed that OBE represented a lowering of academic standards, a "dummying down" of the curriculum, and that materials used in the approach contained values that were not consistent with their beliefs.

The protests against OBE were orchestrated by a national organization of religious right groups. Whenever a local organization's protests about OBE were ignored or rejected by a board of education, the group would set out to influence the election of board members. Many such efforts were successful, and the governance of the school systems was affected. Clearly, the last decades of the century brought conditions that demanded a more effective approach for addressing school issues. After working with the two projects described in this book, we believe that the key to discovering creative and effective solutions rests in reframing the issues and problems confronting public schools.

RESTRUCTURING THE HIGH SCHOOL

In Arizona, the most complex problems associated with multiage, multigrade classrooms were found in the high schools. Traditional academic departments, Carnegie units, and general support for the 6- or 7-period school day together served to form a wall of resistance to proposals for individual progress plans, interdisciplinary study, and the like.

The directors of the Arizona project attempted to influence the high school members through workshops, retreats, and individual persuasion. It was felt that a strategy that brought students of all ages together would be the best way to gain entry to the high schools. To this end, the schools were encouraged to establish teacher-advisor programs in place of traditional homeroom programs. In these programs, students from all grade levels made up the advisory groups. Each advisory group was headed by a teacher-advisor, a volunteer who had been given special training in conducting such groups. The efforts of the teacher-advisors were coordinated by a member of the school's counseling staff.

Students would enter the advisory groups as freshmen and remain there until they graduated. The dynamics of the process worked so that older students were available to help induct the younger students into the mysteries of class work, student activities, and so forth. Above all, the program was designed to ward off the problem of students getting lost and "falling through the cracks," as so often happens in modern high schools.

The directors hoped that the teacher-advisor programs would encourage the high schools to explore the possibilities of multiage, multigrade groupings in the academic areas. They recognized that experimentation, should it be undertaken within a high school, would be done on a smaller scale, such as that found in a school-within-a-school format.

Most of the schools that experimented with the teacher-advisor programs found the programs to be successful in inducting and encouraging students to participate in the activities of the school. Only one of the schools, however, was able to use its teacher-advisor program as a bridge to multiage, multigrade academic classrooms.

Cholla High School is located in Tucson and serves a multiethnic population of Hispanics, African Americans, and Caucasians. At the beginning of the Arizona project, Tom Scarborough was serving as the assistant principal of the school, and Deborah Cunningham was a faculty member. Both attended organizational meetings of the project schools and workshops related to teacher-advisor programs. The teacher-advisor workshops included reframing exercises in which the participants hypothetically restructured their schools. The hope of the workshop

directors was that such exercises would encourage the school representatives to develop projects that featured multiage, multigrade academic classes. Such was the case with the Cholla representatives.

A great deal of creativity and planning went into the Cholla plan.
Deborah wrote the original paper after hours of discussion with Tom and
other school representatives. The plan called for the creation of a
school-within-a-school for 100 volunteer students. All grades and ages in
the school were to be represented in the group. The group would be composed of one third at-risk students, one third average students, and one
third advanced students.

The program was focused on students mastering the Arizona Essential Skills, an extensive list of accomplishments that state officials required of all Arizona students. Portfolio evaluations were to be used to
measure the students' progress as they acquired mastery of the essential
skills. Students would progress through the program individually and
at their own pace. Furthermore, the students could take any level of
the core academic components (i.e., math, social studies, science, and
English) that they chose. Their work would be approved and evaluated
by one of the four teachers (representing each core area) assigned to
the project.

A key component of the Cholla program was a community service
project. During each student's time in the program, he or she would plan
and conduct a project for the benefit of the community. Supervision of
the service projects was the responsibility of the Cholla program coordinator.

It took about a year to get approval of the concept paper for the
Cholla plan and to marshal the necessary resources for the program. The
third year of the Arizona Restructuring Project was the first year of the
Cholla project. While the school was waiting for approval of the plan,
Tom was appointed as principal of Cholla, and Deborah was appointed
as the project coordinator.

Even after only 1 year, the successes have been many. Students are
taking responsibility for their own learning. They are mastering the
state's essential skills and are providing the staff with evidence of such
mastery. Assessment of student progress includes verbal and written
evidence, which is then included in the students' portfolios.

New lessons regarding the dynamics of this type of education have
been identified and are in the process of being learned. Perhaps the
most difficult lesson for the teachers has been to trust the decisions the
students make for themselves regarding subject matter levels, pacing,
and so forth. Another difficult lesson has been the enormous effort
such teaching requires. Even with additional planning time during the

summer and an additional planning period during each school day, the workload never eases.

The program is expensive. Additional personnel, space, and planning time place a strain on the school's resources. Yet the attainments of the students makes such expenditures worthwhile. Tom is already planning additional schools-within-schools at Cholla that are based on the original concept. Each new school will have 100 students and a core teaching faculty of four.

Clearly, Deborah and Tom's school-within-a-school is a clear example of reframing. They and their colleagues were willing to look at the high school structure and its pattern of operation that had existed for about 100 years and see that the structure and operation were not adequate for their students. The students required something more meaningful, and they needed to have a hand in developing it.

REMOVING TRADITIONAL SCHOOL BOUNDARIES

Educational administration textbooks present a rather clear picture of the school and its community. Most instructive are the descriptions of public relations programs. Such descriptions state clearly the importance of keeping parents and other members of the school community informed of happenings at the school. They then typically list the multitude of activities a school can conduct to keep the community informed (Ubben & Hughes, 1992).

Although this is perhaps the most specific description of the relationship between a school and its community, it is by no means the only one. Throughout such textbooks, readers can find reference after reference that highlights the distance existing between a school and its community. Parents, citizens, and business leaders are resources to be tapped as the need arises.

To ensure that these resources are available when needed, the school must keep them informed by various communiqués, parent–teacher meetings, advisory groups, and social occasions such as carnivals and picnics. This school–community model has been the traditional approach advocated for administrator use. If the model did not work, it was because insufficient effort was put into the activities. The validity of the model was not questioned in the literature. It is as though educators were saying, "Even though our citizens' interest in public education is totally different from the interest of citizens 30 years ago, the old public relations approach that has always been used is still sufficient." Stated in this manner, the case for reframing the school–community relationship should become clear.

REFRAMING SCHOOL ISSUES

A visitor to Abraham Lincoln High School in Denver today would find a school filled with activity. Students and faculty members would likely be found chatting around benches in the lobby and wide entry hall. Parents and other adults would be coming and going from the parents' lounge and office located off the lobby near the school's main office. (The parents' office serves as a headquarters for the volunteer program, an information center where parents and visitors may find descriptions of the school's programs and activities, and a meeting place for parent committees.) As the visitor wandered down the halls of the school, he or she would come upon the health clinic, which is staffed continuously by professional health-care providers and volunteer parents. Students are able to obtain a variety of medical services in the clinic. Severe problems are referred to other health-care facilities.

Other activities involving members of the community are scheduled throughout the day. A student court, sponsored by the Denver Bar Association, meets regularly to hear cases of students who have not observed the school's conduct regulations. The work of student attorneys litigating the cases is carefully supervised by volunteer attorneys. The student credit union is run by students and supervised by banking specialists from the community. The credit union serves as a banking facility for students and provides a rich experience for those who are involved in its operation.

Case Study One in Chapter 5 mentioned the think tank composed of community leaders and teachers that was instrumental in establishing goals for the school based on student needs. From the think tank deliberations came 12 committees of parents, teachers, business people, and school administrators that were responsible for making recommendations to the steering board, the governance body of the school. The steering board was composed of the chairs of the 12 committees and the principal, Christine Johnson. There were no teacher, parent, or business seats on the steering board. The membership was dictated by the makeup of the committee chairs.

A careful review of the Abraham Lincoln High School story reveals a reframing process that was conducted during the think tank's first year, when the mission and goals of the school were established. The heavy involvement of community leaders and business people from the beginning, and the willingness of the think tank members to read and discuss various ideas and approaches in the literature, almost guaranteed that reframing of some sort would take place.

What emerged was a totally different conception of the school and its community. There was never a point of demarcation between the school and the community; instead, they appeared to be a seamless garment. Members of the school were members of the community;

members of the community were members of the school. Each institution shared the responsibility for the other's success.

Abraham Lincoln High School's inclusion of its school community is a model for today's contentious times. Controversies and differences of opinions or values are addressed as issues arise. Accommodations for differences result, and the school moves on without losing sight of its first responsibility: the student.

CLASSICAL VERSUS OPEN-SYSTEMS THEORY

The differences between classical theory and open-systems theory are manifested in the contentious nature of many community debates on public school issues and the reframing efforts of Abraham Lincoln High School to become a part of the community. Classical theorists writing about industries at the turn of the 20th century were not concerned with the environment. In the early years of the Industrial Revolution, the American public was so eager for the new products of American industry that being sensitive to the wishes and needs of citizens was not an issue. Henry Ford's comment that the American public "can have any color of Model T it wants, so long as it's black" illustrates the thinking of the leaders of American industry at the time. What was important was to create the perfect organizational structure that was most effective (i.e., achieved its goals) in the most economical manner: the bureaucracy.

Classical theory, because it gave little, if any, thought to the environment, was characterized as a closed system. Schools characterized in the literature as having public relations approaches to the community reflect closed-system, bureaucratic thinking. According to this approach, it is important to keep the community happy through a series of communications and other activities. Nevertheless, such public relations initiatives serve to maintain the distance between the school and the community. The community learns only what the school wishes it to learn about school operations. As shown by the controversy surrounding outcome-based education, this standoffish, arbitrary approach to working with the community no longer is appropriate, if indeed it ever was.

Open-system organizations are the opposite of closed-system organizations. An organization viewed from the open-system perspective influences its environment and, in turn, is influenced by the environment (Katz & Kahn, 1978). It is from the environment that the organization receives its resources to operate. In turn, the organization's products affect the environment and encourage the environment to continue to provide the organization's resources.

Reframing the school and its environment as parts of a seamless garment is very much in keeping with open-systems thinking. The bottom line of open-systems thinking, just as it was with classical theory thinking, is to make the organization a success. The problem is that many educators have not recognized that a closed-system, "tell them what we want them to know" approach simply is not good enough for today's communities.

INTERAGENCY PERSPECTIVE

Although Abraham Lincoln High School's reframing of the relationship between the school and its community included interagency collaboration, this collaboration occurred between the school and the agencies; the agencies did not interact with one another. True interagency collaboration occurs among the agencies themselves, as well as with the school. A better example is a project initiated by President and Mrs. Carter called the Atlanta Project.

The Atlanta Project is a massive community project focused on the needs of some 500,000 people who live in the inner city. The number represents approximately half of the disadvantaged families in Georgia. The problems being addressed within the project include poverty, homelessness, unemployment, teen pregnancy, lack of health care, inability to complete high school, and life in neighborhoods with crime and drug sales. The approach to these problems is to help communities develop the necessary structures and processes that will ensure long-term successes. Just pouring financial resources into the neighborhoods has been rejected because it produces only temporary and short-term results.

The target area of the Atlanta Project has been divided into clusters that roughly approximate the attendance areas of high schools. These clusters are known as the Grady Cluster, the Crim Cluster, and so on. Each cluster is coordinated by a cluster coordinator, a full-time paid employee who lives in the cluster.

The Atlanta Project is a good example of interagency collaboration because one of its objectives is to coordinate the efforts of several hundred federal, state, and local agencies. Up to this time, the agencies have operated largely independently, without regard to what other agencies were doing. The Atlanta Project is attempting to end this approach for the benefits of the target population.

The Atlanta Project is cited here because it is the largest example of interagency collaboration we know of. According to newspaper reports, when President Carter met with President Bush and congressional leaders, they were stunned to learn that he had not come to seek funding for the Atlanta Project. Instead, he was seeking help in cutting the red tape of the Washington bureaucracy that prohibited federal agencies from working with each other and with state and local agencies on common problems.

The Atlanta Project reflects the Carters' reframing of the issue of how to improve the lives of inner-city residents. Their solution was a bold initiative that has hope of success simply because it is so big. A single or several agencies working on one or two problems would be overwhelmed by the magnitude of the needs. The Atlanta Project, however, mobilized all of the concerned agencies along with foundations and private industry. It also incorporated the volunteer efforts of hundreds of educational, religious, governmental, and business leaders who volunteered their time to participate.

There is great hope for the success of the Atlanta Project. Perhaps its greatest benefit, however, will be that it will serve as a pilot study for similar projects in cities throughout the country.

LEADERSHIP ISSUES AND REFRAMING

Reframing is not without its critics. Many would wish for conditions of yesteryear, when the school educated the community's children in basic skills, and then perhaps did a little bit more. Communities of that long-ago age are remembered as being generally well satisfied with their public schools that provided "universal education." If such an idyllic time was ever a part of American education, it certainly exists no longer. Today the schools are filled with rancor and debate as various publics vie for more power and control of the education process.

This chapter has discussed the reframing phenomenon, which appears to have promise for identifying strategies that may eliminate the we/they mentality that characterizes so many schools and their communities. Yet some of the strategies frighten educators as well as community members. A few of the issues raised by the reframing efforts of the empowerment and Arizona projects are discussed in the following sections.

Community Involvement in Setting Goals

For many years, schools have used citizens on their self-study committees when preparing for accreditation visits. Presumably these representatives ensure citizen input in the statement of school goals. Probably this is true, although citizen suggestions would most likely be seriously questioned if they required the school to change course or to adopt goals that would require new programs and activities.

As demonstrated in the Abraham Lincoln High School vignette, citizen participation in setting school goals means something quite different from serving on self-study goal committees. It means educators must allow parents and other members of the community into their inner sanctums, where the real mission and goal statements are hammered out. Such inclusion could be perceived as threatening to many in the education establishment.

Developing Structures for Business and Industry Involvement

Involvement with industry might be perceived as a less urgent issue than that of goal setting, because the business partnership movement has become an accepted element in schools throughout the country. Most such programs came into existence because they conformed to the conventional model for community involvement. It benefits the school to have a partnership with one of the community's businesses or industries, since such a relationship results in the company's resources being made available to the school. Normally, such resources are human resources—employees voluntarily working with students of the school, providing training for staff members, and so forth. What characterizes the partnership program in most schools is that the school receives what the company wishes to provide. Such services are usually helpful and, if nothing else, sensitize the company's leadership to the needs, as well as the accomplishments, of the school.

The issue that arises when businesses are encouraged to participate in the goal setting and basic operations of the school is quite a different matter from a simple partnership. Many educators would describe the situation as analogous to inviting the wolf into Red Riding Hood's grandmother's cabin.

Business leaders have been critical of the ways educators organize and lead schools. The common refrain is that the schools should be run more like businesses. Today a number of private companies are being employed to run both school districts and individual schools. It is too early to assess how successful such companies will be in meeting the challenges of inner-city schools and the needs of diverse student bodies.

Nevertheless, business leaders believe and are quick to point out that schools could be improved by using methods they use in their companies. The questions that arise when the school–community relationship is restructured to include business people, therefore, make educators nervous. Too often they are afraid that the schools will be taken over by the business people, and they will lose control. This did not happen at Abraham Lincoln High School, but largely because Christine Johnson's decision to include two community leaders in the original think tank was a careful strategy that began with the inclusion of a few highly respected leaders who would participate fully in the mission-setting process. Thereafter, additional business leaders were added to the various committees that advised the steering board. Occasionally, these business leaders would chair their committees and therefore sit on the steering board. By that time, however, the structures governing the school already had been established.

Fostering Meaningful Parent Participation

If ever a school faced all the difficulties associated with involving parents in the school operation, it was Abraham Lincoln. As mentioned earlier, the school serves a racially and ethnically diverse neighborhood in south Denver. For the most part, parents have immigrated to this country, and their educational attainments are low. They are people of modest incomes earned largely in service industries of one sort or another. The area is a blue-collar neighborhood where the parent or parents work long hours away from the home.

As is so frequently the case, parents are hesitant to participate in school activities. Some are embarrassed by their own personal lack of education and do not feel welcome in a school where all the students are better educated than they. Others are involved in small businesses or work at two or more jobs. These parents simply do not have the time or energy to be involved in the school. Such were the problems facing the school as its leaders thought of strategies to involve parents meaningfully in its work.

From the beginning of her tenure as principal, Christine Johnson and her fellow administrators were out meeting parents and other patrons of the school in the community. Such activities served as a type of recruiting program for hesitant parents, making them feel more comfortable about coming to the school. At the school, the parent office and lounge had been prepared for them. The information center, the volunteer program, and parents' meetings, however, were managed by the parents. Building parent involvement in the school was a long, slow process. Even today, parent participation is not as good as the school would like it to be.

The parents who are involved participate in a variety of activities, ranging from helping to staff the clinic to assisting teachers in classrooms and the media center. As mentioned earlier, parents also serve on the school's goals committees.

CASTING EDUCATIONAL ISSUES
IN THE LIGHT OF REFRAMING

Reframing is a finding of the projects described in this book. It probably cannot be described as a process so much as an insight. Reframing casts the issue of educational improvement in a different light and encourages unique and creative solutions. Reframing is a skill that probably could be developed. Case studies and other simulated materials could provide materials for administrators to develop the techniques associated with reframing. If such were the case, administrators would be in a better position to find creative solutions to the problems and issues of today's schools.

∞ CASE STUDY

Turning It into an Opportunity

As principal of Washington High School for the past 5 years, Ms. Akins had enjoyed considerable success. Through concentrated efforts at establishing a shared common vision with faculty members, parent representatives, and key stakeholders from the community, many positive changes had occurred. Key indicators related to student attendance, school climate, and academic performance had shown positive trends over the past 3 years.

Demographic shifts in the community were now taking place. Large numbers of lower-income families, many of whom had recently immigrated from Spanish-speaking countries, were moving into the community, and an increasing percentage of upper middle class families were moving to outlying suburban areas. The result was a vastly different student population from the one that existed when Ms. Akins became principal at Washington High.

The school district had developed a long-range plan including provisions for meeting the needs of a rapidly changing student population. One component of this newly developed plan involved the adjustment of school boundaries within the school district. The boundary adjustments were to take effect the following year and would result in nearly 20% of the students who previously had attended Washington being reassigned to another district high school. Washington would receive another group of students who had attended a neighboring high school that was to be closed the following year. Teacher reassignments would be required in order to meet the resulting staffing needs at each district high school.

Akins was frustrated as she pondered the prospect of having to, in essence, start all over with so many students, parents, and community members who would be new to Washington High School the following year. Despite her earnest efforts to facilitate involvement of a large number of stakeholders, she knew that many of the teachers, parents, and community members who had helped develop the vision for the school would no longer be a part of it.

Conversations About the Case Study

1. What are the major leadership issues facing Ms. Akins?
2. What are the community issues that she must consider?
3. How can she reframe this situation into an opportunity?
4. Where must she start?

JAMES MACHELL

REFERENCES

Katz, D., & Kahn, R. L. (1978). *The social psychology of organizations* (2nd ed.). New York: Wiley.

Ubben, G. C., & Hughes, L. W. (1992). *The principal: Creative leadership for effective schools* (2nd ed.). Boston: Allyn and Bacon.

CHAPTER 8

ℰℭ

Empowering Teachers

Reports commissioned by foundations and legislatures, and some of the reform literature, have advocated the empowerment of school staff (Frymier, 1987; Lightfoot, 1985; Maeroff, 1988). The assumption is that a positive work environment, brought about by school participants who are able to initiate and carry out new ideas, results in enhanced learning opportunities for students. In particular, according to Maeroff (1988), key empowerment components for teachers are increased status, a highly developed knowledge base, and autonomy in decision making.

REDESIGNING TEACHER ROLES AND RESPONSIBILITIES

Problematic Nature of Teachers' Work

Problematic aspects of teachers' work have been noted in much of the literature on teaching. Some of these problems have their roots in the historical development of the teaching profession, and others are a result of the bureaucratic structure of schools.

Teachers are isolated in most school settings, and their work is rarely collegial in most typical schools (Little, 1982). According to Rosenholtz (1985), this professional isolation is the greatest impediment to learning to teach. Experienced teachers often are isolated from each other and from those in authority (Zielinski & Hoy, 1983). Exemplary role models are not accessible, so teachers are inhibited from assisting one another. Thus, left alone, they must rely on their own abilities to detect problems and discern solutions. The consequence is that they tend to fall back on models they recall from their own student days. The isolation that results from teachers working alone results in competition and feelings of inadequacy and insecurity and discourages information sharing. The lack of social interaction keeps teachers from helping and seeking help from colleagues and getting valuable feedback. It also prevents them from having access to the interaction that is the medium by which recognition can be given and received (Sergiovanni, 1991).

According to Ashton and Webb (1986), this isolation also can promote the need to conform to prevailing norms and avoid questioning the assumptions on which those norms are based. When teachers have to accept their own lack of power, something vital is missing from their workplace. Frase and Sorenson (1992) stated that what is lost is the creativity, commitment, and energy that teachers could contribute to the school organization. The interaction among personnel in schools is necessary for promoting and institutionalizing change (Sergiovanni, 1991). Researchers have noted the centrality of collegial relationships in schools identified as unusually effective and the importance of collegiality as an aspect of school climate (Anderson & Iwanicki, 1984; Little, 1982).

Together, two separate but important changes in the teaching profession have resulted in a narrowing of what it means to teach. The development of teaching into a profession has resulted in teacher training and certification that is increasingly specialized. Teachers are, for example, certified in high school science, elementary special education, or secondary music. The notion of the teacher as one who works with the whole child and is able to relate knowledge from several traditional disciplines has been lost in the process. At the same time, a long-standing and pervasive push to reduce teaching to a technical process in which the aims can be specified and the outcomes measured has narrowed what it means to be a teacher. While professionalization and accountability are not necessarily problematic in themselves, we know that together they have reduced and limited the work of teachers in ways that are potentially harmful to both teachers and students.

Finally, teachers have little say in what happens in schools outside their own classrooms. Teachers are expected to be in complete control of students, class content, teaching strategies, and evaluation in the classroom, but decisions on the overall operation of the school are outside their realm of influence. In most cases, teachers have no say in who is hired, in setting their own schedules or those of other teachers, or in selecting administrators. While collective bargaining has benefited teachers in many ways, an additional effect has been to centralize deci-sion-making processes in school districts and to limit the number of de-cisions made at the local school level, where individual teachers might expect to participate (Frymier, 1987). Teachers often find themselves teaching in situations in which important decisions are made by persons far removed from the actual activities of the school—decisions that limit the teachers' abilities to meet the educational needs of students and their own need for feelings of significance and self-worth.

Three key issues identified in the literature on teacher work life (Little, 1982) that are associated with teachers' work in traditional Amer-ican schools are:

1. Teachers are isolated from colleagues in most of their daily work.

2. The work of teachers has been narrowed and reduced by the combined forces of professional certification and account-ability.

3. Teachers have not been significantly involved in many of the decisions that affect the nature of their work, particularly in decisions made outside the classroom or the school.

Self-Managing Teams

In recent years, the concept of self-managing work groups has been utilized in business and industry to further the cause of employee em-powerment (Manz & Sims, 1987). Hackman (1986) stated that in self-managing teams employees take personal responsibility for the out-comes of their work, manage and monitor their own performance, seek needed resources, and take the initiative to help others improve.

Hackman (1986) defined self-managing work groups by placing them on a continuum extending from management-led groups at one end to self-governing groups at another. Hackman and Oldham (1980) have identified the following minimal criteria for self-managing groups: (1) that the group be an intact and identifiable—if sometimes small or temporary—social system; (2) that the group be charged with generating an identifiable product whose acceptability is potentially measurable; and (3) that the group has the authority to determine how members will go about working together to accomplish their task.

Conditions that foster self-management in individuals and teams (Cummings, 1978) include task differentiation, boundary control, and task control. Lawler (1986) noted that two kinds of training are essential for members of self-managing work groups, training in the task and training in interpersonal skills. Hackman (1986), in a more extensive list, developed five conditions that foster and support self-management:

1. Clear direction from management that identifies the goals of the organization without specifying the means for obtaining those goals is necessary.

2. Performance-unit structures must be developed that are enabling. These structures must include task design that ensures that a meaningful task is defined for which employees can take personal responsibility and have knowledge of the results. Units must be appropriately sized, balanced between homogeneous composition and heterogeneous composition, and include employees who are competent in working together. Units must be aware that they are responsible for self-regulation and for assessing their own performance.

3. The organizational context must be supportive by providing a nondivisive reward structure, an education system, and an information system.

4. Expert coaching and consultation must be available.

5. The teams must have adequate material resources.

While self-managing teams are generally portrayed as a way to increase worker autonomy and responsibility, organizational context is an important variable. Manz and Angle (1987) studied the introduction of self-managing work groups into an organization that traditionally had relied on individual self-management. In the context of an independent property and casualty insurance firm, self-managed work groups were found to threaten the personal control and autonomy of employees and to result in reduced services to customers. Self-managed work groups were introduced in this firm without worker participation or approval and were used as a means of increasing management control. Manz and Angle concluded that additional research is needed on the effects of introducing self-managing work groups into service occupations, particularly when employees have a history of individual autonomy. This would seem to apply to schools.

Most writers on the role of leadership in self-managing teams have concluded that leadership is at least as important in organizations with self-managing work groups as it is in traditionally structured organizations (Cummings, 1978; Hackman, 1986; Lawler, 1986; Manz & Sims, 1987). Leadership in such organizations is, however, different. Manz and Sims (1984) described the leader in an organization with self-managing work groups as an "unleader, ... one who leads others to lead themselves" (p. 411). Hackman (1986) noted that "leadership is both more important and a more demanding undertaking in self-managing units than in traditional organizations" (p. 119). Leaders must monitor the work of the group by diagnosing and forecasting from available data, and leaders must take action to create or maintain favorable conditions for the group. According to Manz and Sims (1987), the most important leader behaviors are encouraging self-reinforcement and encouraging self-observation and self-evaluation.

Organizations that use self-managing work groups operate from a bottom-up perspective, and "the leader's job is to teach and encourage subordinates to lead themselves effectively" (Manz & Sims, 1987, p. 121). In the organization that Manz and Sims studied, top-level managers called themselves "the support group." Skills that leaders working with self-managing groups must develop were listed by Cummings (1978), Hackman (1986), and Lawler (1986). While their particular lists differ, human relations skills are emphasized over technical skills, including the ability to build trust, understand group dynamics, develop group members' capacities for autonomy, and empower others.

Nature of Teacher Empowerment

Empowerment is a complex construct. It has been defined as a process whereby school participants develop the competence to take charge of their own growth and resolve their own problems. Empowered individuals believe they have the skills and knowledge to act on a situation and improve it. Empowered schools are organizations that create opportunities for competence to be developed and displayed.

Frymier (1987) stated that "in any attempt to improve education, teachers are central" (p. 9). Rosenholtz (1991) suggested that "the culture of a school changes significantly when experienced teachers stop functioning in isolation and start solving problems related to students' learning collectively" (p. 51). In any attempt to improve schools, attention must be given to roles in decision making and increased opportunities for meaningful collective participation in the critical areas of activity that focus on organizational goals.

Research from community psychology is informative. Two community psychologists, Zimmerman and Rappaport (1988), have described empowerment as a construct that ties personal competencies and abilities to environments that provide opportunities for choice and autonomy in demonstrating those competencies. Although the construct can be applied to organizations, persons, and social policies, it appears to be a procedure whereby persons gain mastery or control over their own lives and democratic participation in the life of their community (Katz, 1984; Rappaport, 1987; Zimmerman & Rappaport, 1988).

Maton and Rappaport (1984), in a study of a large number of individuals in a religious community, found that a sense of community and commitment related to empowerment. Zimmerman and Rappaport (1988), studying large numbers of college students and community residents who were participating in various community organizations, again found a consistent dimension of empowerment. They described this dimension as "a sense of civic duty, political efficacy, and perceived personal competence [that] was negatively related to alienation and positively related to willingness to be a leader" (p. 136).

Dunst (1991) suggested that empowerment consists of two issues: (1) enabling experiences provided within an organization that fosters autonomy, choice, control, and responsibility, and (2) allowing the individual to display existing competencies as well as learn new competencies that support and strengthen functioning.

One of the components of school restructuring is the empowerment of teachers, administrators, and students (Murphy & Evertson, 1990; Short, Greer, & Michael, 1991). In fact, the restructuring paradigm of Murphy and Evertson includes empowerment as an integral part of reform. Lortie, in his seminal work (1975), depicted teachers as performing their craft in separate rooms, working in isolation from other teachers with little collegial contact. Teachers are busy completing reports and maintaining orderly classrooms rather than interacting with colleagues in creative ways. These tasks tend to absorb available time for collegial interaction and contribute to teacher isolation.

Research by Gruber and Trickett (1987), conducted in an alternative school, identified the importance of control over decision making in empowering participants in school organizations. Rinehart and Short (1992), in a study of empowerment of teacher leaders in the national program called Reading Recovery, found that teacher-leaders saw opportunities for decision making, control over their daily schedule, a high level of teaching competency, and growth and development as empowering aspects of their work.

Six Dimensions of Teacher Empowerment

Short and Rinehart (1992) identified six empirically derived dimensions of teacher empowerment: involvement in decision making, opportunities for professional growth, teacher status, teacher self-efficacy, autonomy, and teacher impact.

Decision Making. This dimension of empowerment relates to the participation of teachers in critical decisions that directly affect their work. In many cases, this means participation in and responsibility for decisions involving budgets, teacher selection, scheduling, curriculum, and other programmatic areas. Providing teachers with a significant role in school decision making is a key element in empowerment in that teachers gain the opportunity to increase control over their work environment. However, for teacher involvement in decision making to happen, they must believe that their involvement is genuine and that their opinion has a critical impact on the outcome of the decision (Short & Greer, 1989b).

A school climate that encourages involvement in decision making is characterized by openness and risk taking and an environment that encourages teachers to try new ideas and approaches. However, Short, Miller-Wood, and Johnson (1991) found that teachers were less willing to participate in decision making if they perceived that their principals sought their opinions but made the final decision themselves instead of allowing teachers that opportunity. Teachers in their study expressed dismay and frustration over their inability to influence the process of decision making. They felt that they were not consulted and were made to feel that they could not make good decisions. However, being given the final responsibility to make decisions confirms to teachers that they have good ideas and are trusted to make good decisions (Short, Miller-Wood et al., 1991).

Perhaps one of the greatest strengths of shared decision making in schools is the improved quality of teachers' problem solving. Decisions become conscious, well-reasoned choices (Rosenholtz, 1985). In shared decision making that has focused on evaluative insights about the overall quality of a school's instructional program, the dialogue that ensues creates a tremendous opportunity for a school to grow, change, and become more effective. Teachers feel ownership and commitment to the process (Rosenholtz, 1985).

Smylie (1992) expressed the belief that the more teachers perceive that they are responsible for student learning, the more strongly they perceive that they should be held accountable for their work. In turn, this perception leads to a greater interest and willingness to participate in decision making.

A word of warning. Increasing the level of teacher participation in decision making can create the perception of a less positive school climate. This may be attributed to the increased opportunities for conflict when involvement increases and teachers' varying ideologies and perceptions are disclosed. Also, as teachers feel more empowered, they recognize that they have the power to identify problems, institute change efforts and, ultimately, take responsibility for solving those problems. In other words, empowered teachers are more willing to take ownership of problems and find solutions than teachers who are omitted from involvement in decision making. Teachers involved in school decision making assume the roles of problem finder and problem solver (Short, Miller-Wood et al., 1991).

Professional Growth. As a dimension of empowerment, professional growth refers to teachers' perceptions that the school in which they work provides them with opportunities to grow and develop professionally, learn continuously, and expand their own skills through the work life of the school. Glenn (1990) suggested that the real power behind the concept of empowerment is authority derived from command of the subject matter and essential teaching skills. Maeroff (1988) believed that helping teachers become more knowledgeable about teaching and assisting them in developing a repertoire of teaching strategies is requisite for empowering teachers. According to Firestone (1993), efforts to professionalize teachers (i.e., to empower them) builds teacher commitment and improves instruction through increased teacher skill.

Status. Status, as a dimension of empowerment, refers to teachers' perceptions that they have professional respect and admiration from colleagues. In addition, teachers believe that they have colleagues' support and feel that others respect their knowledge and expertise.

Lortie (1975) stated that "the economic realities of teaching play an important role in its nature; they undergird its social position and the shape of careers within the occupation" (p. 8). Maeroff (1988) claimed that the meager salaries and other disenfranchising circumstances of teaching cause teachers to not respect themselves. Teachers worry that their status claims are being eroded further by the public's declining faith in education in general. In addition, teachers face growing public questions about their competence. The combination of high public expectations and poor working conditions, as perceived by teachers, creates the tension that erodes what little status teachers now enjoy. Poor facilities, heavy paperwork unrelated to instruction, interference with teacher time, low opinions of and conflict with the community and boards of education, inadequate parental support, and being involved in daily activities unrelated to teaching (e.g., bus and cafeteria duty) enhance teachers' feelings of low status. Ashton and Webb (1986) also found that status is affected by the powerlessness that is characteristic of bureaucratic organizations. Teachers feel left out and unimportant in the critical decisions affecting their work life in schools.

Self-Efficacy. Self-efficacy refers to teachers' perceptions that they have the skills and ability to help students learn, are competent in building effective programs for students, and can effect changes in student learning. Blase (1982) stated that the primary rewards in teaching result from the teacher's positive self-evaluations of performance with students in instructional, moral, and counseling terms. Self-efficacy develops as an individual acquires self-knowledge and the belief that he or she is personally competent and has mastered the skills necessary to effect desired outcomes. According to Rosenholtz (1985), teachers' sense of self-efficacy and professional certainty relates to their subsequent decisions to remain in teaching. Teacher certainty about professional abilities and skills is highly correlated to student achievement (Rosenholtz, 1985). Because teaching enjoys no professionally sanctioned goals and agreed-upon techniques, teachers are left vulnerable to self-doubt and arbitrary criticism (Ashton & Webb, 1986). Receiving little assurance that their decisions about instruction are effective, or that their actions relate directly to student success, feeds teachers' sense of uncertainty about their competence.

Autonomy.   Autonomy, as a dimension of empowerment, refers to teachers' beliefs that they can control certain aspects of their work life, such as scheduling, curriculum, textbooks, and instructional planning. The hallmark of autonomy is the sense of freedom to make certain decisions.

Schools that create environments that support risk taking and experimentation by teachers also build teachers' sense of autonomy. Autonomy is a necessary prerequisite for a sense of accomplishment (Firestone, 1991). In this environment, teachers shape the educational environment of the school (Lightfoot, 1986). Rosenholtz's (1987) research indicated that the traditional bureaucratic organizational structure of schools prevents teacher autonomy and leads to teachers' defection from the profession.

Impact.   Impact refers to teachers' perceptions that they have an effect and influence on school life. Ashton and Webb (1986) posited that teachers' self-esteem grows when they feel that they are doing something worthwhile, that they are doing it in a competent manner, and that they are recognized for their accomplishments. Lightfoot (1986) added that teachers in her study of good schools grew from the respect they received from parents and community as well as the support they felt for their ideas. Teachers, like all other adults, require challenges and support in order to grow personally and professionally.

Feedback from colleagues is important to teachers' sense that they are having an impact. Blase (1982) stated that low levels of work motivation are the result of achieving outcomes with little or no reward for individual effort. The result for teachers is that they become less involved with students. Teachers believe that they do not receive the recognition that they deserve. Complaints are many; compliments are few. Teachers desire success in the classroom but find few tangible signs of accomplishment. Thus, they feel unsupported by administrators, colleagues, and the community (Ashton & Webb, 1986).

Organizational and Personal Empowerment Variables

Organizations create environments that give employees enabling experiences that lead to empowerment. These enabling experiences are opportunities to display existing competencies and to learn new competencies in ways that support and strengthen their function. In schools, enabling experiences may focus on roles and responsibilities, the culture of the school, the way problems are identified and solved, or the structure of the organization. The level or extent to which teachers perceive their own involvement and participation in the activities of the school that are meaningful to them relates to their sense of either empowerment or alienation.

Teachers' sense of empowerment in schools relates to the degree to which they can make decisions controlling events that are critical to their work. It also relates to their perception that they can make happen what they wish to have happen through their abilities and competence. One personal indicator of empowerment is the perception that the individual has, in the past, had successful experiences. Another indicator of a high level of personal empowerment is being an active problem solver. Displaying competencies and abilities leads to personal empowerment. A final indicator of the level of an individual's personal empowerment is the degree to which that individual is a self-evaluator.

LEADERSHIP ISSUES AND TEACHER EMPOWERMENT

Providing leadership to both create and sustain an empowering school environment for teachers requires attention to a number of issues. These include:

1. Helping teachers frame a definition of teacher empowerment.
2. Building a climate that is supportive of teacher risk taking and experimentation.
3. Creating shared decision making.

4. Developing teacher collaborative problem-solving and conflict-management skills.

5. Building trust and communication within the school.

6. Giving up the need to control.

Framing a Definition of Empowerment

Early in the empowerment process, teachers may not understand clearly
what is meant by teacher empowerment. Having a knowledge base about
the concept of empowerment is critical in framing a definition of empowerment that makes sense to a group of teachers in a particular
school. Initially, teachers need to read about the concept and learn what
writers and researchers are saying about empowerment. It is helpful to
provide extensive readings to teachers throughout the initiation process.
Teachers in the Empowered School District Project pleaded for more
and more articles to read on empowerment.

While knowledge about empowerment from literature is important, teachers also need to develop a definition and understanding of
empowerment that is meaningful and specific to them as a particular
school faculty. A powerful strategy to begin building an understanding of
empowerment is to foster teacher-led meetings or informal gatherings to
address two simple questions: "What makes you feel empowered in this
school?" and "What would make you feel more empowered?" Several
schools in the project held teacher-initiated and teacher-led gatherings in
the evenings to discuss and debate these questions. From these meetings
a working definition of empowerment evolved that had relevance and
importance to that particular faculty. This process proved important in
several ways. First, it provided a common understanding of empowerment that made subsequent efforts to define changes that needed to occur in the schools much easier and meaningful. Second, the agreed-upon
definition provided guidance in establishing strategies and processes for
creating enabling experiences for teachers in the schools. Understanding what would help teachers feel more empowered meant knowing
where to begin.

Building a Risk-Taking Environment

Establishing new patterns of involvement in an empowered school requires change. Research by Leithwood and Montgomery (1982) highlighted the impact that a climate of experimentation has on establishing
norms for trying out new practices and engaging in renewal strategies.

Hall and Griffin (1982) suggested that school climates that encourage innovative thinking and openness among members of the organization provide a positive context for increased member involvement.

Researchers (Berman & McLaughlin, 1977; Little, 1982) have suggested that teachers engage in greater innovative efforts and change their classroom practices when they perceive that experimentation is encouraged and expected. A climate of experimentation is critical for new approaches to surface in schools. Barth (1990) related that "considerable research suggests that risk taking is strongly associated with learning ..." (p. 513) and that a climate of experimentation involves risk taking. Principals can encourage risk taking and build an environment that is supportive of experimentation by modeling risk taking and creating processes for collecting new ideas.

Lightfoot (1986) noted that a climate of experimentation and risk taking provides empowering opportunities for teachers to shape the educational environment. Furthermore, empowerment builds teacher commitment and involvement (Lightfoot, 1986). In the empowerment project, principals found that specific actions facilitated the creation of a more risk-taking environment in their schools. One principal spent a great deal of time encouraging teachers and teacher teams to set their own goals. He helped teachers to establish their own task goals and establish goals for performance. Another principal encouraged self-critique of performance, programs, educational assumptions, and collaborative decisions. He set up processes to facilitate self-evaluation. Teachers began to observe each other and to spend time discussing instructional ideas. Peer observations became a major strategy to establish experimentation and risk taking.

Creating Shared Decision Making

Although it is commonly understood that greater teacher involvement in decision making increases support for subsequent implementation of the decision, the manner in which teachers are involved may be complex. Research by Schriesheim and Neider (1988) suggested that participants may perceive their involvement or noninvolvement in decision making in an organization in one of the following seven ways:

1. The principal makes decisions by himself or herself with no input from the teacher.

2. The teacher is asked for information but is not involved in the decision.

3. The principal shares school problems with the teacher and invites opinions, but the teacher is not involved in the decision.

4. Problems are shared, and teacher and principal jointly arrive at a mutually acceptable decision.

5. Problems are shared, but the teacher makes the final decision.

6. The teacher makes the final decision upon obtaining information from the principal.

7. The teacher makes decisions without any input from the principal.

In a study of models of leader motivating behavior, Tetrick (1989) found that "leaders who provide information to their subordinates rather than exerting control will be more effective in increasing intrinsic motivation" (p. 956). In addition, Tetrick suggested that this effect is mediated by subordinate perceptions of self-competence and self-determination—perceptions influenced by work environments that are structured to foster the participants' sense of control and competence or, in other words, by environments that empower participants through participative decision making (Short & Greer, 1989a).

Dawson (1984) found that certain contextual variables influenced the involvement of teachers in school change efforts, including administrative commitment to change. Furthermore, teacher involvement in change was related to the degree to which they felt that their input had an effect and that administrative desire for their involvement was genuine (Dawson, 1984; Grindle, 1982).

A good way to involve teachers is to establish problem-solving teams. For example, one high school, as mentioned in Chapter 5, established seven problem-solving teams, one for each period of the day. These teams were made up of all teachers who had common planning times each period. They identified problems that needed solving and gathered problem and solution ideas from their colleagues in their respective departments. The seven teams brought the problems and solution ideas to the Principal's Advisory Council, which was composed of all department heads as well as additional teacher representatives and counselors. This council brought the problems and alternative solutions to the entire faculty, which debated issues and agreed on priorities regarding which problems to address. The seven teams oversaw the implementation of the solutions and gave feedback to the Principal's Advisory Council. One of the many problems solved through this extensive use of problem-solving teams and shared decision making was chronic student tardiness.

Developing Teacher Problem-Solving and Conflict-Management Skills

Clearly, helping teachers to become good collaborative problem solvers involves both training in problem-solving skills and the implementation of problem-solving structures and processes that provide for teacher involvement in issues of critical importance to them. Teachers want to be involved in problem solving concerning issues that directly impact the nature of the work they do and the experiences they have in the school organization. Teachers in the empowerment project, once they realized that their decisions were final and not just advisory, eagerly assumed responsibility for finding solutions to problems including scheduling, discipline, parent involvement, innovation in teaching, professional development, teacher morale, programs for students at risk, inadequate resources, and many other issues.

Several of the schools provided teacher training in problem solving using team effectiveness trainers from private industry. Various problem-solving models were taught to the entire faculty and administration. This training alleviates the usual problems that occur when implementing group problem-solving teams; it teaches teachers how to identify the causes of problems and not merely to focus on solutions, which is the tendency of untrained groups. Teachers also learned how to function effectively in groups. Training in group dynamics gave them the skills to assume productive group roles and to identify problems in the group process that impede the success of the group work. It is very empowering to know that one has the skills to function successfully in group problem-solving experiences. One high school was so successful in training teachers in problem solving and team effectiveness that it began to provide the same training to its students.

In addition to training in collaborative problem solving, schools that created more empowering environments for teachers provided some type of training in conflict management. In most cases, some of the faculty were trained, and they, in turn, provided additional training to the other faculty members. Because discourse becomes much more open in an empowered school, opportunities to expose conflicting ideologies and beliefs in the collaborative problem-solving and decision-making processes increase tremendously. Teachers are working together more intensely, and opportunities for conflict are great. If teachers also have skills in conflict management—if they know how to identify the sources of conflicts and understand conflict management styles and their use—conflicts that might otherwise destroy their ability to collaborate are dealt with in an effective manner.

Building Trust and Communication

Building trust in the school environment involves understanding the complexity of the concept of trust in operation. Building trust within a school involves a number of individuals in a number of ways: teachers must trust the principal; teachers and principal must trust the central administration, including the board of education; the principal must trust the teachers; and the teachers must trust one another. Trust building is a slow process that requires disclosure, authenticity of work and action, follow-through in meeting each others' needs, respect for diversity, enabling teachers to take action in a risk-taking environment without fear of reprisal, and basic ethical actions that demonstrate a concern for the well-being of others.

Giving Up the Need to Control

While it is difficult to understand without having experienced it, the principals in the empowerment project who were willing to eventually relinquish control of decision making and other issues related to running a school found that they had not given up power in the way they had expected. When teachers have a decision-making role in issues affecting their own work life, they feel more responsible for the quality of the work of the school (Short & Rinehart, 1993). Thus, teachers assume the leadership role in identifying school problems and structuring the problem-solving process to address those problems. In one school in the empowerment project, the principal finally allowed teachers to take leadership in addressing the scheduling for the coming year. They appointed a scheduling committee, dealt with problems when special education teachers complained that they were being taken advantage of in covering for general education teachers to plan, and, in the end, constructed a better schedule than the principal could have devised. One principal worked early to relinquish control of the process by encouraging teachers to meet at the beginning of the empowerment effort *without him* to define empowerment as it meant to them. The principal struggled with being absent, and the teachers wondered whether it was right to have these discussions without him, since they had never before tackled anything without his direction and attendance. Later, the principal said that it was like "more feet running in the same direction" to see the faculty acting on common goals and common concerns.

∞ CASE STUDY

How did one school structure and focus its efforts to help teachers feel greater empowerment? How did the leadership implications discussed earlier play out in this school's work? The case study that follows should provide the basis for conversations about leadership issues surrounding teacher empowerment.

Becoming an Empowered Faculty

When you arrive at this elementary school, you will find a student population of approximately 480 students: 51% white and 49% from different racial and ethnic groups. Changing demographics have led some community members to believe that excellence has been compromised in attempts to meet the needs of a changing student population.

The instructional staff consists of 35 certified and 6 noncertified members. The male principal, who has been at the school for the past 6 years, is assisted by a part-time assistant principal and a full-time counselor. The principal initiated the school's involvement in the empowerment effort by contacting one of the project directors and requesting the opportunity to participate.

While participation in the Empowered School District Project was received well by the principal and a few of the teachers, not all of the faculty immediately endorsed the idea. However, several teachers at the school already were planning a cross-age grouping arrangement to change instruction, and they viewed student empowerment as a natural outcome of cross-age grouping.

The first challenge that faced the principal and the teachers who really were interested in the project was building a climate for empowerment. A school climate survey conducted at the end of the previous year had indicated that five teachers perceived a negative climate. These teachers, who were not in favor of the project, were mostly those who had been at the school for several years and had seen many new fads come and go. To provide a context, it is important to note that although the school entered the project believing it was functioning well, it lost that complacency by the end of the first year. During that time, the school began to acknowledge areas of need in empowerment. One faculty member stated early in the project, "We're fine. We do a great job. We're already empowered here." She spoke for many of the faculty. In fact, 2 months into the new school year, the staff was not motivated by the opportunity to participate in this national project.

There were some troubling signs that continued to hang on and seemed to drain the enthusiasm of the staff. A second climate survey, conducted toward the end of the second month of the first year of the project, verified that the staff was dissatisfied with some areas of the principal's performance. When asked, "If you could do one thing to improve working conditions at the school, what would it be?" the staff responded with suggestions to replace the current administrator, have more collaborative support from the administration, develop effective leadership, and improve the relationship between staff and supervisor.

The results of the survey were discussed at a night meeting held at a local business, with all but two teachers in attendance. The principal decided not to attend in order to demonstrate faith in their efforts to hold such a dialogue in his absence. The main agenda topic was "What Makes a Teacher Feel Empowered?" The idea of empowerment intrigued some of the staff members. Although there was no overt support for the project, there were glimmers of hope that the idea would catch on. After this meeting, several teachers formed a committee with the purpose of getting more information about empowerment. Several weeks later, they arrived at a definition of what empowerment meant to them: "A shared confidence and recognition of each other and ourselves in a safe, healthy environment in which there are opportunities for growth and cooperative decision making."

At this point, the principal expressed concerns about the following issues:

- How do we solve problems?
- How do we develop a rationale for becoming better problem solvers and what would that rationale be?
- How can we develop a process by which we examine our options?
- What is important to us?
- How can we find a systematic process by which we deal with our concerns?

These concerns became a focus for empowering the teachers at the school.

By midyear, a faculty meeting was held in which the teachers brainstormed about their needs, wants, ideas, projects, and thoughts concerning empowerment. Although some teachers felt that the staff already was empowered and therefore there was no reason to become involved with the empowerment project, others wanted to try and see whether problems could be worked out. During the brainstorming session, the teachers filled three chalkboards with comments. At this time, a teacher volunteered to become the chronicler for the project. Also, the teachers decided to vote on participation in the project. The vote, by secret ballot, resulted in 13 votes for participation and 9 votes against.

Later in the year, nine teachers formed what was known as the Empowerment Committee. The committee began to work on the three issues that seemed to be the most important to the staff: implementing whole language, intervening for students at risk, and scheduling. In addition, the full implementation of the cross-age team began as an approach to restructure instruction to meet students' needs. The teacher-chronicler, a teacher chosen to document the change process, made articles available to the teachers that would provide helpful information for decision making. The teachers found the articles useful in planning solutions to the problems that were of interest to them.

The teachers wanted to inform the parents about the project. In a memo written to the faculty, the teacher-chronicler stated: "I know it's important that everyone be informed about the process of teacher empowerment and that everyone have the opportunity for input into this process." The Empowerment Committee decided that the way to inform the parents about the empowerment efforts was to role play in a PTA meeting. Teachers were asked whether they wanted to volunteer to participate in a "fish bowl" activity in which they would brainstorm ideas with the parents. The topic was "How Can We Improve Communications Between the School and the Home?" Those teachers who volunteered to participate in the PTA meeting planned and prepared for the encounter. The PTA meeting was held, with the teachers as presenters. Parents now had an idea of what was happening at the school and expressed great interest in the idea of empowerment.

The work of the teacher-chronicler became more involved as she provided a focus for the energy being created by the empowerment effort. The teacher-chronicler stated: "If teacher empowerment doesn't come from the teachers themselves, it's not empowerment." During early spring of the first year of the project, the chronicler was granted a day of professional leave for the purpose of surveying the teachers to find answers to the following questions:

- What does teacher empowerment mean to you?
- How do you feel about teacher empowerment?
- What makes you feel empowered?
- What makes you feel unempowered?
- What ideas do you have for increasing teacher empowerment at this school?

Among the responses were that (a) empowerment means teachers having more involvement in things that directly impact their jobs, such as textbook selection, scheduling, and decisions about finance, and (b) empowerment means looking at the relationships that exist in the building that promote professionalism and a sense of well-being.

During the spring, the staff decided to work on the Intervention Program, which was designed to assist students who were at risk for failure. The direction that the school district was headed was contrary to the direction that the staff felt was productive for their students. The district was seriously considering implementing an intervention program that would group students by ability. The faculty worked together and collected educational articles that supported heterogeneous grouping for instruction. They prepared a position paper based on research on ability grouping that was to be sent to the district meeting. However, prior to that meeting, the decision to group the students homogeneously was dropped. The teachers expressed the belief that if they truly were an empowered school, then they would know what was best for the students. The principal had served in a facilitative role during this period, providing teacher release time to prepare the position paper, meeting with the school facilitator and several teachers to develop a strategy for making a presentation to the district intervention committee, and expressing verbal support for the school philosophy against ability grouping. A faculty member expressed concerns that the principal would ultimately give in to district pressure and weaken their efforts. Later, she was thrilled at the position taken by the principal. She stated that at that point she felt empowered.

In late spring, the teachers were asked to compare their attitudes from the time the empowerment effort first began with their present feelings. Of the 16 teachers responding to the survey, 11 reported that initially their attitude was either negative or they had no opinion, while only 5 responded that their attitude at the beginning of the project was positive. This survey revealed that a significant change had taken place. Three teachers still had negative opinions, while 12 felt either positive or very positive about the project. One teacher had no opinion.

The faculty felt that factors that accounted for this change in attitude included increased awareness of the value of empowerment accomplished through distribution of articles from the literature, faculty discussions, debate and reflection concerning empowerment, and increased teacher involvement. Actually, many teachers became actively involved as empowerment leaders, and they persuaded others of the value of empowerment. Another factor was an emphasis on voluntary participation in empowerment activities. Teacher leaders served to build trust among the faculty.

CHAPTER 8

During this time in the project a fundamental shift occurred in the roles assumed by the principal and the teachers. The teachers saw that they could have an impact on the decisions made at the school, and they became more interested in the entire decision-making process. At the same time, on the recommendation of one of the project facilitators, the principal eased his control and allowed the teacher-leaders and teacher-chronicler to assume leadership in the decision-making activities. The principal did not have to be the one who identified areas for collaborative decision making, with teachers feeling left out of the process. Instead, teachers began to identify areas in which the school could improve and, by forming committees, began to take responsibility for finding solutions to problems.

Before the second year of the project, a retreat was held at a state park. Twenty-one of 26 teachers attended the meeting. The entire faculty planned the agenda. The retreat focused on whole language instruction, and a university consultant selected by the teachers worked with them on strategies for its use. There was a high degree of satisfaction regarding the retreat, according to the responses given by the teachers on a retreat evaluation.

The second year of the project, several teachers from another school district came to visit the school. The agenda for the visiting teachers, prepared cooperatively by the principal and the teachers, included a discussion of school accomplishments to date. According to the staff, these included the following:

- Improved communications.
- Involvement in budget matters.
- More effective curriculum design such as intervention for students at risk and whole language instruction.
- Improved decision making.
- Responsibility by all school participants for decisions made.

Areas needing attention were also discussed with the visitors, including:

- Establishing boundaries for decisions.
- Misusing the concept of empowerment to justify inappropriate decisions.
- Structuring an environment supportive of teacher risk taking.
- Sustaining a level of motivation for the empowerment process.

In the fall of the second year, the teachers decided that they wanted to provide duty-free lunch periods for homeroom teachers. They scheduled meetings in which this was the main agenda. At one of the meetings, a teacher became upset with the discussion about the homeroom teachers having so much more to do than the special-area teachers. This teacher was afraid that the goodwill that had existed before was vanishing with all the talk about everyone not carrying their fair share of the workload. The teachers talked through this and worked out a schedule that allowed homeroom teachers to have some time off during lunch throughout the week. Teachers who did not have a homeroom provided supervision in place of teachers with a homeroom. Everyone approved this decision. With this turn of events, the Empowerment Committee met and developed their plan for solving problems: the "Problem-Solving Sequence." This sequence involved inviting teachers to express concerns or identify problems to the Empowerment Committee, which, in turn, passed these problems to the Problem-Solving Committee, which would create smaller teams to develop alternative solutions. These smaller teams would pass solutions back to the Problem-Solving Committee, which brought the problems and solutions to the faculty. The faculty would discuss the issues and vote on possible solutions. The smaller problem-solving teams would implement the solutions and provide follow-up and monitoring of results. This sequence was implemented immediately, and it was successfully employed to address a wide variety of faculty concerns.

In December, four staff members went to visit another project school in another state and had an opportunity to discuss and exchange ideas with the other school's faculty. These discussions reinforced a sense of collaboration.

During the spring of the second year of the project, some teachers applied for and received a grant providing the school with technical assistance and stipends for teachers working with a consultant to implement whole language instruction. A retreat was held during the summer, with the superintendent, the two assistant superintendents, and the special education director in attendance. Again, the majority of the staff attended the retreat. As a result of the feedback from the year before, this retreat was held for 2 days, with the option of staying overnight at the state park. The presenter for the second day was one of the third-grade teachers.

In the third year, many plans were implemented. The faculty identified a growing sense of authentic involvement in decisions as a critical factor in a change in climate. The problem-solving sequence had produced better solutions and helped teachers grow into better problem solvers. The principal admitted, "The faculty identified scheduling as a problem. We took it to the Problem-Solving Committee, and they came up with a better schedule than I could have devised." Many of the changes realized by the third year stemmed from the problem-solving abilities developed during the project. For example, a major issue that arose during year 3 was teacher concern about student discipline. These concerns were funneled to the Empowerment Committee and, subsequently, to the Problem-Solving Committee. The committee met over a 6-week period to discuss discipline problems and possible strategies to reduce student behavior problems, gather input for the entire faculty, and develop a proposal for a modified "Assertive Discipline Program" to be adopted by the faculty. The Problem-Solving Committee made a presentation at a faculty meeting, and discussion followed. The faculty decided to adopt the program, and a committee was formed to conduct a staff training session to prepare the faculty to implement the plan. The program was implemented, and early assessment of its impact was positive.

As a result, teachers expressed the need to focus on more issues of concern and asked the Problem-Solving Committee to develop possible ideas for addressing the various concerns of the faculty. The faculty identified scheduling problems, especially the need for some release time for teams of teachers to plan together. The Problem-Solving Committee asked for volunteers to work on a new schedule. Within 3 weeks, two proposed schedules were presented to the faculty and one was adopted.

Many changes occurred in the instructional program during the third year. Many of the changes emanated from teacher identification of significant issues and concerns about meeting students' needs. Instead of complaining about those concerns, the faculty shifted their efforts toward generating solutions and brought them to the Empowerment Committee.

This was a radical change from the manner in which teachers addressed concerns early in the project. It appeared that involvement in the decision process created more of a sense of problem ownership on the part of the faculty. For example, teachers implemented the portfolio assessment process. They had experimented with the concept through a project minigrant the past year and found strategies that made portfolios useful to them. In particular, they discovered that, although individual videos prepared for portfolios were expensive, parents were eager to contribute blank videos at the beginning of the year to be used in the year-long videotaping of children for individual portfolios. The faculty saw videos as valuable in documenting students who exhibited some of the characteristics of an empowered child: responsibility, creativity, and group leadership. In addition, the faculty sought an increased emphasis on whole language instruction, and the strategy was adopted by additional grade levels. Finally, the multiage team adopted cooperative learning strategies with great success.

Conversations About the Case Study

This section is intended to provide you with ideas for conversations regarding the case study and its focus on the empowerment of teachers. As you discuss teacher empowerment and explore the leadership issues related to it, use the following questions to spark debate, develop further questions, critique current practice, and guide your leadership assumptions.

1. Why are processes for the involvement of teachers so critical in teacher empowerment?
2. What mechanisms were put in place that allowed the development of each of the six dimensions of empowerment in this school?
3. To what extent did the principal understand the leadership issues involved in creating enabling experiences that empower teachers?
4. Why was building trust such an issue in this school?
5. How can a principal work with "key influentials" to encourage empowerment of teachers?
6. What are the key leadership lessons learned by the principal in this school relative to teacher empowerment?

REFERENCES

Anderson, M. B. G., & Iwanicki, E. F. (1984). Teacher motivation and its relation to burnout. *Educational Administration Quarterly, 20*(2), 109–132.

Ashton, P. T., & Webb, B. W. (1986). *Making a difference: Teachers' sense of efficacy and student achievement.* New York: Longman.

Barth, R. S. (1990). A personal vision of a good school. *Phi Delta Kappan, 71,* 512–516.

Berman, P., & McLaughlin, M. W. (1977). *Federal programs supporting educational change: Volume VII. Factors affecting implementation and continuation.* Santa Monica, CA: Rand.

Blase, J. J. (1982). A social-psychological grounded theory of teacher stress and burnout. *Educational Administration Quarterly, 18*(4), 93–113.

Cummings, T. (1978). Self-regulating work groups: A socio-technical synthesis. *Academy of Management Review, 3,* 625–634.

Dawson, J. A. (1984, April). *The principal's role in facilitating teacher participation: Mediating the influence of school context.* Paper presented at the annual meeting of the American Educational Research Association, New Orleans, LA.

Dunst, R. (1991, February). *Issues in empowerment.* Paper presented at the annual meeting of the Children's Mental Health and Service Policy Convention, Tampa, FL.

Firestone, W. A. (1991). Merit pay and job enlargement as reforms: Incentives, implementation, and teacher response. *Educational Evaluation and Policy Analysis, 13,* 269–288.

Firestone, W. A. (1993). Why "professionalizing" teaching is not enough. *Educational Leadership, 50*(6), 6–11.

Frase, L. E., & Sorenson, L. (1992). Teacher motivation and satisfaction: Impact on participatory management. *NASSP Bulletin, 76*(540), 37–44.

Frymier, J. (1987). Bureaucracy and the neutering of teachers. *Phi Delta Kappan, 69,* 9–14.

Glenn, E. (1990). Teacher empowerment. *Music Educator's Journal, 77*(2), 4–6.

Grindle, B. W. (1982). Administrative team management: Four essential components. *Clearing House, 56,* 29–33.

Gruber, J., & Trickett, E. J. (1987). Can we empower others? The paradox of empowerment in an alternative public high school. *American Journal of Community Psychology, 15,* 353–372.

Hackman, J. R. (1986). The psychology of self-management in organizations. In M. S. Pollack & R. O. Perloff (Eds.), *Psychology and work: Productivity change and employment* (pp. 85–136). Washington, DC: American Psychological Association.

Hackman, J. R., & Oldham, G. R. (1980). *Work redesign.* Reading, MA: Addison-Wesley.

Hall, G. E., & Griffin, T. (1982, March). *Analyzing context/climate in school settings: Which is which?* Paper presented at the annual meeting of the American Educational Research Association, New York, NY.

Katz, R. F. (1984). Empowerment and synergy: Expanding the community's healing resources. *Prevention in Human Services, 3,* 201–226.

Lawler, E. E., III. (1986). *High involvement management: Participative strategies for improving organizational performance.* San Francisco: Jossey-Bass.

Leithwood, K., & Montgomery, D. J. (1982). The role of the elementary school principal in program improvement. *Review of Educational Research, 52,* 309–339.

Lightfoot, S. L. (1985, March). *On the goodness of schools: Themes of empowerment.* Paper presented at the Macyie K. Southall Distinguished Lecture on Public Education and the Futures of Children, Vanderbilt University, Nashville, TN.

Lightfoot, S. L. (1986). On the goodness of schools: Themes of empowerment. *Peabody Journal of Education, 63*(3), 9–28.

Little, J. (1982). Norms of collegiality and experimentation: Workplace conditions of school success. *American Educational Research Journal, 19,* 325–340.

Lortie, D. C. (1975). *Schoolteacher.* Chicago: University of Chicago Press.

Maeroff, G. I. (1988). A blueprint for empowering teachers. *Phi Delta Kappan, 69,* 472–477.

Manz, C. C., & Angle, H. (1987). Can group self-management mean a loss of personal control? Triangulating a paradox. *Group and Organizational Studies, 11,* 309–334.

Manz, C. C., & Sims, H. P., Jr. (1984). Searching for the "unleader:" Organizational member views on leading self-managing groups. *Human Relations, 37,* 409–424.

Manz, C. C., & Sims, H. P., Jr. (1987). Leading workers to lead themselves: The external leadership of self-managing work teams. *Administrative Science Quarterly, 32,* 106–128.

Maton K. I., & Rappaport, J. (1984). Empowerment in a religious setting: A multivariate investigation. *Prevention in Human Services, 3,* 37–72.

Murphy J., & Evertson, C. (1990, April). *Restructuring schools: Capturing the phenomena.* Paper presented at the annual meeting of the American Educational Research Association, Boston, MA.

Rappaport, J. (1987). Terms of empowerment/exemplars of prevention: Toward a theory for community psychology. *American Journal of Community Psychology, 15,* 121–148.

Rinehart, J. S., & Short, P. M. (1992). Reading recovery as an empowerment phenomenon. *The Journal of School Leadership, 1,* 379–399.

Rosenholtz, S. J. (1985). Effective schools: Interpreting the evidence. *American Journal of Education, 93,* 352–388.

Rosenholtz, S. J. (1987). Education reform strategies: Will they increase teacher commitment? *American Journal of Education, 95,* 534–562.

Rosenholtz, S. J. (1991). *Teachers' workplace: The social organization of schools.* New York: Teachers College Press.

Schriesheim, C. A., & Neider, L. N. (1988, August). *Distinctions among subtypes of perceived delegation and leadership decision making.* Paper presented at the annual meeting of the American Psychological Association, Atlanta, GA.

Sergiovanni, T. J. (1991). *The principalship: A reflective practice perspective* (2nd ed.). Boston: Allyn and Bacon.

Short, P. M., & Greer, J. T. (1989a). *The Empowered School District Project.* Grant funded by the Danforth Foundation, St. Louis, MO.

Short, P. M., & Greer, J. T. (1989b, April). *Increasing teacher autonomy through shared governance: Effects on policy making and student outcomes.* Paper presented at the annual meeting of the American Educational Research Association, San Francisco, CA.

Short, P. M., Greer, J. T., & Michael, R. (1991). Restructuring schools through empowerment: Facilitating the process. *Journal of School Leadership, 1*(2), 5–25.

Short, P. M., Miller-Wood, D. J, & Johnson, P. E. (1991). Risk taking and teacher involvement in decision making. *Education, 112*(1), 84–89.

Short, P., & Rinehart, J. (1992). School Participant Empowerment Scale: Assessment of the level of participant empowerment in the school. *Educational and Psychological Measurement, 54,* 951–960.

Short, P. M., & Rinehart, J. (1993). Teacher empowerment and school climate. *Education, 54,* 598–602.

Smylie, M. A. (1992). Teacher participation in school decision making: Assessing willingness to participate. *Educational Evaluation and Policy Analysis, 14*(1), 53–67.

Tetrick, L. E. (1989). The motivating potential of leader behaviors: A comparison of two models. *Journal of Applied Social Psychology, 19,* 947–958.

Vroom, V. H., & Yetton, P. W. (1973). *Leadership and decision making.* Pittsburgh: University of Pittsburgh Press.

Zielinski, A., & Hoy, W. L. (1983). Isolation and alienation in elementary schools. *Educational Administration Quarterly, 19*(2), 27–45.

Zimmerman, M. A., & Rappaport, J. (1988). Citizen participation, perceived control, and psychological empowerment. *American Journal of Community Psychology, 16,* 725–750.

CHAPTER 9

℘

Empowering Students

The major thrust in empowering school participants appears to take the form of providing teachers with (a) a significant role in school decision making, thereby developing a sense of shared governance; (b) control over their work environment and work conditions; and (c) opportunities to contribute to the school in a range of professional roles: teacher, administrator, curriculum developer, mentor, and learner.

However, a critical area that often is overlooked in the restructuring movement is student empowerment. The empowerment of teachers will facilitate the empowerment of students; teachers who are empowered will in turn give students more opportunities to become empowered through shared decision making and increased choice and responsibility for their own learning.

CREATING LIFE-LONG LEARNERS

Revolutions in the technological base of our society are altering the knowledge, skills, and values that people need to be successful in the workplace. With the advent of self-managing teams and problem-solving networks in the workplace, the collective knowledge, skills, and creative energy of a group of individuals will be the structure used for task completion in effective organizations (Peters, 1987). Future jobs will demand organizational participants who are flexible in both thinking and action, as knowledge expands and job requirements shift. Participants must be able to work in collegial, collaborative problem-solving teams that function with great independence (Dede, 1989).

Participative Management and Decision Making

The popular notion of participative decision making was defined by Crane (1976) as a management approach that allows and encourages subordinates to participate in decisions that will affect them. Lowin (cited in Dunstan, 1981) found that participative management is an organizational operation by which decisions are reached by including the persons who are to execute those decisions. According to Patterns, Purkey, and Parker (cited in Rice, 1987), putting decision-making power as close to the point of delivery as possible makes implementation of those decisions not only possible, but successful. Erickson and Gmelch (1977) noted that the overall benefits of adopting a team-management approach to school governance include improved quality of communication and decision-making practices, increased staff motivation, and enhanced coordination of tasks and plans.

Self-Managing Work Groups

The concept of the self-managing work group has its origin in business and industry literature (Hackman & Oldham, 1980). In self-managing work groups, employees take personal responsibility for the outcomes of their work; manage their own performance; and monitor, reinforce, and reward the work of the group (Hackman, 1986). Kasten, Short, and Jarmin (1989) observed that interdisciplinary teaching teams in middle schools are an example of self-managing teams.

Empowerment

Empowerment, although described mainly in the literature on teacher empowerment, also can be defined as the opportunities *students* have for autonomy, choice, responsibility, and participation in decision making in organizations (Lightfoot, 1986). Jenkins (1988) stated that "to empower others is to give a stakeholder share in the movement and direction of the enterprise" (p. 149). Students who are able to initiate and carry out new ideas by involvement in decision making should, in turn, take more responsibility for their learning and exhibit higher levels of engagement in learning experiences (Jenkins, 1988; Short & Greer, 1989). Traditionally, students are passive participants in their learning activities, growing increasingly detached from any substantive involvement in school experiences. Lortie (1975) depicted teachers as working in isolation from other teachers with little collegial contact. Likewise, schools provide little opportunity for students to develop skills in group interaction and problem solving, responsibility for their own learning, flexibility in thinking, and life-long learning values. The opportunities to display competencies such as these are few, with schools treating students as "products" instead of workers with a vested interest in the learning experiences in which they participate (Murphy & Evertson, 1990; Short, Greer, & Michael, 1991).

Rappaport and his colleagues have described empowerment as a construct that ties personal competencies and abilities to environments that provide opportunities for choice and autonomy in demonstrating those competencies (Zimmerman & Rappaport, 1988). Dunst (1991) has suggested that empowerment consists of two factors: (1) enabling experiences, provided within an organization that fosters autonomy, choice, control, and responsibility, which then (2) allow the individual to display existing competencies, and learn new competencies that support and strengthen functioning. Research in the Empowered School District Project found that indicators of an empowered student include functioning as an active problem solver, being a creative and productive group member, being competent, engaging in self-evaluation, and experiencing success in the activities in which he or she engages.

LEADERSHIP ISSUES AND STUDENT EMPOWERMENT

Five themes are critical in implementing student empowerment efforts in schools:

1. Early identification of a definition.
2. Intense focus on students.
3. Flexibility and resourcefulness.
4. Risk taking and experimentation.
5. Facilitative leadership by the principal.

The three cases at the end of this chapter serve to clarify and illustrate how these themes evolved from the research conducted in the schools.

Theme One: Early Identification of a Definition

The three empowerment project schools described in the case studies in this chapter that experienced greater success in establishing measures to empower students did not frame student empowerment as a power struggle, fearing that students would take over the school. Instead, within the first year of the project, these three schools developed a working definition of student empowerment that focused on developing student responsibility, successful student experiences, student competence, and student choice.

Theme Two: Intense Focus on Students

All three schools centered their empowerment work, formally and informally, on students. These schools seemed to be comfortable with the notion of student as team member and student as worker rather than student as product. Specific ways in which they made these values operational included (a) developing student problem-solving skills, (b) giving students a stake in the success of the organization, and (c) developing student academic skills.

Developing Problem-Solving Skills

Case Study One provides an example from the secondary level of a high school that trained its students in problem-solving and leadership skills. Interviews with some of these students indicated that they felt an increasing sense of self-efficacy in facing decisions. Teen Court, implemented in Case Study Two, provided students with many opportunities to solve problems in situations that were relevant to them.

Having a Stake in the Organization

Faculty at the three schools saw student input into planning, both in instructional areas and organizational issues, as an important mechanism for increasing the students' stake in school effectiveness. Students participating in the Leadership Retreat in Case Study One felt a greater need to act responsibly as team members in all school functions. One student said, "I have a responsibility to make school activities, both in the classroom and outside the classroom, successful." This team concept facilitated the notion of student as worker.

The school in Case Study Two involved students on teams of faculty, parents, and community members who were involved in making explicit the values and beliefs undergirding the school organization. The Student Pride program implemented in Case Study Three gave students a critical role in changing the physical environment of the school as well as a responsibility to drive the school in the direction of excellence.

Developing Academic Skills

The Student Pride program in Case Study Three illustrates a specific school strategy to encourage academic achievement. Integral to this program was the recognition given to students who made gains in academic arenas. The school in Case Study Two restructured the delivery of instruction to better meet the learning needs of its diverse student population. The reorganization of the school into schools-within-schools was an attempt to create a learning environment more conducive to student academic success by meeting individual needs.

Theme Three: Flexibility and Resourcefulness

Characteristic of these three schools was their resourcefulness in finding expertise, funds, manpower, and time to support their innovation. All drew on their communities, whether from a university, business and industry, outside consultants, or funding sources, in order to implement changes. One school gained from the expertise of industry trainers who volunteered to conduct the Leadership Retreats on weekends. The school in Case Study Two gained industry assistance in conducting an environmental audit prior to its think-tank activities. The faculty wrote grants that funded numerous school projects. In some cases, school and outside environmental boundaries disappeared, creating a sense of school–community collaboration and responsibility for helping every student succeed. This openness created a flood of opportunity for implementation of new ideas.

The three schools demonstrated great flexibility in thinking about how to construct an effective learning environment for each child, how the school day should look, how roles and responsibilities should be restructured to give students greater choice and autonomy, and how to interact and utilize resources within and outside the school.

Theme Four: Risk Taking and Experimentation

Critical to creating environments in which all students have the opportunity to become empowered is participant belief that it is all right make mistakes, take risks, and experiment with new ideas. As students and teachers become more and more involved in making basic decisions in the school, they must be encouraged to experiment; in so doing, sometimes they will fail. Principals in such schools must set the climate for risk taking by becoming facilitators. Teachers in such schools must establish the climate for risk taking in their classrooms by also becoming facilitators.

Theme Five: Facilitative Leadership by the Principal

The principals in these three schools exercised facilitative leadership within their own schools in varying degrees. The principal in Case

Study Two developed a management team approach to administration and leadership, with faculty, assistant principals, students, and parents having decision-making opportunities and responsibility for making the school effective for its diverse student population. The team approach adopted by the school in Case Study One illustrates how the principal viewed himself as yet another member of a number of teams. He saw his role as resource finder, innovative thinker, and student advocate. All of the principals functioned as the "conscience" of their schools, providing a continuing focus on students. Also, they were able to grapple with their own egos and felt secure enough to share leadership. For one principal, this did not come easily at first. However, he followed the advice of a project facilitator and, even though it was hard, gave others more control. By doing so he learned that teacher leadership and initiative made his job much easier in terms of attaining the changes that would create a more empowered school environment for faculty and students. As he said, "Empowerment is more feet running in the same direction."

IMPLICATIONS FOR PRACTICE

These findings from the empowerment project schools have implications for change efforts within the school context in general. In particular, the following three measures are critical to student empowerment: (1) building trust and the principal's facilitative leadership, (2) creating a culture that supports experimentation, and (3) enhancing student leadership and problem-solving skills.

Building Trust and the Principal's Facilitative Leadership

It is evident that staff commitment to substantive change processes that heighten student and teacher interaction demands considerable time for staff to build trust within the organization. Participative decision making and problem-solving teamwork require greater teacher and student collaboration and concomitant priority setting and problem solving. Teachers must come to believe that students can take responsibility for the direction that the school takes in most areas. Principal and teacher interaction becomes more collegial in an empowered school, intensifying the interactions between these parties. Principals must reflect on their own leadership styles and adopt a more facilitative style in working with teachers.

Creating a Culture That Is Supportive of Experimentation

Risk taking and participant experimentation are necessary ingredients in empowering students. Mistakes are accepted and viewed as learning experiences. Students and teachers are encouraged to try new ideas and experiment with new approaches.

Enhancing Student Leadership and Problem-Solving Skills

Those who are attempting to empower schools will need to consider the complexity of communication channels in such organizations. In the past, traditional hierarchical patterns have predicted the contact points. However, teaming, networks, cooperative problem solving, participative decision making, collaboration, and inquiry learning are all practices that force communication to occur among people who are not normally included in the communication channels of bureaucratic organizations. One such group is students, who must be viewed as being invested in the learning processes that occur in the school.

In addition, these new structures and processes for doing the work of the empowered organization force communication to occur for characteristically different purposes. Instead of communication carrying the dictates of the upper hierarchy to those lower in the organization, all participants will communicate in order to make major decisions about the organization, structure the organization's work, and develop strategies for accomplishing the organization's goals. Skills in group dynamics, group process, verbal and nonverbal communication, group-task goal setting, and strategic planning become important for everyone. Students especially require these skills in order to function as empowered school participants.

❧ CASE STUDIES

Case studies of three of the empowerment project schools are presented here to illustrate school efforts at empowering students. The questions that follow should provide the basis for conversations about leadership issues surrounding student empowerment.

CHAPTER 9

Case Study One: Empowering Students—Leadership Development

Can a school with over 2,700 middle to upper class students afford to empower students? Can the school even do it? Do the school's 175 faculty members believe that student empowerment is an important venture?

The second year of involvement in the Empowered School District Project marked the beginning of Leadership Retreat, a weekend retreat for students and any faculty who wished to attend conducted by four team-effectiveness trainers from Xerox, Boeing, Otis Engineering, and GTE. The first Leadership Retreat was conducted in the spring of the year. The first 50 students who volunteered and several faculty members were participants in this first retreat. The training focused on the leadership, problem-solving, and group-process skills needed by team members.

Upon their return, students were enthusiastic about their experience. One student said, "I learned that I must take responsibility for the success of my team. Just this week, I was messing around in the hall before a class and it was as if a light went off in my head reminding me that I am responsible for my positive behavior and the effectiveness of all of the teams on which I work." Another student stated, "I learned leadership skills that I now use in my classes and in the clubs in which I belong. I help get decisions made, and I feel better about handling conflict. Most of all, I feel responsible for making good things happen." Finally, one of the members of the football team said, "I thought I understood how a team should work together. Now I see my role as a team member even within my classes."

By year 3, all teachers had participated in the team effectiveness training. The focus shifted to training the students at the Leadership Retreat. In order to find additional funding for the venture, a student–faculty team developed a video to show to potential supporters in the business community. It is important to note that students attend the retreats at no charge. The school supports the entire venture. The team effectiveness trainers from the four corporations donate their time during the weekend retreats.

In the spring, students who had participated in Leadership Retreat made a presentation at the American Association of Quality Control. Their presentation featured discussions about responsibilities of team members, new skills learned, and the new relationship with teachers that evolved in the retreat. One student stated, "We learned to really talk and communicate."

By the end of the third year, four Leadership Retreat sessions had been held.

Case Study Two: An Engaging, Learning Place for Students

This urban school and its surrounding community enjoy a high concentration of Asian Hmong, Vietnamese, and Hispanic populations. Early meetings were directed toward creating a school environment conducive to student needs.

One of the major innovative programs begun the first year was the Lincoln Alternative Milestone Program (LAMP), a school-within-a-school that was designed to help selected students be successful in school. Students could enroll for as few as four or as many as six classes during the day. Classes were geared to individual needs, abilities, and academic credit requirements. Lessons related academic skills to everyday living situations. Many units also emphasized the interdisciplinary nature of the academic subjects. Teachers served as advisors to a group of about 15 students to monitor grades, attendance, and school progress. The program provided many resources for students through its mentor program. Business people acted as mentors to provide students with positive role models, help them stay in school, and introduce them to the business world.

Parents were contacted frequently and encouraged to be an active part of their children's education. The LAMP teachers tried a variety of techniques to reach these students at risk. Variable credit could be given for work completed in order to give the students as much success as possible. The experiential program enjoyed a teacher-pupil ratio of 15 to 1. Efforts were made to totally individualize the educational program for each student.

Over the following summer, many committees met and several new programs were readied for experimentation during year 2. The successful implementation of the LAMP program during year 1 seemed to give the school members confidence and fire to take risks with even more creative ideas.

The school implemented the "School of Global Studies" in the second year, a team-taught seminar that focused on providing a nontraditional, interdisciplinary approach to education from a global perspective. The focus for the school was interdisciplinary, with English, math, science, and social studies taught in a 4-year curriculum. The students worked with their teacher-advisors in a variety of activities and experiences designed to help students understand more about themselves and the world in which they live. The program explored course material in the context of an overriding theme or issue (e.g., environment, health, conflict), and students were expected to participate in community-service learning experiences as well.

CHAPTER 9

The School of Global Studies was designed primarily to encourage students to think critically and become more aware of the variety of perceptions, values, and priorities that exist locally and worldwide. Students were provided with the analytical and organizational skills necessary to help them appreciate and understand the world in which they live. They were encouraged to challenge themselves and others when considering world issues and the impact of those issues on their lives. The program's goal was to help prepare students to live successfully and productively as adults in a rapidly changing world. Students were considered for the program based on an application and interview process.

During the second year, discussions were held about forming four divisions that would make the curriculum more relevant to the needs of the 21st century. Additionally, the faculty wanted to create smaller groups of students so that the students would feel a greater sense of belonging, a feeling that is easily lost in a large student body of 1,800. The four divisions were the School of Technical Arts, School of Business Education, School of Fine Arts, and School of Global Studies.

By now, the students understood the notion of empowerment. They took the initiative to form the Student Coalition on Responsible Education. This committee structured many activities to give students responsibility and opportunities to exercise leadership. During year 2, the students in the coalition planned a statewide conference on student empowerment. This conference was held during the following summer.

Also during the second year, the faculty began developing a Guaranteed Graduate philosophy. The purpose of the philosophy was to ensure that graduates would possess the skills needed for entry into the workplace and postsecondary education.

In the third year of the project, the school opened the Student Credit Union, where students could open their own savings accounts and secure loans. A Teen Court with a jury of peers was implemented, and an area judge volunteered his time to it. Teen Court was held in the evening in one of the local courtrooms, with students serving as lawyers. The school also established a Health Based School Clinic to provide for the students' needs. Students could have physical examinations and get counseling for emotional problems in the clinic.

Partnerships were formed with a grocery store chain, and store employees served as tutors in the school. In return, the employees could use the school's recreational facilities. From this partnership, the school founded the Learning Connection, a program that provided tutoring, job placement, and assessment programs for students. The Learning Connection was supported by grants and the grocery store chain. The school attendance records, reviewed at the end of the third year, indicated that attendance was up. The number of college-bound students rose from 25% to 69%. In addition, drop-out rates were down and test scores were up.

Case Study Three: Commitment and Empowerment

The school in this case study is located in the suburbs of a large western city noted for its Mormon religious faith. So pervasive is the religious influence that the school enjoys a special relationship with its community based on the strong family focus found in the Mormon faith. Also heightening this community bond is the fact that the school is the only high school in the district.

The school facility had problems. The faculty felt very unempowered working in such a run-down environment. The teachers felt that the physical plant was in disarray and that they would feel more empowered if they could make the environment better. In addition, the faculty felt that students would benefit from the changes. After discussions with various faculty committees, the faculty decided to focus on building student pride in the school. With the physical changes creating a new pride in the school, the faculty wanted to build student commitment and involvement.

In the spring of year 2, the principal formed the Principal's Advisory Committee, comprising three juniors, three seniors, and three students from various other grades. The students rotated each time the committee met. The committee discussed student concerns and problems. Many issues previously handled by the principal were delegated to the student government during year 2. It was felt that, for greater student empowerment, students must be meaningfully involved in identifying and solving issues of relevance to them. The principal stated at the end of year 2 that the students solved problems more effectively than he did previously.

The formal Student Pride program was developed and initiated during the spring of year 2. The purpose of the formal program was to recognize students who were good citizens in the school. Each week a drawing was held to see who would win $10. Names of students who had not been tardy or absent during the week would be placed into the drawing. Also, the principal would pass out cards for free meals at a local fast-food restaurant to students he "caught doing something good." In addition, the faculty decided to require citizenship credits for graduation to reinforce the norm of student responsibility and leadership within the school.

During year 3, the faculty decided to give parents a display case to use in any way they wished. Parents could recognize any person or program of their choice. Students designed and opened a new restaurant in the school and planned remodeling changes in the student cafeteria.

In other areas, 18 teachers adopted cooperative learning as a model of instruction in their classrooms. This grew out of the growing team-collaborative ideas developing among the faculty. Teachers developed a program on drug awareness that brought national recognition to the school. The school received the Drug Prevention Excellence Award from Washington, DC. Finally, the school was selected as one of four high schools in the state to be designated as an Outstanding School. For this, the school received $10,000.

Conversations About the Case Studies

This section is intended to provide you with ideas for conversations regarding the case studies and their focus on empowerment of students in schools. As you discuss student empowerment and explore the leadership issues related to it, use the following questions to spark debate, develop further questions to explore, critique current practice, and guide your leadership assumptions.

1. Why empower students?
2. How did each school in the three case studies frame a definition of student empowerment?
3. Some teachers are afraid that to empower students is to relinquish control to students. How do you think the schools in the case studies dealt with this issue? Why might it not have been an issue at all?
4. What roles were played by the principals in these three schools relative to empowering students?
5. What are the key leadership lessons learned by the principals in these schools relative to student empowerment?

REFERENCES

Crane, D. P. (1976). The case for participative management. *Business Horizons, 19*(2), 15–21.

Crossland, B. (2000). *The relationships between teacher empowerment, teachers' sense of responsibility for student outcomes and student achievement.* Unpublished doctoral dissertation, University of Missouri - Columbia.

VOICES FROM THE FIELD

Reflections of a Practitioner

Teacher empowerment is a term that is often misunderstood. Often, teacher empowerment is perceived as freedom of choice — to teach what and how one chooses — that is, academic freedom. Yet this definition of empowerment without concomitant responsibility is not true empowerment at all. An important element of teacher empowerment is a common vision or goal combined with the commitment to do whatever is necessary to reach that goal.

A study conducted by B. Crossland (2000) correlating elementary teachers' perceptions of empowerment levels, degree of responsibility for student outcomes, and student achievement revealed a statistically significant correlation between empowerment and responsibility ($r = 0.180$). Interestingly, however, only those schools involved in Missouri's Accelerated Schools project also showed a significant relationship to student achievement.

The major premise of Missouri's Accelerated Schools project is empowerment with responsibility. Apparently, without the commitment to common goals and a sense of personal responsibility for reaching that goal, the results of empowerment are superficial and do not necessarily reach students.

If we want to affect students' learning, teachers must understand that empowerment without a strong sense of personal responsibility for the outcome is ineffective.

BARBARA J. CROSSLAND

Dede, C. (1989). The evolution of information technology: Implications for curriculum. *Educational Leadership, 47*(1), 23–26.

Dunst, R. (1991, February). *Issues in empowerment.* Paper presented at the annual meeting of the Children's Mental Health and Service Policy Convention, Tampa, FL.

Dunstan, J. F. (1981). *An ethnographic study of decision-making processes and leadership behavior at the school wide level in selected secondary schools* (Tech. Rep. No. 572). Madison: University of Wisconsin-Madison, Wisconsin Research and Development Center for Individualized Schooling.

Erickson, K. A., & Gmelch, W. H. (1977). *School management teams: Their structure, function, and operation.* Arlington, VA: Educational Research Service.

Hackman, J. R. (1986). The psychology of self-management in organizations. In M. S. Pollack & R. O. Perloff (Eds.), *Psychology and work: Productivity change and employment* (pp. 85–136). Washington, DC: American Psychological Association.

Hackman, J. R., & Oldham, G. R. (1980). *Work redesign.* Reading, MA: Addison-Wesley.

Jenkins, K. (1988). Metaphor and mindset for educational leadership. *The Educational Forum, 52,* 143–151.

Kasten, K. L., Short, P. M., & Jarmin, H. (1989). Self-managing work groups and the professional lives of teachers: A case study. *The Urban Review, 21*(2), 63–80.

Lightfoot, S. L. (1986). On the goodness of schools: Themes of empowerment. *Peabody Journal of Education, 63*(3), 9–28.

Lortie, D. C. (1975). *Schoolteacher.* Chicago: University of Chicago Press.

Murphy J., & Evertson, C. (1990, April). *Restructuring schools: Capturing the phenomena.* Paper presented at the annual meeting of the American Educational Research Association, Boston, MA.

Peters, T. (1987). *Thriving on chaos: Handbook for a management revolution.* New York: Knopf.

Rice, K. (1987). *Empowering teachers: A search for professional autonomy.* Unpublished master's thesis, Dominican College of San Rafael, CA. (ERIC Document Reproduction Service No. ED 282 845)

Short, P. M. & Greer, J. T. (1989, April). *Increasing teacher autonomy through shared governance: Effects on policy making and student outcomes.* Paper presented at the annual meeting of the American Educational Research Association, San Francisco, CA.

Short, P. M., Greer, J. T., & Michael, R. (1991). Restructuring schools through empowerment: Facilitating the process. *Journal of School Leadership, 1*(2), 5–25.

Zimmerman, M. A., & Rappaport, J. (1988). Citizen participation, perceived control, and psychological empowerment. *American Journal of Community Psychology, 16,* 725–750.

🎵

Evaluation of Empowering Leadership

As school organizations move toward greater participant empowerment, the role of leadership and the organizational climate and culture of the school are restructured. As Sirotnik and Clark (1988) stated, "Schools should be both the objects of and the arenas for educational improvement and change" (p. 660). Schools that promote participant empowerment become centers of renewal and shared decision making (Sirotnik & Clark, 1988). Moreover, teachers and principals engage in reflective thinking and inquiry in a collaborative setting that thrives on change and growth.

With the restructuring of roles and responsibilities that occurs in an empowered school, it is evident that traditional ways of assessing change, student growth and learning, and school leadership fall short (Coladarci & Donaldson, 1991). The focus on knowledge creation and problem solving that characterizes an empowered school invites new ways of viewing evaluation and how the school provides for the development of its participants in the educational process. What is required are new ways of looking at students, leadership, and the school change process.

ASSESSMENT OF ORGANIZATIONAL CHANGE AND EMPOWERMENT

Marshall (1988) suggested that the culture of a school comprises the "rules of the game, organizational climate, norms, dominant values, and informal structure—the basic pattern of assumptions" (p. 262). These

dimensions of culture change as the school becomes a more empowering environment for its participants. As teachers and schools become
more empowered, one obvious change that occurs is their refocus on inquiry through the problem-solving processes and structures they have
established. Instead of having answers brought in from the outside and
imposed on them, teachers, through participation in the problem-
framing and problem-solving process, generate alternative solutions.
Sirotnik and Clark (1988) suggested that, for significant and long-lasting
change to occur in a school, educators at the school site must be involved in developing "their own understandings if we expect to see
awareness translated into action" (p. 662). To bring about change
through the problem-framing and problem-solving activities of empowered teachers, the focus must be on inquiry into what teachers need.
Berman and McLaughin (1978) suggested that innovative programs have
the best chance of implementation and success if teachers play a major
role in the decision-making process.

A key process for empowering schools is shared decision making.
Assessment of this activity in the school requires an examination of the
types of decisions in which teachers are being involved. Russell, Cooper,
and Greenblatt (1992) used eight dimensions of decision making to develop the Teacher Involvement and Participation Scale, an instrument
that can give educators an understanding of how the shared decision-
making process is evolving in a school. These eight key dimensions in
shared decision making (Russell et al., 1992) assess the degree to which
teachers:

1. Are involved in setting the goals and the mission of the school.
2. Have the time, reduced teaching load, changed schedules, and
   waivers to participate in collaborative work.
3. Participate in decisions determining the school's program, curriculum goals, classroom pedagogy, and textbooks and other
   materials.
4. Are involved in decisions relating to designing and implementing the school budget.
5. Participate with administrators in decisions regarding recruiting, hiring, and assignment of school personnel.
6. Design and implement professional development activities for
   the school.
7. Are involved in decisions about managing building use and
   maintenance.
8. Are involved in setting standards for their own performance
   and for student performance.

The assessment model developed by Russell and his colleagues (1992) provides for the collection of baseline data on shared decision making and identifies issues in the collaboration process that need attention in the school. The instrument allows for the collection of data that may indicate areas in shared decision making that the teachers feel carry more importance than other areas. Table 10.1 shows a partial sample of the Teacher Involvement and Participation Scale–Version 2. This instrument can be purchased through RBG Associates, P.O. Box 182, New City, NY 10956.

To assess the overall level of empowerment in the school, Short and Rinehart (1992) developed the School Participant Empowerment Scale (see Table 10.2), an instrument through which data can be gathered on the overall perception of participant empowerment in the school; it also measures teacher perception of the following six dimensions, identified in Short and Rinehart's research (1992), that underlie the construct of empowerment:

1. *Professional growth*—the level at which the school environment is perceived as supportive of teacher growth and development. Includes perceptions that teachers have opportunities to expand their knowledge and skill level on an ongoing basis.

2. *Self-efficacy*—the belief that one has the skills and ability to help students learn because of one's competency.

3. *Decision making*—the level of opportunity to participate in decisions that are of importance to the teacher.

4. *Status*—teachers' perception that they have the respect and admiration of school personnel, that their expertise is acknowledged and valued, and that they are fully supported as professionals.

5. *Autonomy*—the degree to which teachers perceive that they have control over daily schedules, choices relative to the teaching and learning processes, and other decisions that are important to them.

6. *Impact*—the extent to which teachers perceive that they have an effect and influence on educational programs as well as administration, students, parents, and the community.

Leithwood, Jantzi, Silins, and Dart (1993) have suggested that if change is to be substantive and sustained in restructured schools with greater teacher empowerment, second-order change must be considered. According to these researchers, *second-order change* (Leithwood et al., 1993) refers to attention to changes in principal appraisal procedures. They argue that traditional appraisal processes and instruments are

CHAPTER 10

Table 10.1
Teacher Involvement and Participation Scale

T.I.P.S. 2
Teacher Involvement and Participation Scale—Version 2

VII. Facilitating Procedures and Structures

39. Teachers have access to the information they need to make school-wide decisions.	1	2	3	4	5
40. Teachers are represented on a council or group that makes school-wide decisions.	1	2	3	4	5
41. Sufficient time is provided for teachers to share in decision-making activities.	1	2	3	4	5
42. It is possible to obtain waivers from the teachers' contract for school-based decisions.	1	2	3	4	5
43. Teachers working together arrive at decisions on the basis of majority rule.	1	2	3	4	5
44. We would not make a decision until almost everyone is in agreement.	1	2	3	4	5
45. Decisions are not made until everyone can accept the proposal to some extent.	1	2	3	4	5

VIII. Staff Development

46. Teachers have access to current research on effective programs and practices.	1	2	3	4	5
47. Teachers help to determine the staff development they will receive.	1	2	3	4	5
48. Teachers have opportunities to share their expert knowledge.	1	2	3	4	5
49. Teachers participate in staff development activities.	1	2	3	4	5
50. Teachers have access to special training when necessary.	1	2	3	4	5

NOTE. From John J. Russell, Bruce S. Cooper, and Ruth B. Greenblatt (March 1992).

Table 10.2
School Participant Empowerment Scale

Directions: Please rate the following statements in terms of how well they describe how you feel. Rate each statement on the following scale: 1—Strongly Disagree (SD), 2—Disagree (D), 3—Neutral (N), 4—Agree (A), and 5—Strongly Agree (SA).

	SD	D	N	A	SA
1. I am given the responsibility to monitor programs.	1	2	3	4	5
2. I function in a professional environment.	1	2	3	4	5
3. I believe that I have earned respect.	1	2	3	4	5
4. I believe that I am helping kids become independent learners.	1	2	3	4	5
5. I have control over daily schedules.	1	2	3	4	5
6. I believe that I have the ability to get things done.	1	2	3	4	5
7. I make decisions about the implementation of new programs in the school.	1	2	3	4	5
8. I am treated as a professional.	1	2	3	4	5
9. I believe that I am very effective.	1	2	3	4	5
10. I believe that I am empowering students.	1	2	3	4	5
11. I am able to teach as I choose.	1	2	3	4	5
12. I participate in staff development.	1	2	3	4	5
13. I make decisions about the selection of other teachers for my school.	1	2	3	4	5
14. I have the opportunity for professional growth.	1	2	3	4	5
15. I have the respect of my colleagues.	1	2	3	4	5
16. I feel that I am involved in an important program for children.	1	2	3	4	5

NOTE. From School Participant Empowerment Scale by P. M. Short and J. S. Rinehart. Copyright © 1992 by P. M. Short and J. S. Rinehart.

inconsistent with the types of leadership that are helpful for restructuring schools that are empowering. A flatter social structure, inherent in an empowering organization that invokes the kind of problem-framing and problem-solving capacities demanded of teachers, requires a high level of commitment to these purposes (Leithwood et al., 1993). Therefore, analyzing the culture of such a restructured school may require a look at commitment strategies. Leithwood and his colleagues (1993) have devised a model for thinking about and assessing the conditions and processes associated with restructuring. These conditions and processes, modified for locally initiated restructuring projects, are as follows:

1. Out-of-School Conditions and Processes
   - *State educational agency*—the extent to which teachers value the directives and initiatives (policy) from the state education agency related to curriculum, funding, personnel.
   - *District*—the degree to which teachers perceive the leadership in the district, including district staff and educational organizations, to be helpful; professional development opportunities to be valued; and district policies to support the restructuring effort.
   - *School community*—the degree to which teachers perceive support or opposition from parents and the community on policy, use of community resources, and parent involvement.

2. In-School Conditions and Processes
   - *Goals*—the degree to which teachers perceive that the goals of the restructuring have clarity and compatibility with their own goals and school goals.
   - *Teachers*—the level of commitment of teachers to their own professional development, the level to which restructuring is compatible with their own views, and the level of teacher commitment and motivation to be involved in the restructuring process.
   - *School culture*—the degree to which teachers perceive themselves to be collaborating to implement the restructuring processes.
   - *School programs* the extent to which restructuring is seen to be compatible with teachers' views of acceptable programs and instruction.
   - *School policy, organization, and resources*—the degree to which teachers perceive that school policies, finances, materials, and teacher release time support the restructuring program.

3. Teacher-Perceived Outcomes
- Teachers' perceptions of the nature of change, due to the restructuring process, that has occurred in students, teachers, school culture, and school policies and organization.

ASSESSMENT OF THE PRINCIPAL'S LEADERSHIP

As early as the mid-1950s, March and Simon (1958) suggested that participative decision making, a dimension of empowerment, "can be viewed as a device for permitting management to participate more fully in the making of decisions, as well as a means for expanding the influence of lower echelons in the organization" (p. 51). Bartolke, Eschweiler, Flechsenberger, and Tannenbaum (1982) pointed out that "the control that members exercise within the company is, after all, exercised over other members. Thus, if the likelihood of exercising more control is one of the benefits of participation to members, the likelihood of being subject to greater control is perhaps one of the costs" (p. 395). These notions suggest that school governance in empowered schools has implications for rethinking the evaluation of principals (Glasman & Heck, 1992). These implications (Smylie & Crowson, 1993) include the following:

1. Persons to whom the principal is accountable.
2. Subjects of the principal's accountability.
3. Level of the principal's accountability.

As Smylie and Crowson (1993) suggested, in schools with greater shared decision making—a component of empowerment—principals may be accountable for the "integrity of shared governance processes" (p. 67). In addition, principals also "remain accountable for products-decisions that are made with or by others" (p. 67).

Another issue centers on the new relations between stakeholders created by the problem-framing and problem-solving process in an empowered school. As Smylie and Crowson (1993) pointed out, principals may be held accountable by the central office for developing "productive working relationships with teacher leaders and for teacher leaders' job performance. The district office may also turn to teacher leaders to gather information to assess principals' job performance" (p. 68). According to Elmore (1987), the empowerment of teachers is in direct opposition to the traditional culture of authority whereby "teachers are given clearly subordinate status in a hierarchy that rewards status in direct proportion to distance from direct contact with students" (p. 68).

CHAPTER 10

Thus, the changes in duties, powers, responsibilities, perspectives, and administrative style (Smylie & Crowson, 1993) of principals in empowered schools produce changes in evaluation outlook. For instance, Smylie and Crowson (1993) found that there is a need for a processed-produced form of evaluation to adapt to the reform reality. The movement toward shared decision making and the role of the principal in making that happen, including training faculty in the process, facilitating acceptance of decisions, and sharing accountability while giving up control, suggest that evaluation of principals must change (Smylie & Crowson, 1993).

Creating schools in which participants experience an increased sense of empowerment requires that the principal simultaneously lose some position power while engaging others in decision making and problem solving. In addition, more people have a voice and a stake in the problems framed and solutions identified. According to Smylie and Crowson (1993), the tension created by decreased position identity, increased accountability with more players in the decision-making process, pressure to make reform happen, and expanded stakeholders creates the need to reconceptualize the "Who's in charge?" or "The buck stops here" notion of principal evaluation and accountability. They suggested that one way to think about principal evaluation is to consider a wider assessment of the community of players in the problem-framing, problem-solving process. Smylie and Crowson (1993) went further to posit that the process of principal evaluation may need to move to a "carefully planned opening up of evaluative structures towards the much broader formal representation of the stakeholders who now impact informally upon principals' work lives" (p. 83).

Ebmeier (1991) suggested that principals' performance be evaluated using a model consisting of the following four role domains: (1) maintenance, or monitoring the value structure; (2) goal attainment, or achieving outcome goals; (3) adaption, or understanding and making consideration for external demands; and (4) integration, or organizing and coordinating the diverse school tasks necessary for the teaching and learning process.

The principal's abilities to initiate and carry out the culture-changing procedures necessary to create an empowered school are revealed by use of the Ebmeier model (1991). Building trust throughout the organization, developing and maintaining the complexity of communication necessary for people to feel empowered, risk taking, problem solving, and building commitment and support for change—all components of principal leadership in empowered schools (Greer & Short, 1993)—may be placed within the model. The challenge becomes how to assess the level to which a principal can accomplish these functions and lead the evolutionary process toward greater teacher and student empowerment.

Leithwood and his colleagues (1993) studied the type of leadership capable of transforming a school in terms of outcomes and in-school processes. The kind of leadership identified, *transformational leadership*, consists of the following dimensions:

- Visioning.
- Modeling.
- Supporting group goals.
- Giving individual support.
- Exhibiting high expectations.
- Being intellectually stimulating.
- Managing by exception.
- Giving contingent reward.

In an investigation of the relationship between transformational leadership variables and outcomes and in-school processes, in-school conditions and processes were the best predictors of student outcomes. Out-of-school conditions were the next strongest predictors. However, when in-school conditions and processes were held constant, leadership variables had a significant effect on changes in teachers, programs and instruction, and student outcomes (Leithwood et al., 1993).

Rallis and Goldring (1993) suggested that restructured schools that empower participants and embrace innovation and change are called "dynamic schools." According to these researchers, principals in dynamic schools behave differently than principals in traditional schools, requiring a different approach to evaluation (p. 4). They suggested a "school-based accountability model for dynamic schools" (p. 10) that has merit for thinking about schools that focus on participant empowerment (see Figure 10.1). In the Rallis and Goldring model, a school-based team engages in collaborative data gathering, focusing on the principal and on school processes and products. As Rallis and Goldring (1993) stated, "The evaluation coordinating team's responsibility is drawing information from appropriate sources and seeing that information gets to appropriate audiences. Horizontal accountability supports the inquiry ethic of the school by recognizing everyone's responsibility for success and by providing opportunity for reflection" (p. 13). They went on to say that "because process and product surface as mutual components of leadership, they are mutual components of evaluation. Product, or outcomes, are due to process" (p. 15). Rallis and Goldring posited that a

Targets of Evaluation

Uses of Evaluation	Principal	School
Informative	Process	Process
Formative	Process	Process and Product
Summative	Process	Product

Figure 10.1 School-Based Accountability in Dynamic Schools

NOTE. From "Beyond the individual assessment of principals: School-based accounta-bility in dynamic schools" by S. F. Rallis and E. B. Goldring, 1993, *Peabody Journal of Education, 68*(2), 3–23: Copyright © 1993 by the *Peabody Journal of Education.* Reprinted with permission.

productive evaluation of principals should look at those activities for which principals are responsible in empowering schools. The evaluation team would then formulate a set of questions to ask throughout the school and outside the school. Specific examples (Rallis & Goldring, 1993) might be:

- Do people understand what the school is trying to do?
- Is teacher leadership emerging?
- What decision-making structures have been established in the school?
- What opportunities exist for professional growth?
- How do people feel about participation?
- Do students effectively handle conflict management?
- Do teachers engage in creative problem solving when issues arise?
- Are students taking responsibility for their learning?

Rallis and Goldring suggested that responses to these kinds of questions should provide a rich source of documentation on which to un-derstand the work of the principal. Evidence such as this will indicate whether the principal is engaging the processes that create a more em-powering environment in the school for all participants.

According to Rallis and Goldring (1993), the other set of data for evaluating the success of the principal comes from assessment of school outcomes, which are the products of processes, the results of participant interactions and collaborative ventures taking place in the school environment. The principal is instrumental in facilitating the development of this school environment. Thus, the school context must be factored into the assessment process. Examples of the kinds of questions that might be asked are as follows (Rallis & Goldring, 1993):

- What programs have school-based teams developed?
- What solutions for school problems have teams developed and implemented?
- What new policies have collaborative teams produced? How have they been implemented and evaluated?
- What are students learning?

Rallis and Goldring (1993) suggested that the school evaluation coordinating team might develop a school portfolio, which could be used as a "descriptive review" (p. 17). This portfolio could produce "a summative evaluation with solid, defensible data to document the school's record of accomplishment" (p. 18). Use of the portfolio could lead to the formation of a picture of the school by asking the following questions (Rallis & Goldring, 1993, p. 18):

- What kind of school are we? Are we pleased with this picture?
- What kind of work do we do, and what kind of learning occurs? Again, are we pleased with this picture?
- What forces, individuals, and groups are contributing to or responsible for the picture?
- What kind of changes are occurring in this school? Are they changes that improve the school environment?
- Are we moving in the direction we want?
- What forces, individuals, and groups are contributing to or responsible for these changes?
- How can we reinforce the positive aspects?
- What might be barriers or potential barriers to school improvement changes?
- What do we need to strengthen our processes and outcomes?

ASSESSMENT OF STUDENTS

In rethinking the role of students from passive to active participants in their own learning experience in schools, the valued outcomes for student learning can be redefined. One of the schools in the Empowered

Figure 10.2 Characteristics of the Empowered Child[*]

1. Decision maker

2. Self-assessor

3. Responsible

4. Strong self-esteem

5. Independent

6. Articulate

7. Mastery of basic skills

8. Planner

9. Organized

10. Compassionate

11. Cooperative spirit

12. Social skills

13. Adaptable

14. Self-disciplined

[*]Developed by the faculty at Enota Elementary School.
NOTE. From "Restructuring schools through empowerment: Facilitating the process" by
P. M. Short, J. T. Greer, & R. Michael, 1991; *Journal of School Leadership, 1*(2), p. 133.
Copyright © 1991 by Technomic Publishing Co., Inc., Lancaster, PA. Reprinted with per-
mission.

School District Project developed a set of characteristics of the empowered child, as shown in Figure 10.2 (Short, Greer, & Michael, 1991).

Along with new ideas about the characteristics of empowered
children, the movement away from the behaviorist model of learning
(Mitchell, 1992) toward constructivist psychology brings forth new ways
of viewing children's learning experiences. Constructivist psychology
(Mitchell, 1992) focuses on the "mind's operations in terms of schemata,
patterns of understanding into which new information is assimilated and
which either reinforce the existing patterns or modify them" (p. 38). As
is found in schools that structure learning to empower children, cognitive psychology suggests that children can reason and think long before
they acquire basic skills. Also, as Mitchell (1992) pointed out, "a good
deal of learning is in fact not the acquisition of new concepts but the
modification of naive conceptions" (p. 38). Hypothesis testing, exploration, reasoning, problem solving, communication, connections, and
writing and reading that are meaning centered have supplanted compu-

tational drill, phonics, grammar, vocabulary drill, terminology, and paper-and-pencil drill (Mitchell, 1992).

Assessment of the learning of students and their developing characteristics as empowered learners cannot be accomplished in the traditional manner. As Mitchell (1992) stated, "performance assessment in all its manifestations—open-ended questions, portfolios, group projects, observations—was inevitable given the constructivist model of cognition" (p. 38).

The creation of appropriate criteria and assessment tasks is different in an empowered school. Evaluators must begin to ask questions such as the following: What does a responsible child look like? What evidence will indicate that a child is a good problem solver? How can one assess creativity? Standardized modes of assessment and testing fit another paradigm of student outcomes and how children and students learn and participate in their learning experiences. What is needed in empowered schools is authentic assessment.

Authentic assessment requires that performance be assessed in a "real context" under conditions more like those that would normally exist when the behavior is performed. Authentic assessment does not take place in a contrived setting. Meyer (1992) suggested that new facets of authenticity include "stimuli, task complexity, locus of control, motivation, spontaneity, resources, conditions, criteria, standards, consequences" (p. 40). According to Meyer, in traditional performance assessment, the student demonstrates the behavior that the assessor wishes to measure with little interference from the surrounding environment; in authentic assessment, the student completes the required behavior but does so in a real-life context.

Portfolios, as part of authentic assessment, show promise for providing evidence of student outcomes for the empowered child. Portfolios "tell a story . . . put in anything that helps tell the story" (Paulson, Paulson, & Meyer, 1991). One such use of portfolios might fall under the outcome of "student as collaborator." Indications of a high level of collaboration for a fifth-grade student might be as follows: "Monitors own behavior in a group activity, clearly communicates with those in the group activity, and shows consideration for other's opinions in the group activity." A videotape of the child's interactions in several group activities could serve as evidence of how well he or she is developing in the area of collaboration. The video would be included in the child's portfolio along with other evidence of progression toward selected empowered-student outcomes.

Portfolios invite reflection, a systematic interrogation of one's experiences, how and why one chooses among alternative responses, and, if faced with the same scenario, how one might reframe the experience and find other responses (Short & Rinehart, 1993).

A NEW MODEL OF ASSESSMENT

It is clear that traditional approaches to assessment of the organization, students, teachers, and teaching and learning do not work in empowered schools. The changes that occur in roles, responsibilities, learning outcomes, and approaches to change and improvement in empowered schools necessitate a new assessment paradigm. This new paradigm must focus on authentic assessment of learning and horizontal assessment of leadership and organizational processes, while broadening the locus of responsibility for processes and products within the empowered school.

Expectations for these processes and products differ substantially from those in traditional schools. Instead of problem blaming, the empowered school engages in problem/opportunity framing and problem solving. Instead of the principal assuming all responsibility for program success, principal stakeholders hold responsibility for the quality of the problem solutions and their implementation. Students move from passive recipients of knowledge to active participants (i.e., workers), taking leadership in the learning process as well as responsibility for outcomes. Indeed, new ways of viewing evaluation become part of the evolution of the empowered school, with old, traditional methods of assessment becoming inappropriate. Part of the problem-framing, problem-solving activity of an empowered school is to identify and try more appropriate ways of asking, "How are *we* doing?"

REFERENCES

Bartolke, K., Eschweiler, W., Flechsenberger, D., & Tannenbaum, A. S. (1982). Workers' participation and the distribution of control as perceived by members of ten German companies. *Administrative Science Quarterly, 27,* 380–397.

Berman, P., & McLaughlin, M. (1978). *Federal programs supporting educational change: Vol. VII.* Santa Monica, CA: Rand.

Coladarci, T., & Donaldson, G. A. Jr. (1991). School climate assessment encourages collaboration. *NASSP Bulletin, 75,* 111–119.

Ebmeier, H. (1991, April). *The development of an instrument for client-based principal formative evaluation.* Paper presented at the annual meeting of the American Educational Research Association, Chicago, IL.

Elmore, R. F. (1987). Reform and the culture of authority in schools. *Educational Administration Quarterly, 23*(4), 60–78.

Glasman, N. S., & Heck. R. (1992). The changing leadership role of the principal: Implications for principal assessment. *Peabody Journal of Education, 68*(1), 5–25.

Greer, J. T., & Short, P. M. (1993). Restructuring schools. In L. Hughes (Ed.), *The principal as leader* (pp. 143–160). New York: Merrill.

Leithwood, K., Jantzi, D., Silins, H., & Dart, B. (1993). Using the appraisal of school leaders as an instrument for school restructuring. *Peabody Journal of Education, 68*(2), 85–109.

March, H., & Simon, J. G. (1958). *Organizations.* New York: Wiley.

Marshall, C. (1988). Analyzing the culture of school leadership. *Education and Urban Society, 20,* 262–275.

Meyer, C. (1992). What's the difference between authentic and performance assessment? *Educational Leadership, 49*(8), 39–41.

Mitchell, R. (1992). Measuring up: Student assessment and systemic change. *Educational Technology, 32*(11), 37–41.

Paulson, F. L., Paulson, P. R., & Meyer, C. (1991). What makes a portfolio a portfolio? *Educational Leadership, 48*(5), 60–63.

Rallis, S. F., & Goldring, E. B. (1993). Beyond the individual assessment of principals: School-based accountability in dynamic schools. *Peabody Journal of Education, 68*(2), 3–23.

Russell, J. J., Cooper, B. S., & Greenblatt, R. (1992). How do you measure shared decision making? *Educational Leadership, 50*(1), 39–40.

Short, P. M., Greer, J. T., & Michael, R. (1991). Restructuring schools through empowerment: Facilitating the process. *Journal of School Leadership, 1*(2), 127–139.

Short, P. M., & Rinehart, J. S. (1993). Reflection as a means of developing expertise. *Educational Administration Quarterly, 29,* 501–521.

Short, P. M., & Rinehart, J. S. (1992). School Participant Empowerment Scale. Instrument available from authors.

Sirotnik, K. A., & Clark, R. W. (1988). School-centered decision making and renewal. *Phi Delta Kappan, 69,* 660–664.

Smylie, M. A., & Crowson, R. L. (1993). Principal assessment under restructured governance. *Peabody Journal of Education, 68*(1), 64–84.

CHAPTER 11

✖

Reflection in Empowered Schools

Principals who desire to create empowered schools must constantly strive to create processes and structures that support empowerment of students and teachers. For many principals, this requires a change in behavior as well as growth and development of abilities to respond to unclear, unique, and ill-structured problems and issues.

Osterman (1991) proposed *reflection* as a means for changing principals' behavior through analysis of theories-in-use (a person's beliefs, position, culture, and action theories). Osterman (1998) suggested that the primary agenda for reflective practice is behavior change and "specifically change in the dimensions of professional practice" (p. 1). Reflective practice can facilitate organizational change by bringing about changes in the behaviors of individuals in organizations. Reflection upon theories-in-use may add to an individual's understanding and knowledge base about how and why the individual takes certain actions. According to Osterman (1998), change and improvement in leader practice can be achieved only by reflecting on and modifying existing theories-in-use. Behavior change occurs because new information gleaned from the reflection on the individual's actions leads to the development of new theories-in-use (Osterman, 1991). We believe that this is critical to efforts to provide empowering leadership in schools.

Change is not an easy, well-defined process. The complexities involved in changing the school environment toward greater empowerment for students and teachers create "gray-area" issues and problems for school leaders. Schon (1987) suggested that as principals experience gray area problems in their work, reflection serves as a means to assist them in rethinking them in different ways. This analysis of the two worlds of thought and action is a dialogue of thinking and doing through which principals become more skillful at addressing ill-defined problems (Schon, 1987).

Osterman and Kottkamp (1993) suggested that reflective practice can be placed within the constructivist paradigm. They further (1993) posited that reflective practice is a learning cycle consisting of four stages: experience, assessment, reconceptualization, and experimentation. Osterman (1998) reported that when confronted with a troublesome issue, the principal (reflector) steps back to examine the experience "looking at intentions, actions, and outcomes" (p. 3). In the process of analyzing this experience, problems may emerge (Osterman, 1998). A problem is defined as "a discrepancy between intended and actual behavior or between goals and actual outcomes" (Osterman, 1998, p. 3). On reflection, the problem becomes a stimulus for learning, since the reflector is face to face with actions that are not consistent with values or are ineffective in reaching stated goals. This analysis can lead to new understanding and new strategies (Osterman, 1998). Finally, Osterman (1998) has suggested that "the new ideas that emerge in this process then become hypotheses to be tested in action" (p. 3). As the principal's (reflector) experiences become successful, "new behaviors and ideas then become integrated into patterns of action" (Osterman, 1998, p. 3).

Schon (1987) stated that unique problems require unique answers in which the practitioner must go beyond the rules and technical knowledge and devise new methods of reasoning, constructing and testing new categories of understanding, strategies of action, and ways of framing problems. Schon (1983; 1987) further suggested that experts tend to interpret problems at a more abstract level and are better able to integrate multiple sources of information in a context.

According to Smyth (1989), reflection requires the following four processing actions: (1) Clearly describe what one does; (2) consider what it means to practice professionally; (3) confront how the practice evolved; and (4) reconstruct the practice for improvement.

MODELS FOR REFLECTION

Moallem (1998) proposed a reflective thinking model that is comprised of the following five phases: (1) problem recognition; (2) problem clarification; (3) hypothesis or suggestion formation and modification;

(4) mental elaboration of suggestions; and (5) actions taken based on the best-supported hypothesis. Reflection is not the same as simply thinking. Moallem (1998) explained that the nature of reflection is evident only if the person who is reflecting is willing to consider his or her beliefs within the context in which he or she is operating. How do an individual's beliefs interact or conflict with the context in which the individual is working as a principal or teacher? In addition, the reflector must be able to understand the context in which assumptions are formed (Moallem, 1998). The reflector must be able to explore alternatives and options and explore multiple perspectives. A principal in an empowered school must be able to see issues from others' perspectives in order to understand how to create an environment that is supportive of empowerment for both students and teachers.

Three types of reflection are often discussed: technical reflection, practical reflection, and critical reflection. Hatton and Smith (1995) described technical reflection as "concerned with the efficiency and effectiveness of means to achieve certain ends, which themselves are not open to criticism and modification" (p. 35). These researchers also suggested that practical reflection "allows for open examination not only of means, but also goals, the assumptions upon which these are based, and the actual outcomes" (p. 35). They went on to say that "this kind of reflecting, in contrast to the technical form, recognizes that meanings are not absolute, but are embedded in, and negotiated through, language" (p. 35). The third level of reflection, critical reflection, includes parts of the first two levels, but also "calls for considerations involving moral and ethical criteria" (Hatton & Smith, 1995, p. 35). Making judgments about the fairness and justness of decisions and actions falls into this level of analysis.

Interestingly, Schon (1987) included these three levels of reflection in his notions about reflection-in-action and reflection-on-action (Hatton & Smith, 1995). Reflection-in-action takes place as the person engages in the professional activity. Hatton and Smith (1995) suggested that this activity may be part of intuitive knowledge and "includes engaging in reflective conversation with oneself, shaping the situation in terms of the reflector's frame of reference, while consistently leaving open the possibility of reframing by employing techniques of holistic appraisal" (p. 35).

According to Short and Rinehart (1993), reflection can relate to levels of thinking in developing principals' expertise. These levels of thinking relate to the leader's ability to describe problems only from surface characteristics of the problem (little expertise) to viewing problems by describing their underlying principles, theories, and underlying deep structures (high expertise). Short and Rinehart (1993) pointed out that reflective writing can be analyzed for levels of thinking. Principals keep a reflective journal in which they reflect on a critical event by writing about the event, the action they took, and why they took that action based on culture, action, position, and tradition, and identifying alternative ways to react to the event. Reflective journals can be analyzed using a model for reflection developed by Sparks-Langer, Simmons, Pasch, Colton, and Starks (1990) for analyzing preservice teachers' journal writing about their clinical experiences. These levels of analysis include

Level 1—Simple, layperson descriptions.

Level 2—Events labeled with appropriate terms.

Level 3—Explanation with tradition.

Level 4—Preference given as the rationale.

Level 5—Explanation with principle or theory.

Level 6—Explanation with principle/theory and consideration of context.

Level 7—Explanation with consideration of ethical, moral, and political issues.

Analysis of reflective journals can highlight whether reflectors are developing characteristics of experts relative to their identification of the underlying deep structures of the issues and problems they addressed in their journal entries (Short & Rinehart, 1993).

Francis (1995) tied a similar model for reflective journaling to personal and professional empowerment, describing the stages as follows:

Describing—What do I do?

Informing—What does this mean?

Confronting—How did I come to be this way?

Reconstructing—How might I view/do things differently?

Challenging—What action will I take?

Group reflection can be an effective approach to building a culture of reflection within a cohort program. However, students must build a sense of trust and communication to make this effective. Training in feedback and listening skills is essential. Twale and Short (1989) offered the following description of the goals of group reflection:

> Critical [group] reflection means adapting a strategy through which the participants and practitioners make sense of unique or unclear situations using reflective thinking and analysis to develop an understanding of the complexities of schooling. After the group has

identified a real experience and recounted what happened, the group analyzes and reflects upon it. Meanwhile, the group facilitator continually critiques, analyzes, and challenges the group to consider what is important, to whom it is important, and what actions lead to which responses within the school's context. This model forces the self-examination of the student's position and its base in one's value system, school tradition, and importance of these positions on action. (pp. 151–152)

The purpose of the procedure is to enhance the students' abilities to use critical reflective thinking in examining their position on an incident or problem, the basis of the position in culture and tradition, and the impact of these on action within the administrative role of the principal. The process for reflection is based on the assumption that any action or experience is the result of the interaction of four sources of influence: action, position, culture, and tradition. *Action* involves what a person does to deal with the critical incident. *Position* includes the underlying beliefs and values that facilitate taking a specific action in a critical incident. *Culture* includes the mores, values, beliefs, and assumptions emanating from a person's culture. *Tradition* is the collective wisdom and knowledge of the culture, including the formal knowledge base of a discipline. The process is conducted within a group setting with one student consenting to present a real, critical incident in which the individual has had to take action in order to solve the problem. The entire group interacts in doing the following:

- Presenting an incident (presented by one student).
- Focusing on a shift in action.
- Identifying thoughts and feelings at the shift.
- Generating a metaphor for the thoughts or feelings.
- Identifying a leadership perspective in the metaphor.
- Comparing, contrasting, and correlating perspectives from the four sources of influence.
- Identifying insights and questions.
- Determining implications.

The deliberation and hypothesis testing that are a part of this group process provide the foundation for the reflection process that constitutes the individual journals completed by the students during the year-long seminar.

One of the advantages of group reflection is that the students bring different backgrounds, life experiences, professional activities, and frameworks of thought to the same critical incident being analyzed (Bolman & Deal, 1993). This expands the understanding of the incident and supports the analysis and subsequent reflection on action, since more options and alternative perspectives come into the discussion.

REFLECTION AND CHANGE

Substantive change in a school is complex, and attempting to create an empowered school can challenge the very best leader. Senge (1991) suggested that the principal must develop a type of "systems thinking" to manage the type of substantive change required to create an empowered school. Undergirding systems thinking are concepts of personal mastery, shared vision, mental models, and team learning. Additionally, according to Senge, reflection is a critical element of the principal who desires to bring about change in a substantive manner within the school; the leader must be a reflective individual (Senge, 1991). Covey's work (1991) supports this position. He emphasized that leaders must reflect on their personal core beliefs and, in addition, must be able to develop the trust and skills critical to fostering collaborative change—the type of change that is imperative in moving toward a more empowered school.

☺ CASE STUDY
The Role of Reflection in the Empowerment of Teachers

Brad Conrad had always been a risk taker. He observed his mother's success as a small business owner, a true believer in leadership by modeling and inclusion. As principal of a small rural school at age 25, Brad had led the efforts at school reform through teacher empowerment. This was accomplished through shared decision making and meaningful participation by teachers in the site-based management efforts in this small, but innovative district. In 2 years, Brad was offered a position as assistant principal in a large suburban elementary school. After his second year as assistant, Brad returned to graduate school full time to work on his doctoral degree. He had been offered a research assistantship by a university professor who had been impressed by his intelligence and conscientiousness in the educational administration program. Although returning to school would mean a drastic decrease in his income, he explained to his wife that he felt it was an opportunity he could not decline.

As Brad progressed through the doctoral course work, comprehensive exams, and finally the dissertation process, he became more and more convinced that transformational leadership, which concerns itself not with power, but with the empowerment of others, was the true path to school excellence. The doctoral program that meant so much to Brad's intellectual and personal advancement focused on inquiry and reflection on problems in practice that paved the road to becoming a dynamic, scholarly, but practical practitioner. The role of reflection in his professional and personal life became an important one. Brad thought of the time spent in reflection on the actions, reactions, and learning that occurred during his day as a way to "hit the replay button" and consider the success or continuing challenges facing him.

When Brad graduated and became Dr. Conrad, he accepted a position in a large, wealthy district that neighbored his previous district. His new school, Timberwood Elementary School, had been headed by the same principal, Mr. Barnes, for the past 18 years. Mr. Barnes was a prominent, quite traditional member of the community who appeared to have been successful with his top-down approach to leadership. A majority of Timberwood teachers had been there as long as the principal, and Brad knew that the change in leadership would be difficult for these veterans. But as it turned out, "difficult" was an underestimation.

As Brad talked to the superintendent and investigated the recent history of the school, he discovered a picture of student achievement that, although far from low, had not improved significantly over the past 5 years. Brad also discovered that younger teachers typically did not stay at the school longer than 2 years. He knew the teacher shortage was a real threat to every district trying to attract and maintain quality educators, and he felt this exit of young teachers was interfering with potential school improvement. Brad felt compelled to address this problem from the beginning of his tenure at this new position, and at his first faculty meeting he assured his teachers that he did not intend to run the school by himself. "I wouldn't even want to try to run this school. This is our school, and we all should take part in the leadership."

These were not hollow words to Brad, who knew that only through a collaborative school culture could teachers become truly empowered. He committed himself to shaping this type of culture by (a) providing teachers with opportunities to share in leadership by taking part in meaningful decisions, (b) providing professional development opportunities designed to create a path toward empowerment, and (c) establishing teacher-led focus groups to address the school's challenges. He felt his relationship with the teachers was a good one, and although he realized that not all the staff members were as enthusiastic about his expectations of their leadership, the year ended with no loss of the younger teachers.

Although his second year began smoothly, it quickly became stressful and disconcerting to Brad. The Curriculum and Instruction focus group had recommended hiring an outside expert to visit their school and to report on the types of instruction going on in the classrooms. When the data were returned from the expert, the focus group presented the findings at a faculty meeting. "According to data our focus group has collected, we have only 15% of our instruction in the 'active' range," the group's chair began. "To ready our students for achievement tests, we are going to have to change our classroom strategies to reflect a more authentic, real-world type instruction. I propose we begin by our reliance on worksheets and end-of-the-chapter questions. We need to limit the number of copies each teacher uses per semester so we won't be tempted to fall back on bad habits."

After an awkward silence, a teacher of 14 years at Timberwood spoke for what seemed to be the majority of the teachers in the room. "Telling us how to teach should not be the purpose of your focus group. You need to provide us with information and let us decide for ourselves what is best for our classrooms. I use worksheets, and my test scores are not bad. To count how many copies we make is juvenile and shows us that there is very little trust left in this school." Another chimed in, "Not everyone on the Curriculum and Instruction committee is a classroom teacher. I don't see how they can tell us anything about classroom practices. You can't criticize something that you don't know about!" At this remark, the chair, who was a reading specialist, looked angry and hurt. "I have just as much knowledge about what goes on in the classrooms as you do, Brenda. Actually, probably more since I'm in the position to see what goes on in all the rooms in this building, and let me tell you, some of it is not pretty!"

As the tension grew, Brad stood and asked the teachers if they would go home and reflect upon the meeting, their feelings, and what they felt could be possible recommendations to improve instruction for the benefit of the students at Timberwood. "After all," Brad tried to remind the teachers, "they are why we are all here. We're on the same team, you know. We just need to work together for our school's sake." Brad heard an under-the-breath comment from the back: "Yea right, our school." Brad suggested the faculty meeting be continued the following week.

That evening, as Brad sat at his computer, he reflected upon the happenings of the day and the disintegration of the faculty meeting. Reflection had always allowed Brad not only to stay in touch with his knowledge base and beliefs, but also to review his actions and either remain committed to them or plan how to revise them. He was sure he was right about the involvement of teachers in running the school by participating in decisions and planning. As he added this written reflection to his professional journal, Brad felt reassured that although it was not a comfortable process, empowerment of the teaching staff would eventually empower students.

During the next week, Brad felt the animosity and negativity toward him and among the teachers growing, but he resisted the urge to become involved. He felt sure the teachers could come to a consensus and solve the problem themselves. The day before the faculty meeting, Brad received a call from the superintendent, Dr. Wilson, asking him to come to the central office for a "visit."

As Brad walked into the office, he had no idea what was waiting. Dr. Wilson had been district superintendent for 10 years. He was viewed by the community as the savior of the district, seemingly single-handedly rescuing it from bankruptcy after years of incompetent fiscal management. Dr. Wilson was popular and accepted by teachers and most patrons of the district. After some small talk, Dr. Wilson got down to the real reason for the meeting. "Dr. Conrad, I have a list here of comments I have received from teachers over the past week. I think you need to explain to me what is going on in your school." The superintendent handed Brad a typewritten list of comments that included the following:

> "Someone needs to teach Dr. Conrad how to be an effective leader."

> "We never had to take on the responsibility of running the school before. If we're doing that, what's his job?"

> "Mr. Barnes was never afraid to take care of this type of situation."

> "I think, 'If it ain't broke, don't fix it.'"

> "He should just tell us what to do, and we'll do it. But we don't want to be bossed around by teachers who have no business in our business!"

> "You pay him the big bucks to be the leader, now tell him to lead."

> "That's why he's the principal and we're just the teachers."

Brad was shocked at the tone of these comments and told the superintendent he had no idea why the comments were even made, much less so critical. The superintendent looked over his glasses and said, "I think that's part of the problem, Dr. Conrad. You don't really know what's going on with the teachers, and they feel you want them to do your job." "I don't want them to do my job, I just want them to help run the school," Brad tried to explain. "That's their school, too. And I'm a believer in shared leadership and the empowerment of teachers." "I know that's all well and good in graduate school, Brad. But this is the real world, and in the real world not everyone wants to be empowered. Most of these teachers have been teaching in this district for a long time and are set in their ways. I know we need to change with the times, but this is not the group to ask to do that. You have young teachers you can empower, but you're going to have to be a stronger leader to the rest of the staff, or you're putting your job in jeopardy."

As Brad drove home that night, he considered all that had happened during the last week. Dr. Wilson had asked him to come back the following day with a plan as to how to improve relations with the teachers in his building. Brad knew there would be very little sleep that night, but he vowed to have an answer, one way or the other, in the morning.

Conversations About the Case Study

1. The reflective principal combines theoretic and practical knowledge and applies that to practice. Has Brad succeeded?

2. Not all teachers are comfortable with the notion of shared leadership. What model of reflection might Brad use with his faculty to help them understand what an empowered school might look like and how roles and responsibilities are different in empowered schools?

3. How might reflection help a principal in a situation like Brad's to better understand how to grow and change as a leader?

CAROL MAHER

REFERENCES

Bolman, L. S., & Deal, T. E. (1993). Everyday epistemology in school leadership: Patterns and prospects. In P. Hallinger, K. Leithwood, & J. Murphy (Eds.), *Cognitive perspectives on school leadership* (pp. 21–33). New York: Teachers College Press.

Covey, S. (1991). *The seven habits of highly effective people.* New York: Simon & Schuster.

Francis, D. (1995). The reflective journal: A window to preservice teachers' practical knowledge. *Teaching and Teacher Education, 11*(6), 229–241.

REFLECTION IN EMPOWERED SCHOOLS

Hatton, N., & Smith, D. (1995). Reflection in teacher education: Towards definition and implementation. *Teaching and Teacher Education, 11*(1), 33–49.

Moallem, M. (1998). Reflection as a means of developing expertise in problem solving, decision-making, and complex thinking of designers. In *Proceedings of selected research and development presentations at the national convention of the Association of Educational Communications and Technology.* (pp. 281–289). Bloomington, IN: AECT.

Osterman, K. F. (1991, August). *Reflective practice: Linking professional development and school reform.* Paper presented at the annual meeting of the National Council for Professors of Educational Administration, Fargo, ND.

Osterman, K. F. (1998). *Using constructivism and reflective practice to bridge the theory-practice gap.* New York. (ERIC Document Reproduction Service No. ED 425 518)

Osterman, K. F., & Kottkamp, R. B. (1993). *Reflective practice for educators: Improving schooling through professional development.* Newbury Park, CA: Corwin.

Schon, D. A. (1983). *The reflective practitioner: How professionals think in action.* New York: Basic Books.

Schon, D. A. (1987). *Educating the reflective practitioner.* San Francisco: Jossey-Bass.

Senge, P. M. (1991). *The fifth discipline: The art and practice of the learning organization.* New York: Doubleday Currency.

Short, P. M., & Rinehart, J. S. (1993). Reflection as a means of developing expertise. *Educational Administration Quarterly, 29*, 501–521.

Smyth, J. (1989). Developing and sustaining critical reflection in teacher education. *Journal of Teacher Education, 10*(2), 2–9.

Sparks-Langer, G. M., Simmons, J. M., Pasch, M., Colton, A., & Starks, A. (1990). Reflective pedagogical thinking: How can we promote it and measure it? *Journal of Teacher Education, 41*(4), 23–32.

Twale, D., & Short, P. M. (1989). Shaping school leaders for the future: Innovation in preparation. *Planning and Changing, 20*(3), 149–157.

INDEX